The Equity Risk Premium

Wiley Frontiers in Finance
Series Editor: Edward I. Altman, New York University

Corporate Financial Distress and Bankruptcy, 2nd ed., Edward I. Altman
Pension Fund Excellence: Creating Value for Stockholders, Keith P. Ambachtsheer
  and D. Don Ezra
International M&A, Joint Ventures & Beyond: Doing the Deal,
  David J. BenDaniel and Arthur Rosenbloom
Investment Management, Peter L. Bernstein and Aswath Damodaran
Style Investing: Unique Insight Into Equity Management, Richard Bernstein
Options, Futures & Exotic Derivatives: Theory, Application & Practice, Eric Briys
Managing Credit Risk: The Next Great Financial Challenge, John Caouette,
  Edward Altman, and Paul Narayanan
Managing Derivative Risk: The Use and Abuse of Leverage, Lilian Chew
Valuation: Measuring and Managing the Value of Companies Paper,
  Tom Copeland, Tim Kroller, and Jack Murrin
Investment Valuation, Aswath Damodaran
*Damodaran on Valuation: Security Analysis for Investment and Corporate
  Finance*, Aswath Damodaran
Project Financing: Asset-Based Financial Engineenng, John D. Finnerty
Financial Statement Analysis: Practitioners Guide, 2nd ed., Martin S. Fridson
M&A: A Practical Guide to Doing the Deal, Jeffrey C. Hooke
*Security Analysis on Wall Street: A Comprehensive Guide to Today's Valuation
  Methods*, Jeffrey C. Hooke
New Dimensions in Investor Relations: Competing for Capital in the 21ˢᵗ Century,
  Bruce Marcus and Sherwood Wallace
*Chaos and Order in the Capital Markets: A New View of Cycles, Prices, & Market
  Volatility, 2nd ed.*, Edgar E. Peters
Using Economic Indicators to Improve Investment Analysis, 2nd ed.,
  Evelina Tainer
Investment Timing and the Business Cycle, Jon G. Taylor
Fixed Income Securities: Tools for Today's Markets, Bruce Tuckman
Export–Import Financing, 3rd ed., Harry M. Venedikian and Gerald Warfield
New Financial Instruments: Investor's Guide, Julian Walmsley

Forthcoming:
Risk Arbitrage: An Investor's Guide, Keith M. Moore
The Independent Fiduciary: Investing for Pension Funds and Endowment Funds,
  Russell L. Olson
Credit Risk Management: A Guide to Sound Business Decisions,
  Anthony Saunders
*Relative Dividend Yield: Common Stock Investing for Income and Appreciation,
  2nd ed.*, Anthony E. Spare

The Equity Risk Premium

THE LONG-RUN FUTURE OF THE STOCK MARKET

Bradford Cornell

John Wiley & Sons, Inc.

New York • Chichester • Weinheim • Brisbane • Singapore • Toronto

Library of Congress Cataloging-in-Publication Data:
Cornell, Bradford.
  The equity risk premium : the long-run future of the stock market
Bradford Cornell.
    p.   cm.—(Wiley frontiers in finance)
  Includes index.
  ISBN 0-471-32735-2 (cloth : alk. paper)
  1. Stocks—Prices—United States. 2. Risk—United States.
  I. Title. II. Series.
HG4915.C664 1999
332.63'22'0973   98-51035

Printed in the United States of America

10 9 8 7 6 5 4 3 2 1

Contents

Preface   ix

Acknowledgments   xi

Chapter 1: Measuring and Assessing Stock-Market Performance   1

An Introduction to Stock-Market History   5
    Stock-Market Indexes   6
    Using Investor Returns to Assess Stock-Market Performance   9
    An Overview of Market Performance: Annual Holding-Period Returns   12
The Equity Risk Premium   18
    Definition   18
    Importance   19
Using the Historical Data to Estimate Future Stock-Market Performance   20
Uses of the Equity Risk Premium   27
Inflation and Asset Returns   29
Stock Returns and the Risk Premium: Looking Forward   34

Chapter 2: Evaluating the Historical Record   36

Computing the Average Premium: Arithmetic versus Geometric   36
How Accurately Can the Historical Risk Premium Be Measured?   39

Nonstationarity and Historical Estimates of the Equity
Risk Premium   45
Attempts to Model Changes in the Risk Premium   49
Models Based on the Variability of Returns   51
Models Based on Dividend and Earnings Yield   52
*Does Nonstationarity Really Matter for Estimating the
Long-Run Risk Premium?*   53
*The Impact of Permanent Changes in the Risk Premium
on Stock Prices*   55
The Bottom Line on Nonstationarity   59
Survival Bias   60
The Impact   60
The Bottom Line   69
Stock and Bond Returns   70
Over the Long Horizon   70
The Impact of Inflation   74
A Final Assessment of the Historical Record   77
Appendix 2.1: Monthly Data for Stocks, Bonds, Bills,
and Inflation   79

**Chapter 3: Forward-Looking Estimates of
the Equity Risk Premium**   101

The Discounted Cash Flow Model   102
Forms of the Model   102
Constant-Growth Form   102
Multistage Form   106
*Comparison of the Discounted Cash Flow and Historical
Estimates of the Risk Premium*   113
The Blanchard Extension of the Discounted Cash Flow
Approach   114
The Kaplan–Ruback Study   115
The Fama–French Aggregate Internal Rate
of Return Analysis   117
An Earnings Yield Approach to Estimating the
Market Risk Premium   121
The Welch Survey   122
Summary of the Risk Premium Estimates Produced
by Competing Approaches   125

Chapter 4: Risk Aversion and the Risk Premium Puzzle

Chapter 4: Risk Aversion and the Risk
    Premium Puzzle   126

The Economic Theory of Risk Aversion   126

What Types of Risk Are Rewarded: A Brief Review
    of Portfolio Theory   130

The Market Risk Premium and the Cost of Equity Capital   135

Risk Aversion and the Historical Equity Risk Premium:
    The Risk Premium Puzzle   137

Explanations for the Risk Premium Puzzle

The Puzzle Is an Illusion: The Empirical Data Are Wrong   141
High Risk Aversion   142
Nonstandard Utility Functions   145
Autocorrelation in Returns   149
Time Varies Expected Returns   150
Heterogeneous Investors   151
What about a Stew?   154

What Explanations of the Equity Risk Premium Say
    about the Future   154

Chapter 5: The Risk Premium and the Stock-Market Boom of the 1990s

Chapter 5: The Risk Premium and the
    Stock-Market Boom of the 1990s   158

Determining Whether Stock Prices Are High or Low   159

Explanations for the High Level of Stock Prices   164

*A Decline in the Discount Rate Due to a Drop
    in the Equity Risk Premium*   165
Changing Stock-Market Risk   168
Changing Investors and Changing Investor Demographics   170
*The New Economic Paradigm: Higher Earnings
    and Dividend Growth*   178
Irrational Exuberance: The Market Is Overvalued   183

Summary   194

Appendix 5.1: International Stock Market Indices   196

Chapter 6: The Equity Risk Premium and the Long-Run Outlook for Common Stocks

Chapter 6: The Equity Risk Premium and
    the Long-Run Outlook for Common
    Stocks   201

Weighing the Empirical and Theoretical Evidence   202

What Does the Stock Price Run-Up of the 1990s Augur
    for the Future?   206

*The Impact of a Rational Drop in the Equity Risk
    Premium*   206
The Impact of Permanently Higher Growth   210
The Implications of Overvaluation   211
Summary   213
Implications of a Lower Equity Risk Premium
    in the Future   213
Investment Implications   213
Implications for Corporate Financial Decision Making   215
Implications for Pension and Retirement Planning   216

References   217

Index   223

Preface

Books and articles on the stock market span a wide spectrum between two poles. At one end is the academic literature as published in major scholarly journals, including *The Journal of Finance, The Journal of Financial Economics,* and *The Review of Financial Studies.* This literature is highly complex and sophisticated, yet it is remarkably humble. Despite all the high-powered tools financial economists bring to analysis, they recognize that most of the variation in stock prices is unpredictable, particularly over the short term.

At the other pole are books designed to sell investment strategies to beat the market. These are written in clear, forceful language. They are often aggressively marketed and occasionally become best-sellers. Unfortunately, the messages they convey usually have no scientific validity.

Between these two poles are thousands of books and articles on the stock market and investing. This book lies at a point about three quarters of the way toward the academic-literature pole. The goal here is to summarize the scientific work in a digestible manner for people who are not professional economists. There is a risk in this, of course. If the scientific articles could be fully explained without the technical complexity, the technical complexity would never have evolved in the first place. Any simplification is just that—a simplification. Because some readers, particularly finance students, may not be satisfied with my explanations, this book contains numerous citations of the literature on which it is based. Nonetheless, this book is not a finance textbook. Too many people are interested in scientific work on investing to limit the book's audience to business-school graduates.

The goal of this book is to help the reader understand what can be expected from the stock market in the future over the long run. The path to this goal is through the equity risk premium— the difference between the returns on common stock and the returns on government securities. Be forewarned: There no dramatic tips or secrets revealed here. In fact, if I had such information, I would be exploiting it, not writing about it. In this respect, the scientific literature on investing indicates that I am not alone. When it comes to investing, no one has any dramatic secrets. This does not mean, however, that a thoughtful analysis of the behavior of stock prices cannot help one become not only a better investor but a more relaxed one. Recognizing one's limitations can be as liberating as learning new skills.

Acknowledgments

As regards the preparation of this book, I want first to thank my colleagues at FinEcon. John Haut, John Hirshleifer, Liza James, and particularly Ed Bergstrom helped me bring together all the academic articles and empirical analyses of the equity risk premium. Mina Samuels at John Wiley & Sons was also instrumental in steering the book through the publication process.

Finally, I would like to thank my mother, Barbara June Cornell, for all the encouragement she gave me regarding the project. Her continuing good cheer and enthusiasm, in the face of much personal suffering, was a never-ending source of inspiration.

Chapter 1

Measuring and Assessing Stock-Market Performance

Perhaps the most commonly asked question in finance is "What can I expect from the stock market in the years ahead?" This is obviously a critical question for investors attempting to decide what fraction of their portfolio to commit to equities, but its practical importance extends far beyond that. Every pension-fund manager must have an estimate of future stock-market performance to gauge funding requirements and to set investment policy. Retirees face a similar problem. Expected returns on stocks also play a fundamental role in determining a firm's cost of capital and therefore the hurdle rate the company should employ when making capital budgeting decisions.

There is an immense folklore literature that attempts to answer the question "Where is the market going?" At various times, hugely popular books have been published predicting market booms or crashes. The unfortunate fact is that there is virtually no scientific support for any of the popular publications. Since the late 1960s, hundreds of detailed statistical studies of stock markets throughout the world have reached one common conclusion:

most all of the short-term variation in stock prices is unpredictable.[1] Although booms and crashes have occurred around the globe in the past and are likely to occur in the future, the timing of their occurrence is entirely unpredictable. Even without all the academic articles, a simple thought experiment demonstrates why this must be true. Suppose, for example, that someone were to write a convincing book entitled *The Crash of 2000,* explaining why the new millennium will be accompanied by a dramatic drop in stock prices. If the arguments were truly convincing, then investors who read the book would clearly want to sell their stock before the dawn of the millennium. Assuming that enough investors read the book and acted in accord with its predictions, stock prices would not fall at the start of the millennium but at the time the book was widely distributed—but this would mean the predictions of the book are false. Stock prices would fall when the book was published, not at the start of the new millennium.

The foregoing thought experiment holds not only for books predicting market movements but also for theories that tie major market moves to predictable external events. For instance, assume that it was known that the market always rises sharply following the election of a Republican president. In that case, investors would start buying stock as soon as a Republican candidate took a lead in the polls. Any further indications that the Republican candidate was going to win would be met by increased buying. By the night of the election, the market would already reflect the expected outcome. The only circumstance in which the market would move sharply after the election would be one in which the race was too close to call. In that case, however, knowing that Republican wins are associated with stock price increases would be useless information because the outcome of the election is equivalent to a coin flip.

The foregoing thought experiments illustrate what has come to be known in the academic literature as the efficient market hypothesis. In a nutshell, the efficient market hypothesis says that publicly available information is immediately reflected in the current level of the stock market, so it cannot be used to predict

---

[1] For two partial reviews of this literature, see Fama (1970 and 1991).

where the market will go in the future. The election example illustrates how this works. Assuming again that Republican victories are good for stock prices, the critical information would be the likelihood of a Republican victory. If the Republicans have an overwhelming lead in the polls, as they did with Ronald Reagan in 1984, then stock prices will rise well in advance of the election. The election itself will have no impact on stock prices because the market will have already reflected, or impounded, the Republican victory. Only in those elections in which a Republican victory is at least somewhat unexpected would stock prices rise. The more unexpected the victory, the greater the increase.

From the preceding, it follows that the efficient market hypothesis is a kind of catch-22 of investing. Information that is predictable is worthless because it is already reflected in stock prices. The information that is valuable and can be used to make money is that information which cannot be predicted. As a corporate example, knowing that Microsoft is going to have positive earnings is useless information because virtually every investor makes that assumption. Knowing that Microsoft's earnings are going to exceed the expectations of the most savvy software industry analysts would be valuable information, but how could investors get this information? Because the expectations of analysts reflect careful analysis of available data, how can individual investors expect to produce more accurate forecasts on a consistent basis?

Of course, an investor can always *assume* that he or she knows better. If an investor was convinced that the analysts were wrong and that Microsoft's earnings were going to exceed expectations, then the investor could make extraordinary profits by buying the stock. For the strategy to work in general, however, the investor would have to be correct more than 50% of the time. Unfortunately, a vast academic literature indicates that virtually all investors who have such self-confidence are simply deluding themselves. Furthermore, what holds true for individual stocks is even more true for the market. Although an individual investor may have truly superior information about a company, particularly if he or she works there, it is hard to imagine how an individual could have better information about the future of the market as a whole than the professional investment community[2]—but that is what is required to beat the market. It is the average viewpoint of the professional investment community that determines the level of stock prices. Consequently, the best advice that can be given to someone who believes that he or she can forecast short-run fluctuations in the market is a reminder regarding the Socratic virtues of self-knowledge and humility. To paraphrase economist John Kenneth Galbraith's statement regarding the future of interest rates, "When it comes to the stock market, there are two kinds of investors. Those who don't know where the market is going and those who don't know that they don't know where the market is going."

The foregoing might be interpreted as implying that movements in the market are entirely random. Stock prices are equally likely to rise or fall. However, such a conclusion is incorrect, as another thought experiment illustrates. Suppose that stock prices were equally likely to rise or fall by equal amounts. In that case, the expected investment return on stock (ignoring dividends for the time being) would be zero. With an expected return of zero, no one would buy stock. Risk-free treasury securities are available promising returns typically in the range of 5% to 10%. For investors to be willing to bear the risk associated with owning stock, the expected returns would at least have to equal the returns promised by treasury securities. This means that on average over the long run, stock prices must be expected to rise.

Putting the previous two lines of thought together produces a useful working model of how stock prices move. One component of the movement of stock prices is a slow upward drift necessary to compensate investors for the risk associated with holding stock. Superimposed on this underlying drift is a large amount of unpredictable random noise. A mental image consistent with this is a river with a slow current but many swirls and eddies. If you toss a leaf into the river and watch it for a minute or two, its movements will be dominated by the swirls and eddies. If you

---

[2] Although an individual may possess superior information about a company where he or she works, the individual can run afoul of insider trading regulations by trading on that information.

watch the leaf for an hour, the current will be the main determinant of its course. The same is true of stock prices. Over the short term, time intervals of 1 month or less, the random noise is predominant and stock price movements are virtually unpredictable. Over longer time intervals, however, the random ups and downs tend to cancel out one another and the upward drift becomes relatively more important. Over very long intervals of 20 years or more, the drift becomes predominant. For instance, there is no 20 year period in U.S. history during which stock prices have declined, even the 20 year period beginning in September 1929.

The problem with the popular writing on the stock market is that it all too often focuses on the unpredictable short-run eddies and swirls. The hope, of course, is to predict those random fluctuations, particularly the sharp moves, and make a quick killing. The drawback is that there is no way that this can be reliably done. Consequently, the real key to understanding the stock market and making wise long-term investment decisions is to study the factors that affect the drift. That is the focus of this book.

At first blush, it might seem that this task is trivial. If there is a long-term drift, then it could be estimated by averaging returns provided by stocks over extended periods of time. The problem with that simple approach is that the drift itself can change over time. In fact, much of this book focuses on the question of whether the drift has changed and what it means for the level of stock prices, investment management, and corporate finance. Nonetheless, for understanding what is meant by the equity risk premium and why it is so important for interpreting long-run movements in stock prices, there is no better place to start than with a brief overview of the historical record.

An Introduction to Stock-Market History

An analysis of the historical performance of the American stock market first requires answering two questions: What is meant by *the market*? How should performance be measured?

Ideally, the market should be defined to include all stocks that exist at the beginning of each performance measurement point. For example, if annual data are used to assess market performance, then the market index should include all companies that exist at the beginning of each year. This is not a practical solution. For many small companies, adequate data are not available, particularly in earlier years. Fortunately, this does not make a big difference because most of the value of the American market is accounted for by the 500 hundred largest companies. Therefore, indexes that include 500 or so major stocks provide a valid indicator of the performance of the market as a whole.

Stock-Market Indexes

The most famous stock-market index is the Dow Jones Industrial Average (DJIA), often called the Dow. Despite its fame, however, the DJIA is not a good index to use for assessing market performance. First, the number of companies is too small and the index is not representative. The DJIA includes just 30 large, well-established companies. Adding more companies, particularly newer and smaller companies, would make the index more representative of the overall market. Second, the DJIA is a price-weighted average. Price-weighted indexes are computed by summing the prices of the constituent stocks and dividing by the adjusted number of stocks in the sample. Adjustments to the divisor are required to take account of stock splits and stock dividends.[3] The problem with price-weighted indexes is that

---

[3] As of December 31, 1997, the Dow Jones Industrial Average (DJIA) was computed by adding the prices of the 30 stocks in the index and dividing by 0.25. The divisor is much less than 30 because of adjustments made to take account of stock splits and changes in the sample of companies. Each time a stock splits, the divisor is lowered so that the DJIA is not affected by the split.

movements in the index are not equal to the returns that investors would earn if they bought and held the stocks in the index. This makes price-weighted indexes less than ideal for assessing investment performance.

Because of the foregoing deficiencies, the DJIA is rarely used in scientific studies of the stock market. The two indexes that are most commonly used to measure market performance are the Center for Research in Securities Prices (CRSP) value-weighted index and Standard & Poor's S&P 500 value-weighted index. The term *value weighted* means that each company in the index receives a weight proportional to the market value of its equity. Value-weighted indexes have the useful property of tracking the performance of a buy-and-hold investment in the underlying stocks.

A simple example illustrates the difference between price- and value-weighted indexes. Suppose, as shown in Table 1.1, company A has a price of $20 per share and has 1,000 shares outstanding on day 1. Company B has a price of $80 and 500 shares outstanding. Consequently, the value of the market portfolio is $60,000 on day 1. The next day, the price of company A rises to $25 and the price of company B falls to $70. As the table shows, this has no impact on the value of the market portfolio, which remains at

Table 1.1. Price- and Value-Weighted Indexes

	Day 1			Day 2		
	Price ($)	Shares Outstanding	Value ($)	Price ($)	Shares Outstanding	Value ($)
Company A	20	1,000	20,000	25	1,000	25,000
Company B	80	500	40,000	70	500	35,000
Totals	100		60,000	95		60,000
Price-weighted index	50			47.5		
Value-weighted index	50			50		

$60,000. By definition, it also has no impact on the value-weighted index. Computation of a value-weighted index starts with a given basis value. Here, it is defined to be 50 on day 1. (For the S&P 500, the starting basis value was 10.) Future values of the index are then computed by calculating the value of the constituent stocks on the day in question (price times shares outstanding) and dividing by the value of the same stocks at the starting date. This makes it clear that changes in the index are exactly proportional to changes in the value of the underlying portfolio of stocks. In addition, the calculation procedure eliminates any need to adjust for stock splits because the change in price and change in shares outstanding associated with a split automatically offset each other.

Table 1.1 shows that unlike the value-weighted index, which by definition remains unchanged at 50 on day 2, the price-weighted index drops from 50 to 47.5, a 5% decline. That artificial drop is related to the fact that the less expensive stock is given too small a weight in the index relative to the number of shares outstanding. As a result, the index fails to track the value of the underlying portfolio.

Of the CRSP and the S&P indexes, the CRSP is more comprehensive because it contains all stocks listed on the New York Stock Exchange (NYSE) and the American Stock Exchange (ASE). However, the S&P 500 is much more well known outside academic circles. For that reason, the S&P 500 index is used as a proxy for the market throughout this book. Because both indexes are dominated by the same large firms, this choice does not make much difference.[4] The results presented in this book would be largely indistinguishable if the CRSP index were substituted for the S&P 500.

---

[4] Between 1962 and 1998, the 500 stocks in the Standard & Poor's (S&P) 500 Index have accounted from somewhere between 80% and 95% of the value of the stocks in the more comprehensive Center for Research in Securities Prices (CRSP) index.

Using Investor Returns to Assess
Stock-Market Performance

The basic metrics for assessing stock-market performance are investor returns, which are defined as the percentage change in wealth that results from holding a given investment over a given interval. Most commonly, returns are measured historically, or ex-post, to use economic terminology. In that case, the units of measurement are holding-period returns.

Holding-period returns can be calculated over any time interval ("the period"), but the most common choices are 1 day, 1 month, and 1 year. The holding-period return is defined by the formula

$$\text{Holding Period Return (HPR)} = \frac{(P_1 - P_0 + D)}{P_0} \qquad (1.1)$$

For example, in the case of monthly data, P_0 is the price (or level of the index) at the beginning of the month, P_1 is the price at the end of the month, and D is any dividends received during the month.[5] From Equation 1.1 it is clear that the holding-period return equals the percent change in an investor's wealth that results from holding the stock or index over the prescribed interval (in this case, 1 month).

Returns can also be defined in a forward-looking, or ex-ante, sense. Future holding-period returns are conceptually trickier because they are random variables. Consider, for instance, next period's holding-period return as of time t, HPR_{t+1}. At time t, this future return is unknown. However, it is still possible to speak of

---

[5] When data for longer than 1 day are used to calculate holding period, the compounded return depends on when during the interval the dividend is received. Stock price databases like the one maintained by the Center for Research in Securities Prices (CRSP) credit the dividend on the ex-dividend date. The dividend is then assumed to be reinvested in the underlying stock or index.

the expectation of that return, $E_t(HPR_{t+1})$, where the expectation reflects the information available to the market at time t. The goal of most financial models, including the one used in this book, is to develop reasonable measures of future expected returns.

Ex-ante expected returns can be measured over any horizon. For a variety of purposes, including making long-run investment decisions, it is particularly important to estimate expected future returns over the long run. As is evident throughout this book, this long-run expected return is intimately related to the level of stock prices through the fundamental valuation equation:

$$P = \frac{Div_1}{1+k} + \frac{Div_2}{(1+k)^2} + \frac{Div_3}{(1+k)^3} + \ldots \qquad (1.2)$$

Equation 1.2 states the value of an individual stock or portfolio of stocks equals the present value of the expected stream of future dividends the investment is expected to provide (Div_1, Div_2, etc.), discounted at the relevant cost of capital. However, finance theory teaches that the cost of capital equals the return that investors require (and therefore expect) to earn from holding the investment. Consequently, when Equation 1.2 is applied to the S&P 500, the discount rate is the long-run average expected return on the market.

Equation 1.2 can be employed to illustrate the relation between ex-ante and ex-post returns. To see how, first assume that market conditions are static so that neither expected future dividends nor the discount rate is changing over time. Applying the fundamental valuation equation at both times $t = 0$ and $t = 1$ gives

$$P_0 = \frac{Div_1}{1+k} + \frac{Div_2}{(1+k)^2} + \frac{Div_3}{(1+k)^3} + \ldots \qquad (1.3)$$

$$P_1 = \frac{Div_2}{1+k} + \frac{Div_3}{(1+k)^2} + \frac{Div_4}{(1+k)^3} + \ldots \qquad (1.4)$$

Multiplying Equation 1.3 by *1 + k* and subtracting Equation 1.4 yields

$$(P_0[1 + k]) - P_1 = Div_1 \qquad (1.5)$$

Solving for *k* gives

$$k = \frac{(P_1 - P_0 + Div_1)}{P_0} \qquad (1.6)$$

Equation 1.6 shows that *k* is exactly equal to the holding-period return. This proves that in a static market, the holding-period return always equals the long-run expected return.

Of course, markets are not static. Nonetheless, the basic valuation equation is helpful. Actual holding-period returns will fail to equal *k* when changes in expected dividends or the discount rate imply that Equation 1.5 is no longer true. That is, the expected future dividends and discount rate that go into Equation 1.4 are not equal to those that go into Equation 1.3 because conditions have changed. The new price, P_1, reflects the changed condition, but the old price, P_0, does not. For instance, assume that between periods 0 and 1 a war erupts in the Middle East that causes investors to reduce their expectations for future dividends across the board. In that case, P_1 will be significantly less than *(P_0[1 + k]) – Div_1*. As a result, the holding-period return will be less than *k* (and most likely negative).

The example generalizes directly. Next period's holding-period return will be less than *k* if one of two things happen: (1) investors revise downward their expectations of future dividends or (2) investors increase the expected return that they require for holding common stock. Similarly, next period's holding-period return will be greater than *k* if investors increase their expectations regarding future dividends or decrease the expected return they require for holding stocks.

The fact that stock returns jump around so much is testament to the fact that people are constantly changing their expectations.

To an extent, this is not surprising. Each day, markets around the globe are besieged by new information. As information arrives, minds change and stock prices adjust. Of course, some have argued that prices move too much to be justified by information arrival alone.[6] At this juncture in the book, however, it is too early to address that question. What makes the debate so tricky is that stock values depend on the present value of expectations far into the future. Consequently, events that have little current impact can have a major effect on stock prices if they alter investor expectations regarding future developments.

An Overview of Market Performance: Annual Holding-Period Returns

The starting point for any analysis of the stock market is an examination of ex-post holding-period returns on stock and competing classes of financial assets. Although a discussion of the more subtle statistical issues related to evaluating the historical record is postponed until Chapter 2, it is difficult to go further here without presenting the basic data. In that regard, Table 1.2 presents annual holding-period data for four classes of assets that are central to analyzing the performance of the stock market: stocks (as measured by the S&P 500), long-term government bonds (as measured by the Ibbotson Associates[7] long-term treasury bond index), short-term treasury bills (as measured by the Ibbotson Associates treasury bill index), and consumer goods (as measured by the Consumer Price Index [CPI]). The complete monthly data set that is employed in subsequent analyses is presented in Appendix 2.1. The Ibbotson short-term treasury bill index is based on bills with a maturity of 1 month, and the long-term treasury bond

---

[6] See, for example, French and Roll (1986) and Shiller (1981).

[7] The Ibbotson indexes are taken from Ibbotson Associates (1998). They are the most widely used indexes for recording the performance of long-term government bonds and short-term government bills.

Table 1.2. Annual Returns on Stocks, Bonds, Bills, and Inflation

Year	S&P 500 Return (%)	20-Year Treasury Bond Return (%)	1-Month Treasury Bill Return (%)	Inflation (%)	Stock Path of Wealth (%)	Bond Path of Wealth (%)	Bill Path of Wealth (%)	Inflation Path of Wealth (%)	Bond Premium (%)	Bill Premium (%)
					1.00	1.00	1.00	1.00		
1926	11.61	7.77	3.27	-1.49	1.12	1.08	1.03	0.99	3.84	8.34
1927	37.48	8.94	3.13	-2.09	1.53	1.17	1.07	0.96	28.54	34.35
1928	43.61	0.08	3.23	-0.96	2.20	1.17	1.10	0.96	43.53	40.38
1929	-8.41	3.42	4.74	0.21	2.02	1.22	1.15	0.96	-11.83	-13.15
1930	-24.90	4.65	2.43	-6.03	1.52	1.27	1.18	0.90	-29.55	-27.33
1931	-43.35	-5.32	1.09	-9.52	0.86	1.20	1.19	0.81	-38.03	-44.44
1932	-8.20	16.84	0.95	-10.30	0.79	1.41	1.20	0.73	-25.04	-9.15
1933	53.97	-0.07	0.30	0.51	1.21	1.41	1.21	0.73	54.04	53.67
1934	-1.43	10.02	0.18	2.03	1.20	1.55	1.21	0.75	-11.45	-1.61
1935	47.66	5.00	0.14	3.00	1.77	1.62	1.21	0.77	42.66	47.52
1936	33.92	7.50	0.19	1.21	2.37	1.75	1.21	0.78	26.42	33.73
1937	-35.02	0.22	0.29	3.10	1.54	1.75	1.22	0.80	-35.24	-35.31
1938	31.14	5.51	-0.04	-2.78	2.02	1.85	1.22	0.78	25.63	31.18
1939	-0.42	5.95	0.01	-0.48	2.01	1.96	1.22	0.78	-6.37	-0.43

13

Table 1.2. (Continued)

Year	S&P 500 Return (%)	20-Year Treasury Bond Return (%)	1-Month Treasury Bill Return (%)	Inflation (%)	Stock Path of Wealth (%)	Bond Path of Wealth (%)	Bill Path of Wealth (%)	Inflation Path of Wealth (%)	Bond Premium (%)	Bill Premium (%)
1940	-9.78	6.09	-0.02	0.96	1.81	2.07	1.22	0.79	-15.87	-9.76
1941	-11.58	0.93	0.04	9.72	1.60	2.09	1.22	0.85	-12.51	-11.62
1942	20.33	3.22	0.28	9.30	1.93	2.16	1.22	0.94	17.11	20.05
1943	25.91	2.07	0.35	3.18	2.43	2.21	1.22	0.97	23.84	25.56
1944	19.73	2.82	0.33	2.12	2.90	2.27	1.23	0.99	16.91	19.40
1945	36.41	10.73	0.32	2.25	3.96	2.51	1.23	1.02	25.68	36.09
1946	-8.07	-0.09	0.36	18.16	3.64	2.51	1.24	1.20	-7.98	-8.43
1947	5.70	-2.63	0.50	9.01	3.85	2.44	1.24	1.31	8.33	5.20
1948	5.51	3.38	0.81	2.71	4.06	2.53	1.25	1.34	2.13	4.70
1949	18.79	6.44	1.12	-1.81	4.83	2.69	1.27	1.32	12.35	17.67
1950	31.74	0.05	1.22	5.79	6.36	2.69	1.28	1.40	31.69	30.52
1951	24.02	-3.94	1.49	5.87	7.88	2.58	1.30	1.48	27.96	22.53
1952	18.35	1.16	1.65	0.89	9.33	2.61	1.32	1.49	17.19	16.70
1953	-0.98	3.63	1.83	0.64	9.24	2.71	1.35	1.50	-4.61	-2.81
1954	52.62	7.18	0.86	-0.50	14.10	2.90	1.36	1.49	45.44	51.76

14

1955	31.54	-1.28	1.57	0.36	18.55	2.87	1.38	1.50	32.82	29.97
1956	6.56	-5.58	2.47	2.86	19.77	2.71	1.41	1.54	12.14	4.09
1957	-10.79	7.47	3.15	3.02	17.63	2.91	1.46	1.59	-18.26	-13.94
1958	43.37	-6.11	1.53	1.77	25.28	2.73	1.48	1.62	49.48	41.84
1959	11.98	-2.28	2.97	1.51	28.31	2.67	1.53	1.64	14.26	9.01
1960	0.46	13.79	2.67	1.48	28.44	3.04	1.57	1.66	-13.33	-2.21
1961	26.89	0.96	2.12	0.67	36.09	3.07	1.60	1.68	25.93	24.77
1962	-8.73	6.88	2.72	1.21	32.94	3.28	1.64	1.70	-15.61	-11.45
1963	22.78	1.21	3.11	1.66	40.44	3.32	1.69	1.72	21.57	19.67
1964	16.51	3.51	3.53	1.21	47.12	3.43	1.75	1.74	13.00	12.98
1965	12.45	0.70	3.92	1.93	52.98	3.46	1.82	1.78	11.75	8.53
1966	-10.05	3.64	4.75	3.35	47.66	3.58	1.91	1.84	-13.69	-14.80
1967	23.99	-9.19	4.20	3.04	59.09	3.25	1.99	1.89	33.18	19.79
1968	11.08	-0.26	5.22	4.72	65.64	3.25	2.09	1.98	11.34	5.86
1969	-8.49	-5.07	6.57	6.10	60.07	3.08	2.23	2.10	-3.42	-15.06
1970	4.03	12.10	6.52	5.48	62.49	3.45	2.38	2.22	-8.07	-2.49
1971	14.32	13.24	4.39	3.36	71.44	3.91	2.48	2.29	1.08	9.93
1972	18.98	5.67	3.84	3.42	85.00	4.13	2.58	2.37	13.31	15.14
1973	-14.67	-1.10	6.93	8.78	72.53	4.09	2.75	2.58	-13.57	-21.60
1974	-26.46	4.35	8.01	12.20	53.34	4.26	2.97	2.90	-30.81	-34.47
1975	37.21	9.19	5.80	7.01	73.18	4.66	3.15	3.10	28.02	31.41
1976	23.85	16.76	5.08	4.82	90.64	5.44	3.31	3.25	7.09	18.77

(continues)

Table 1.2. (Continued)

Year	S&P 500 Return (%)	20-Year Treasury Bond Return (%)	1-Month Treasury Bill Return (%)	Inflation (%)	Stock Path of Wealth (%)	Bond Path of Wealth (%)	Bill Path of Wealth (%)	Inflation Path of Wealth (%)	Bond Premium (%)	Bill Premium (%)
1977	-7.18	-0.65	5.13	6.77	84.13	5.40	3.48	3.47	-6.53	-12.31
1978	6.57	-1.18	7.20	9.03	89.66	5.34	3.73	3.78	7.75	-0.63
1979	18.42	-1.21	10.38	13.32	106.17	5.27	4.11	4.28	19.63	8.04
1980	32.41	-3.96	11.26	12.41	140.58	5.06	4.58	4.82	36.37	21.15
1981	-4.91	1.86	14.72	8.94	133.68	5.16	5.25	5.25	-6.77	-19.63
1982	21.41	40.37	10.53	3.87	162.30	7.24	5.80	5.45	-18.96	10.88
1983	22.51	0.69	8.80	3.80	198.83	7.29	6.31	5.66	21.82	13.71
1984	6.27	15.54	9.78	4.02	211.30	8.42	6.93	5.88	-9.27	-3.51
1985	32.17	30.96	7.73	3.77	279.28	11.03	7.47	6.11	1.21	24.44
1986	18.47	24.45	6.15	1.14	330.86	13.73	7.93	6.18	-5.98	12.32
1987	5.23	-2.70	5.46	4.41	348.16	13.36	8.36	6.45	7.93	-0.23
1988	16.81	9.68	6.36	4.42	406.69	14.65	8.89	6.73	7.13	10.45
1989	31.49	18.10	8.38	4.64	534.75	17.31	9.64	7.05	13.39	23.11
1990	-3.17	6.20	7.82	6.10	517.80	18.38	10.39	7.48	-9.37	-10.99
1991	30.55	19.26	5.60	3.07	675.99	21.92	10.97	7.71	11.29	24.95

1992	7.67	9.41	3.51	3.03	727.84	23.98	11.36	7.94	-1.74	4.16
1993	9.99	18.24	2.90	2.75	800.55	28.35	11.69	8.16	-8.25	7.09
1994	1.31	-7.78	3.91	2.67	811.04	26.15	12.14	8.37	9.09	-2.60
1995	37.43	31.67	5.60	2.67	1,114.61	34.43	12.82	8.60	5.76	31.83
1996	23.07	-0.92	5.20	3.33	1,371.75	34.11	13.49	8.88	23.99	17.87
1997	33.37	15.87	5.25	1.70	1,829.50	39.53	14.20	9.04	17.50	28.12
1926–1997										
Average	13.0	5.6	3.8	3.2	11.0%	5.2%	3.8%	3.1%	7.4	9.2
SD	20.3	9.2	3.2	4.5					20.6	20.7
SD of mean	2.4	1.1	0.4	0.5					2.4	2.4
1946–1997										
Average	13.7	5.9	4.9	4.4	12.7%	5.4%	4.8%	4.0%	7.8	8.9
SD	16.5	10.5	3.1	3.8					19.2	19.0
SD of mean	2.3	1.5	0.4	0.5					2.7	2.6

SD = standard deviation; S&P = Standard & Poor's.

index is based on bonds with an average maturity of 20 years.[8]
The data run from the beginning of 1926 through the end of
1997. The starting point reflects the beginning of the database on
which most studies of market behavior are based.

In Table 1.2, the averages for the entire 72-year sample period,
which are reported under each series, are standard arithmetic averages. The average return on common stock is 13% per year. This
represents a premium of 9.2 percentage points per year over the
average return on short-term treasury bills (3.8%) and a premium
of 7.4 percentage points over the average return on long-term
treasury bonds (5.6%). It also exceeds the average rate of inflation
by almost 10 percentage points. Over the postwar period since
1946, the results are largely similar. The average return for the
S&P 500 is 13.7%. This exceeds the inflation rate by 9.3% and
represents a premium of 8.8 percentage points above the average
return on treasury bills (4.9%) and 7.8 percentage points above
the average return on treasury bonds (5.9%).

The Equity Risk Premium

Definition

The difference between the return on common stock and the return on government securities is what is called the equity risk premium. Although the equity risk premium can be measured with
respect to any treasury security, in practice only two securities are
used. The first is short-term treasury bills, which are a popular
choice for assessing risk premiums because they are the closest
thing there is to a risk-free security. The most common bill selected is the 1-month treasury bill because returns on the 1-month

---

[8] The 20-year maturity period is used so that the series can be constructed
back to 1926. The government did not start issuing bonds with a maturity of
more than 20 years until the 1960s.

bill are included in the Ibbotson data. The second choice is long-term treasury bonds. Because the treasury did not start issuing 30-year bonds until 1968, 20-year bonds typically are used to calculate equity risk premiums. As is discussed in detail later in this chapter, this raises some questions because 20-year treasury bonds, although free from default, are not risk-free securities. Over the short term, the prices of long-term bonds can vary quite widely because of changes in interest rates. Over longer periods of time, the value of the payouts on 20-year bonds varies because of unpredictable changes in inflation.

Like stock returns, the equity risk premium is defined in both a historical, or ex-post, sense and a forward-looking, or ex-ante, sense. The ex-post premium is calculated as the difference between the historical average return on common stocks and the average returns on the two treasury securities. The ex-post premium can be calculated over a variety of historical periods using a variety of observation intervals. Unfortunately, as Chapter 2 demonstrates, the estimate of the premium changes significantly when the sample period is altered. The ex-ante premium is the big question mark. Assessing the extent to which common stocks can be expected to outperform treasury securities in the years ahead is the central goal of this book.

Importance

To assess the economic importance of the equity risk premium, Table 1.2 presents data on the path of wealth (POW) for the four asset classes. The POW measures the growth of a dollar invested in any given asset, assuming that all proceeds are reinvested in the same asset. One of the prime reasons for studying the equity risk premium is the dramatic difference between the POWs for the competing asset classes. The table shows that the cost of purchasing the bundle of goods that comprise the CPI rose by a factor of 9.04 over the period. Goods that cost $1 at the end of 1925 cost $9.04 at the end of 1997. Nonetheless, all of the investments outperformed inflation.

One dollar invested in treasury bills grew to $14.20 and $1 invested in treasury bonds grew to $39.53. The stunning fact, however, is that $1 invested in the S&P 500 grew to $1,829.

Beneath the POWs are the average rates of growth in investor wealth over the 72-year period, or geometric averages. Notice that the geometric averages are less than the arithmetic averages, particularly for common stock. The reason for this, and the relation between arithmetic and geometric averages, is explored in Chapter 2. Even in the case of geometric averages, however, stocks markedly outperform the other asset classes. The geometric average return for stocks is 11%, compared with 3.2% for bills and 5.8% for bonds.

As an illustration of how important the equity risk premium is for long-run capital appreciation, the POWs are also presented graphically in Figure 1.1. Figure 1.1A presents a logarithmic plot of the POWs for the four asset classes and Figure 1.1B presents a standard linear plot. A glance at Figure 1.1B clearly illustrates why the logarithmic plot is generally presented in financial texts. The increase in wealth produced by investment in stock is so great that when a linear plot is employed, the lines for treasury bills, treasury bonds, and inflation become invisible.

Using the Historical Data to Estimate Future Stock-Market Performance

To return to the question at hand, how can the historical data be used to estimate the long-run returns that can be expected in the future? As mentioned at the outset of this chapter, one possibility is to extrapolate historical averages. For instance, Table 1.2 shows that over the 72-year sample period, the average returns on stocks was 13.0%. If the past is indicative of the future, it follows that investors can expect to earn about 13% on stock going forward.

Unfortunately, this direct approach has two basic flaws. The first and most important drawback is that it fails to take account of inflation. Numerous academic studies have shown that financial

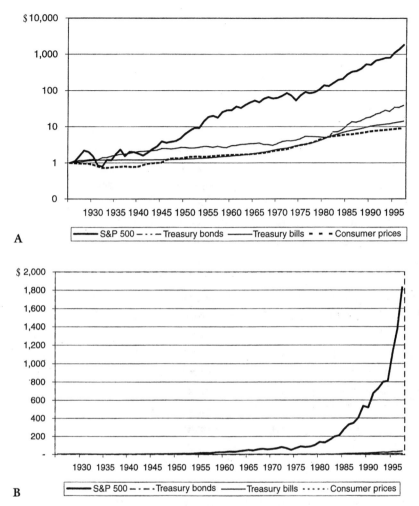

Figure 1.1. The path of wealth from the investment of $1, 1926–1997: **(A)** logarithmic plot; **(B)** standard arithmetic plot. S&P 500 = Standard & Poor's 500 Index.

asset prices reflect expected inflation.[9] This makes perfect sense. To entice an investor to part with his or her funds, an investment must offer the expectation of an increase in purchasing power. For example, assume that when there is no inflation an investor is sat-

[9] See, for example, Fama and Schwert (1977).

isfied with a 3% return on a security. If inflation rises to 10%, the investor has to earn 13% on the security to achieve the same increase in purchasing power.[10] Consequently, the returns that investors require (and expect) on their investments rise and fall with the rate of inflation. During the 72-year history reflected in Table 1.2, there have been periods of deflation (the early 1930s) and periods of relatively high inflation (the late 1970s). Averaging returns from periods with different inflation rates mixes apples and oranges because investors require different ex-ante returns during periods with different inflation rates. Failure to take account of the impact of inflation on expected returns makes the past average a potentially misleading indicator of future expected returns.

A solution to this problem is to use a two-step procedure to take account of inflation. First, the average *real* return is calculated. The real return equals the holding-period return on a security net of inflation. Real returns on stocks, bonds, and bills between 1926 and 1997 are presented in Table 1.3. Arithmetic averages of the returns are shown at the bottom of the columns. Over the full period, the average real return on stocks is 9.8%.

Although the procedure for computing real returns is straightforward, it can lead to a bias. The bias arises because the market prices of common stock at the beginning of each observation interval reflect *expected* inflation over the upcoming interval. However, the actual real return the investors subsequently earns over the observation interval depends on *realized* inflation. As a result, a bias will arise if there is consistent unexpected inflation during the sample period. Fortunately, over long periods of time the errors introduced by not taking account of the difference between actual and expected inflation tend to be canceled out, at least in the case of U.S. data.[11] For instance, unexpected inflation was positive in 1979 but negative in 1982. If it is assumed that the dif-

---

[10] This calculation ignores the impact of taxes.

[11] The fact that the inflation rate in the United States shows no discernible trend over the full 72-year sample period means that the errors must cancel out when averages are computed over the entire period.

ferences between expected and unexpected inflation cancel out over sufficiently long periods of time, the bias disappears and the average return of 9.8% reported in Table 1.3 is a fair estimate of the long-run real return.

Table 1.3. Annual Real Returns on Stocks, Bonds, and Bills

Year	S&P 500 Return (%)	20-Year Treasury Bond Return (%)	1-Month Treasury Bill Return (%)	Stock Path of Wealth (%)	Bond Path of Wealth (%)	Bill Path of Wealth (%)
				1.00	1.00	1.00
1926	13.10	9.26	4.76	1.13	1.09	1.05
1927	39.57	11.03	5.22	1.58	1.21	1.10
1928	44.57	1.04	4.19	2.28	1.23	1.15
1929	−8.62	3.21	4.53	2.09	1.27	1.20
1930	−18.87	10.68	8.46	1.69	1.40	1.30
1931	−33.83	4.20	10.61	1.12	1.46	1.44
1932	2.10	27.14	11.25	1.14	1.85	1.60
1933	53.46	−0.58	−0.21	1.75	1.84	1.60
1934	−3.46	7.99	−1.85	1.69	1.99	1.57
1935	44.66	2.00	−2.86	2.45	2.03	1.52
1936	32.71	6.29	−1.02	3.25	2.16	1.51
1937	−38.12	−2.88	−2.81	2.01	2.10	1.47
1938	33.92	8.29	2.74	2.69	2.27	1.51
1939	0.06	6.43	0.49	2.70	2.42	1.51
1940	−10.74	5.13	−0.98	2.41	2.54	1.50
1941	−21.30	−8.79	−9.68	1.89	2.32	1.35
1942	11.03	−6.08	−9.02	2.10	2.18	1.23
1943	22.73	−1.11	−2.83	2.58	2.15	1.20
1944	17.61	0.70	−1.79	3.03	2.17	1.18
1945	34.16	8.48	−1.93	4.07	2.35	1.15

(continues)

Table 1.3. (Continued)

Year	S&P 500 Return (%)	20-Year Treasury Bond Return (%)	1-Month Treasury Bill Return (%)	Stock Path of Wealth (%)	Bond Path of Wealth (%)	Bill Path of Wealth (%)
1946	−26.23	−18.25	−17.80	3.00	1.92	0.95
1947	−3.31	−11.64	−8.51	2.90	1.70	0.87
1948	2.80	0.67	−1.90	2.99	1.71	0.85
1949	20.60	8.25	2.93	3.60	1.85	0.88
1950	25.95	−5.74	−4.57	4.53	1.74	0.84
1951	18.15	−9.81	−4.38	5.36	1.57	0.80
1952	17.46	0.27	0.76	6.29	1.58	0.80
1953	−1.62	2.99	1.19	6.19	1.62	0.81
1954	53.12	7.68	1.36	9.48	1.75	0.83
1955	31.18	−1.64	1.21	12.44	1.72	0.84
1956	3.70	−8.44	−0.39	12.90	1.58	0.83
1957	−13.81	4.45	0.13	11.12	1.65	0.83
1958	41.60	−7.88	−0.24	15.74	1.52	0.83
1959	10.47	−3.79	1.46	17.39	1.46	0.84
1960	−1.02	12.31	1.19	17.21	1.64	0.85
1961	26.22	0.29	1.45	21.72	1.64	0.87
1962	−9.94	5.67	1.51	19.56	1.74	0.88
1963	21.12	−0.45	1.45	23.69	1.73	0.89
1964	15.30	2.30	2.32	27.32	1.77	0.91
1965	10.52	−1.23	1.99	30.19	1.75	0.93
1966	−13.40	0.29	1.40	26.15	1.75	0.94
1967	20.95	−12.23	1.16	31.63	1.54	0.95
1968	6.36	−4.98	0.50	33.64	1.46	0.96
1969	−14.59	−11.17	0.47	28.73	1.30	0.96
1970	−1.45	6.62	1.04	28.31	1.38	0.97
1971	10.96	9.88	1.03	31.42	1.52	0.98
1972	15.56	2.25	0.42	36.30	1.55	0.99
1973	−23.45	−9.88	−1.85	27.79	1.40	0.97
1974	−38.66	−7.85	−4.19	17.05	1.29	0.93
1975	30.20	2.18	−1.21	22.20	1.32	0.92

(continues)

Table 1.3. (Continued)

Year	S&P 500 Return (%)	20-Year Treasury Bond Return (%)	1-Month Treasury Bill Return (%)	Stock Path of Wealth (%)	Bond Path of Wealth (%)	Bill Path of Wealth (%)
1976	19.03	11.94	0.26	26.42	1.48	0.92
1977	−13.95	−7.42	−1.64	22.73	1.37	0.91
1978	−2.46	−10.21	−1.83	22.17	1.23	0.89
1979	5.10	−14.53	−2.94	23.31	1.05	0.86
1980	20.00	−16.37	−1.15	27.97	0.88	0.85
1981	−13.85	−7.08	5.78	24.09	0.82	0.90
1982	17.54	36.50	6.66	28.32	1.11	0.96
1983	18.71	−3.11	5.00	33.62	1.08	1.01
1984	2.25	11.52	5.76	34.37	1.20	1.07
1985	28.40	27.19	3.96	44.14	1.53	1.11
1986	17.33	23.31	5.01	51.78	1.89	1.17
1987	0.82	−7.11	1.05	52.21	1.75	1.18
1988	12.39	5.26	1.94	58.68	1.84	1.20
1989	26.85	13.46	3.74	74.43	2.09	1.25
1990	−9.27	0.10	1.72	67.53	2.09	1.27
1991	27.48	16.19	2.53	86.09	2.43	1.30
1992	4.64	6.38	0.48	90.09	2.59	1.31
1993	7.24	15.49	0.15	96.61	2.99	1.31
1994	−1.36	−10.45	1.24	95.29	2.68	1.32
1995	34.76	29.00	2.93	128.42	3.45	1.36
1996	19.74	−4.25	1.87	153.77	3.31	1.39
1997	31.67	14.17	3.55	202.47	3.77	1.44
1926–1997						
Average	9.8	2.4	0.6	7.7%	1.9%	0.5%
SD	20.9	10.9	4.3			
SD of mean	2.5	1.3	0.5			
1946–1997						
Average	9.4	1.6	0.5	8.4%	1.3%	0.8%
SD	18.2	11.8	3.8			
SD of mean	2.5	1.6	0.5			

SD = standard deviation; S&P = Standard & Poor's.

Given an estimate of the historical real return, future long-run expected returns can be calculated by adding an estimate of long-run expected inflation. At the beginning of 1998, most economic forecasting firms were predicting that long-run inflation rates would be on the order of 3%. Adding this figure to the 9.8% historical real return gives a future expected return of 12.8%. This estimate is almost identical to the 13% average historical return, without adjustment for inflation, because at the beginning of 1998 the forward-looking inflation rate of 3% was nearly equal to the historical average of 3.2%.

Adjustment for inflation is not sufficient to solve the problem of projecting future returns on the basis of past historical averages. Economic theory teaches that stock returns will vary with the real component of interest rates. (Real interest rates are defined as the return on fixed-income securities net of inflation.) This occurs because stocks compete with fixed-income assets for investor dollars. If the expected real return on a fixed-income asset rises, the expected real return on stocks must also rise by approximately the same amount if equities are to remain competitive. To take account of changes in real interest rates, the same two-step procedure that was used for inflation is employed, but with returns on government securities replacing the rate of inflation. This procedure takes account of variation in both real interest rates and expected inflation because these are the two components that determine the yield on treasury securities.

The first step is to compute the average historical difference between stock returns and the returns on treasury securities—in other words, the historical equity risk premium. The data in Table 1.2 show that on average, between 1926 and 1997, common stocks offered returns that were 9.2 percentage points greater than those offered by treasury bills and 7.4 percentage points greater than those offered by treasury bonds. Compounded over long periods of time, these are huge premiums. That is why $1 invested in common stock has grown so much more rapidly than $1 invested in treasury bills or bonds.

Future expected returns are estimated in the second step by adding the historical risk premium to current yields on government bonds. At the beginning of 1998, the yield on 1-month treasury bills was approximately 4% and the yield on 20-year treasury bonds was about 6%. Adding the respective historical risk premiums to these yields produces expected future returns for common stock of 13.2% and 13.4%, respectively. When this calculation is performed, it is important to use the yield on the same-maturity government security that was used to compute the historical equity premium. It makes no sense, for instance, to add the current treasury bond yield to the historical premium over treasury bills.

As was true for the inflation-adjusted calculation, the two-step procedure produces estimates of future stock returns that are quite close to the simple historical average of 13.0%. This occurs because interest rates on bonds and bills at the start of 1998 were close to the average returns on those securities. Compared with the yields of 4% and 6%, respectively, the average return on bills was 3.8% and the average return on bonds was 5.6% between 1926 and 1997.

A good way to think about the two-step procedure is as follows. Expected returns are the sum of three components: (1) the expected real rate of interest, (2) the expected rate of inflation, and (3) the expected equity risk premium. The first two factors do not have to be forecast because they determine the yield on government securities, which is observable directly. Consequently, forecasting future stock returns amounts to adding an estimate of the future risk premium to the yield on government securities. That is why understanding the risk premium is the key to predicting the long-run future of the equity market.

Uses of the Equity Risk Premium

As the key to estimating long-run stock returns, the equity risk premium plays an important role in a host of financial decisions. The most obvious use of an estimate of the premium is for making asset allocation decisions. A basic decision that every investor must make is how to divide his or her portfolio among stock, fixed-income securities, and other assets. This is commonly referred to as the asset allocation problem. The fundamental data on which this decision is based are estimates of the relative risks and expected returns for the competing asset classes. In the case of stock and fixed-income securities, the relative return is precisely the equity risk premium.

Aside from playing a central role in asset allocation, the equity risk premium is also a critical input into planning decisions for pension funds and retirees. Planning for retirement necessitates approximating the funds that will be available in the future. This requires estimates of the returns on investments. For fixed-income securities, the calculation is straightforward because the yields are known. For equities, however, it requires an estimate of the market risk premium. In the case of fixed-benefit plans, the burden of estimating the equity risk premium switches from the retiree to the company. Funding requirements for fixed-benefit plans depend on the assumptions made regarding investments returns. Those assumptions, in turn, depend on the equity risk premium.

On a different front, the equity risk premium plays an important role in corporate investment decision making. Finance theory teaches that a company should undertake all projects that have a positive net present value. The calculation of present value depends on the firm's opportunity cost of capital, which serves as the discount rate. The opportunity cost of capital, in turn, is greatly influenced by the cost of equity. Modern asset pricing models, such as the capital asset pricing model (CAPM), employ a two-step procedure for estimating the cost of equity. First, the cost of equity is estimated for the market as a whole. Because *cost of equity for the market* is a synonym for *expected return on the market,* that is determined by a forecast of the equity risk premium.

Second, the marketwide cost of equity is adjusted to take account of the risk of the company's equity relative to the risk of stocks generally. Although deciding how the adjustment should be made has been the focus of a great deal of attention in the finance literature, the expected return on the market is perhaps an even more important determinant of the discount rate. In this fashion, the equity risk premium determines in part what investments projects are undertaken in the economy.[12]

Finally, the equity risk premium is a critical determinant of the level of stock prices. Because the equity risk premium determines the expected return on common stock generally, by definition it determines the rate at which investors discount cash payouts on the market portfolio.[13] If the equity risk premium falls, the discount rate falls and the level of stock prices rises. As we shall see, one of the commonly offered explanations for the rise of stock prices in the 1990s is a decline in the equity risk premium.

Inflation and Asset Returns

As noted previously, inflation is not considered explicitly when using the equity risk premium to forecast long-run future stock returns because it is already included in the interest rates that go into the calculation. Nonetheless, the role of inflation is central to understanding many arguments regarding the behavior of the

---

[12] In a controversial article, Porter (1992) argued that one reason America "fell behind" Japan and Germany economically during the 1980s was because the cost of equity capital was higher in the United States. In light of developments in the 1990s, however, that argument had not received much attention at the end of the 1990s.

[13] In equilibrium, the return that investors expect and the return that they require must be the same. If expected and required returns on an asset were not equal, investors would attempt to increase or decrease their holdings of that asset. Because investors as a group cannot increase or decrease their holdings, the price of that asset rises or falls until expected returns and required returns are equal. The returns that investors require to invest in a particular asset is the opportunity cost of capital and therefore the discount rate for that asset.

stock market and possible variation in the risk premium. At the outset, therefore, it is helpful to explain the relation between asset prices and inflation in a little greater depth.

From an investment perspective, the best way to think about inflation is as an externally controlled policy variable that affects the purchasing power of money. As an analogy, assume that governmental actions had the ability to affect the value of the inch and that as a result of current policies the inch was shrinking. The shrinkage would play havoc with the system of measurement. As the inch shrunk, everything would appear to be getting bigger. Pieces of lumber that began as $2'' \times 4''$ would eventually become $5'' \times 10''$. To avoid the confusion caused by the shrinking of the inch, architects, designers, and engineers would probably invent the concepts of normal "nominal" inches and "real" inches, the latter of which are immune from the ravages of distance inflation. One way to do this would be to pick a base year—say, 1990—and use it as the definition of the real inch. Real distances would be measured in terms of 1990 inches, whereas nominal distances would be stated in terms of normal current inches.

Although the foregoing example may seem farfetched, it describes perfectly what is happening in the case of the U.S. measure of purchasing power, the dollar. Actions by the government—specifically, expansionary monetary policy—cause the value of the dollar, measured in terms of goods and services, to shrink. As a result, the price of everything in terms of dollars tends to rise. The rate at which the dollar is shrinking is called the rate of inflation. It is measured by the average rate of increase in prices generally. The government tracks a number of indexes designed to estimate the average rate of increases in prices. Of these, the CPI calculated by the Bureau of Labor Statistics is by far the most widely followed.

To adjust for the shrinkage, economists have invented the term *real,* or inflation-adjusted, *dollars.* Normal dollars, unadjusted for inflation, are referred to as nominal dollars. As an illustration of the distinction, consider the price of gas. Between 1965 and 1997, $1 of regular gasoline rose in price from approximately $0.32 to $1.28, an increase of 400% in terms of nominal dollars.

However, over the same period of time, the CPI increased 508%. As a result, the real price of gasoline, in 1965 dollars, fell from $0.32 to $0.263.[14]

When investors invest, their goal is to increase future consumption. Consequently, the success of an investment is measured not in nominal dollars but real dollars. Put another way, investors are concerned with real returns, defined as the percent increase in purchasing power, not nominal returns.

As a result of investor concern with real returns, expected inflation is reflected in asset prices. The clearest example is the case of interest rates presented earlier. For an investor to expect to maintain a constant real return of 3%, the nominal return on the security must be set to equal 3% plus the expected rate of inflation over the life in the security.[15] Under these circumstances, the 3% is referred to as the ex-ante, or expected, real return. This is distinguished from the ex-post, or actual, real return, which equals the difference between the nominal yield and the actual rate of inflation. For instance, suppose that an investor purchases a security with a 13% nominal yield, reflecting a 3% expected real return and expected inflation of 10%. If the rate of inflation over the life of the security turns out to be 5%, the ex-post real rate would be 8%. The example makes it clear that the difference between the ex-ante real return and the ex-post real return equals the difference between expected and actual inflation. On a period-to-period basis, this difference will be large if there is significant unexpected inflation. By the end of the period, however, investors adjust their expectations to take account of the new inflationary environment. On average over many periods, this adjustment means that actual and expected inflation tend to move together.

---

[14] The real price is computed using the following formula: *Real Price = Nominal Price/(1 + Percent Inflation)*. In this case, the real price equals *$1.28/(6.08) = $0.263.*

[15] The situation becomes more complicated when taxes are considered. Nonetheless, empirical work by Fama (1975) indicated that expected inflation is reflected on a one-to-one basis in asset prices.

Although the impact of expected inflation is most easily analyzed in the case of fixed-income securities, the same effect operates for all financial assets. To ensure the relative constancy of real returns, investors build a premium equal to the expected rate of inflation into the expected returns on financial assets. This inflation premium is immediately observable in the case of fixed-income securities, whose yields are observable. In the case of equities, however, this effect is difficult to observe for two reasons. First, there is no promised yield on equities analogous to the yield on a fixed-income security. Second, equity holding-period returns are so variable, for reasons other than inflation, that changes caused by variation in expected inflation are hidden in the noise. Nonetheless, financial economists universally accept the proposition that the expected returns on equity rise and fall with expected inflation.

In some cases, distinguishing between real and nominal magnitudes is not important. For instance, when the risk premium is calculated, expected inflation cancels out because it is included in both the interest rate and the expected return on equity. There is one case, however, in which the impact of inflation is paramount: determining the risk and real return of long-term fixed-income securities. Consider, for instance, a newly issued 30-year treasury bond. Assume that the nominal yield is 6%, reflecting an expected real return of 2% and expected inflation of 4% over the 30-year horizon. The actual real return that will be earned on the security, if it is held for 30 years, depends on the relation between the actual inflation rate and the expected rate of 4%. Over the course of 30 years, actual inflation may diverge significantly from the expected rate of 4%. If, for example, inflation accelerates to 10% or more, the ex-post real return on the treasury bond will be significantly negative. If, however, inflation jumps to 100% or more, as has happened on numerous occasions throughout the globe, the value of the investment will be largely destroyed. Therefore, the primary risk that investors in long-term high-grade fixed-income securities face is that inflation will deviate sharply from its expected value at the time of issuance.

What makes inflation risk particularly dangerous for fixed-income investors is the nature of the inflation process. Many economic variables are constrained by natural forces that limit their variation. For example, real economic growth is largely determined by the growth rate of population and productivity growth. Because neither of these variables has grown in excess of 2% per year for extended durations, periods of abnormal economic growth tend to be self-limiting. In the long run, economic growth reverts to the mean level determined by growth in population and productivity. Inflation, on the other hand, depends on monetary growth, which is a policy variable without physical constraints. Unlike the population, the money supply can grow at 5%, 100%, or 10,000% per year if that is the government's preference.[16] The fact that governments have routinely made the decision to allow such rapid money growth is what makes long-term fixed-income securities risky. That risk, however, is usually not reflected in day-to-day or month-to-month price changes. As long as the government keeps inflation under control, the risk will not be realized. Unfortunately, history has repeatedly taught that political behavior is unpredictable. Inflation remains a sleeping giant that can awaken at any time.

It is the long-run unpredictability of inflation that complicates analysis of the risk–return tradeoff provided by stocks and high-grade bonds. Because stocks represent control over real assets, they offer a long-run hedge against dramatic changes in the inflationary environment.[17] Consequently, it is possible that in the long run stocks are *less* risky than long-term default-free bonds. Whether this is true and what the implications are for the equity risk premiums are issues addressed in later chapters.

---

[16] During the hyperinflations in Europe after World War II, monetary growth rates exceeded 1,000,000% per year.

[17] This should not be interpreted as implying that common stocks are a good hedge against modest, short-run changes in the rate of inflation. In fact, the empirical evidence indicates that for variation in the inflation rate on the order of magnitude of that experienced in the United States, monthly holding-period returns on common stock are negatively correlated with both expected and unexpected inflation. The first study to report this finding was that of Fama and Schwert (1977). This finding has since been confirmed by many others.

The central point to take away from the discussion here is that the distinction between real and nominal returns is critical. Too many financial reporters blithely talk about market returns without making it clear whether the numbers to which they refer are real or nominal. That oversight is a major mistake. Financial market performance cannot be understood without recognition of the effect of inflation. A good habit to develop is to not use the word *return* without specifying whether it is real or nominal. In this book, the following convention is adopted: When real returns are referred to, the word *real* is always included; if there is no modifier, the returns referred to can be assumed to be nominal.

Stock Returns and the Risk Premium: Looking Forward

Of the two treasury securities used to apply the two-step procedure, long-term bonds are the most popular choice. Despite the fact that long-term treasury bonds are not risk free, they are chosen for two reasons. First, their longer duration makes them more comparable to common stocks. Second, the question of ultimate concern to most investors, pension-fund managers, and corporate financial officers is what future stock returns will be over the long run. Estimates of future long-run returns are best achieved by adding an estimate of the long-run future risk premium over bonds to the current treasury bond yield.

The fundamental issue is whether application of the two-step procedure produces an economically justifiable estimate of future stock returns going forward. Applying the two-step procedure as of July 1998 and using the historical estimate of the risk premium gives the following result for future long-run stock returns:

Expected Future Return (as of July 1998) = Long-Term Treasury Yield (5.7%) + Historical Equity Risk Premium (7.4%) = 12.1%

The 12.1% is a nominal estimate of future stock returns. The associated expected real return is given by subtracting the estimate of long-run expected inflation of 3.1%. Can stocks reasonably be expected to produce returns of 9% above the rate of inflation and more than 7% above long-term treasury bonds in the years ahead? In anticipation of what will come, the brief answer is no. It is highly likely that stocks will not do as well in the future, relative to bonds, as they have done in the past. Investors and corporate finance officers who make decisions based on the assumption that the future will be as rosy as the past are going to be disappointed. This does not mean that equities are a bad investment or that investors should avoid them. It simply means that compared to bonds and inflation, they will not do as well as they have done in the past.

The remainder of this book is designed to illustrate and explain the basis for this pessimistic conclusion. Chapter 2 takes a closer look at the historical record. The goal is to determine why it may or may not be reasonable to extrapolate past averages of the equity risk premium into the future. Chapter 3 examines forward-looking approaches for estimating the equity risk premium. Chapter 4 applies financial economic theory to the problem of determining what the equity risk premium should be if investors behave in the rational fashion assumed by the theory. Chapter 5 analyzes the relation between the equity risk premium and the level of stock prices. In an editorial article published by the *Wall Street Journal* in March 1998, James Glassman and Kevin Hassett of the American Enterprise Institute argued that the dramatic rise in stock prices in the 1990s can be explained by a sharp drop in the equity risk premium (Glassman and Hassett, 1998). The analysis in Chapter 5 makes it possible to assess whether such an argument makes economic sense and, if so, what it implies for the equity risk premium going forward. Finally, Chapter 6 returns to the question of estimating future stock returns, elaborating on the conclusion that the future will not be as rosy as the past and presenting several alternative scenarios.

Chapter 2

Evaluating the Historical Record

Primitive peoples, with no knowledge of modern science, express confidence in the proposition that the sun will rise tomorrow. The reason is that the historical record is unambiguous on this point. Ask whether it will rain tomorrow, though, and doubt arises. Because of random variation in weather, the historical record is a good deal more ambiguous. Rain today does not necessarily mean rain tomorrow.

With respect to the equity premium, the confidence that can be placed in the assumption that the future will be like the past depends on two related characteristics of the historical data: how accurately the historical premium can be measured and the extent to which the measured premium depends on the choice of the sample period. Before those questions can be addressed, however, there is the issue of how the average returns that go into the premium should be computed in the first place.

Computing the Average Premium: Arithmetic versus Geometric

The historical equity risk premium equals the difference between the average return on equities and the average return on treasury securities calculated over a specified time period. It can be seen in Table 1.2, for instance, that over the full sample period between 1926 and 1997, the average return on stocks was 13.0% and the average return on treasury bills was 3.8%, so the equity risk premium over bills was 9.2%. Those are arithmetic averages. They are computed in the standard way: Add up all the annual returns and divide by the numbers of years (in this case, 72).

Although it is familiar, the arithmetic average has a peculiar property. As an illustration, suppose that an investor earns returns of 10%, 20%, −25%, and 15% in 4 consecutive years. The arithmetic average of the four returns is 5%. Now consider an investor who starts with $100. If he or she earns 10%, 20%, −25%, and 15% in each of 4 years, his or her ending wealth will be $113.85. However, if that investor earns 5% per year for 4 years, he or she will end up with $121.55. This is a general problem. Investors who earn the arithmetic average of a series of returns wind up with more money than investors who earn the series of returns that are being averaged.

The geometric average solves this problem. By definition, the geometric average is the constant return an investor must earn every year to arrive at the same final value that would be produced by a series of variable returns. The geometric average is calculated using the formula

$$\text{Geometric Average} = (\text{Final Value}/\text{Initial Value})^{1/n} - 1$$

where n is the number of periods in the average. When the formula is applied to the preceding example, the results are as follows:

$$\text{Geometric Average} = (113.85/100)^{1/4} - 1 = 3.29\%$$

An investor who earns 3.29% for 4 years will end up with $113.85.

There are four properties of arithmetic and geometric averages that are worth noting:

- The geometric average is always less than or equal to the arithmetic average. For instance, in Table 1.2 the arithmetic average stock return is 13.0%, but the geometric average is only 11.0%. (The geometric averages are reported at the bottom of the path of wealth columns in Table 1.2.)
- The more variable the series of returns, the greater the difference between the arithmetic and geometric average. For example, the returns for common stock are highly variable. As a result, the arithmetic average exceeds the geometric average by 200 basis points. For treasury bonds, whose returns are less variable, the difference between the two averages is only 40 basis points.
- For a given sample period, the geometric average is independent of the length of the observation interval.[1] The arithmetic average, however, tends to rise as the observation interval is shortened. For instance, the arithmetic average of monthly returns for the S&P 500 (calculated on an annualized basis by compounding the monthly arithmetic average) over the period between 1926 and 1997 is 13.1%, compared with the 13.0% average of annual returns.
- The difference between the geometric averages for two series does not equal the geometric average of the difference. Consider, for instance, stock returns and inflation. Table 1.2 reveals that the geometric average stock return is 11.0% and the average inflation rate is 3.1%, for a difference of 7.9%. However, Table 1.3 shows that the geometric average real return on common stock was 7.7%. This discrepancy does not arise for arithmetic averages, where the mean difference always equals the difference of the means.

With respect to the equity risk premium, the manner in which the average is calculated makes a significant difference. When compared with treasury bills over the full 1926-to-1997 period,

---

[1] This follows immediately from the fact that the geometric average depends only on the initial and final values of the investment.

the arithmetic average risk premium is 9.2%, whereas the geometric average premium is only 7.2%. Which average is the more appropriate choice? That depends on the question being asked. Assuming that the returns being averaged are largely independent and that the future is like the past, the best estimate of expected returns over a given future holding period is the arithmetic average of past returns over the same holding period. For instance, if the goal is to estimate future stock-market returns on a year-by-year basis, the appropriate average is the annual arithmetic risk premium. On the other hand, if the goal is to estimate what the average equity risk premium will be over the next 50 years, the geometric average is a better choice. Because the ultimate goal in this book is to arrive at reasonable forward-looking estimates of the equity risk premium, both arithmetic and geometric averages are employed where they are useful.

It is worth reiterating that projection of any past average is based on the implicit assumption that the future will be like the past. If the assumption is not reasonable, both the arithmetic and geometric averages will tend to be misleading.

How Accurately Can the Historical Risk Premium Be Measured?

The accuracy with which the historical risk premium can be measured depends on the variability of the observations from which the average is calculated. In an assessment of the impact of that variability, the best place to start is with an expanded version of Table 1.2 that includes monthly returns for the four asset classes over the period between 1926 and 1997. Given this expanded data set, one way to assess the variability of the ex-post risk premium, defined as the difference between the observed returns for stocks and the related treasury securities, is to plot one histogram for stocks versus bonds and another for stocks versus bills. Each bar on the histogram represents the fraction of the 864 monthly observations that fall into the range shown on the x axis. So that the data are easier to interpret, the monthly returns have been annualized by multiplying all of the observations by 12. The arithmetic means for the monthly premiums are 7.2% over treasury bonds and 8.7% over treasury bills.[2] If there is little variation in the equity risk premium, then most of the observations in the histogram for bonds will be bunched near 8.7% and most observations in the histogram for bills will be bunched near 7.2%.

The histograms for the equity risk premium measured with regard to treasury bonds and treasury bills are presented in Figures 2.1A and 2.1B, respectively. The general results hold no matter which treasury security is used to define the premium. In particular, the historical observations are so widely dispersed that the x axis in both histograms runs from −150% to +250% and it still does not contain all the observations.[3] Given this huge range, it is necessary to use intervals of 10% to plot a reasonable histogram. Even so, the two bars that comprise the interval from 0% to +20%, which includes a substantial margin on either side of the mean, account for only about 15% of the observed monthly premiums. Furthermore, in both histograms about 20% of the observed premiums are over 50% per year and another 15% are less than 40% per year.

The huge variability depicted by the histogram is confirmed by estimates of the standard deviation of return. The standard deviations for the annual data are reported at the bottom of each column in Table 1.2. The standard deviations for the annualized monthly data are nearly identical. The table shows that the standard deviation for annual stock returns is about 20%. The standard deviation of the risk premium also is about 21%, whether it is measured with respect to bills or bonds. The finding that the standard deviations of

---

[2] These figures are slightly lower than the annual means reported in Table 1.2 because the monthly returns have been multiplied by 12 and not compounded.

[3] Returns of less than −100% are possible because the data are 12 times the monthly premiums. Obviously, none of the monthly premiums is less than −100%.

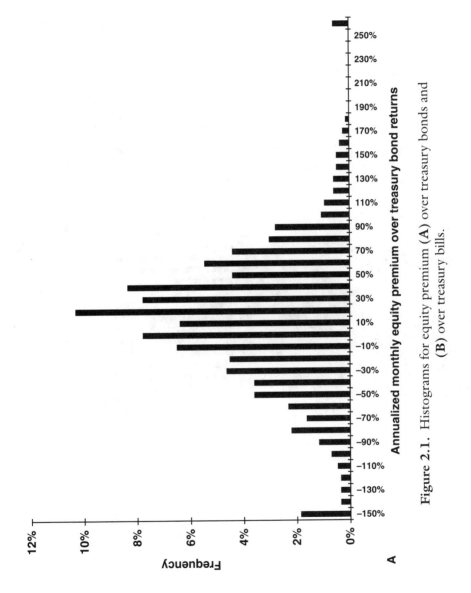

Figure 2.1. Histograms for equity premium (A) over treasury bonds and (B) over treasury bills.

41

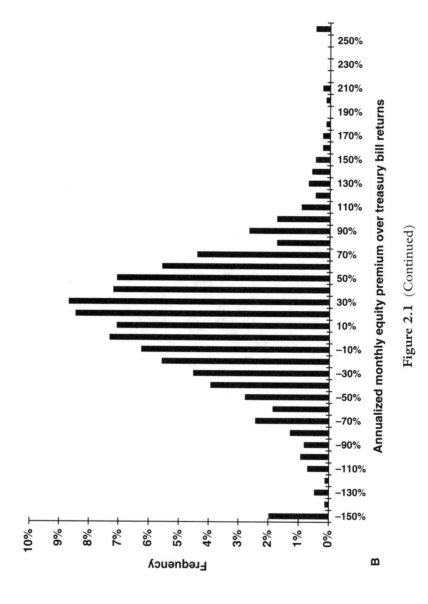

Figure 2.1 (Continued)

stock returns and the risk premiums are nearly equal reflects the fact that most of the variation in the premiums is due to changing stock returns, not to variation in bill or bond returns.

A standard deviation of 21% per year means that a 95% confidence interval for next year's premium runs from approximately –34% to +48%.[4] This is truly a range with which Texans would feel at home. It suggests that returns are so variable that history fails to provide a reasonably accurate guide as to what the risk premium will be the next year.

If only the postwar data are used, the estimated standard deviations fall somewhat. The standard deviation of stock returns drops to 16.5% and the standard deviations of the premiums decline to approximately 19%. This reduces the 95% confidence interval for the next year's premium to a range of –30% to +44%. Such a range is still far too wide to say what the next year's premium will be with any accuracy.

For many purposes, it is not necessary to know the next year's actual risk premium. The key question for long-term investors is what the future risk premium will be over the long run, not what it will be the next year. From the standpoint of corporate investment decision making, what is needed is an estimate of the next year's *expected* return, not the next year's actual return. That is because the discount rate used in capital budgeting is based on the cost of capital, which depends, in turn, on future expected returns.[5] Con-

---

[4] The calculation of the confidence interval assumes that the returns are independent and normally distributed with a constant standard deviation. Neither of those assumptions is precisely consistent with the data. Nonetheless, when more sophisticated analyses are employed, the confidence interval remains largely the same.

[5] To appreciate the difference between the variance of actual returns and expected returns, consider the following example. If a baseball player is a .250 hitter and comes to bat four times each game, he or she is expected to get one hit per game. This expectation will change very slowly over time because it depends only on the player's long-term batting average. The actual number of hits the player gets each game is much more variable. In many games the player is likely to go hitless, whereas in others he or she will get more than one hit.

fidence intervals for these numbers depend not on the standard deviation of individual returns but on the standard deviation of the mean return. Because the standard deviation of the mean declines at a rate approximately equal to the square root of the number of observations, then the longer the sample period, the smaller the confidence interval. For instance, Table 1.2 shows that the standard error of the mean return for Standard & Poor's (S&P) 500 returns over the full 72-year sample period is 2.4%. The standard error for the mean risk premium is the same. This means that a 95% confidence interval for the average risk premium runs from about 2.5% to 14%, depending on which treasury security is used. This is still a huge range. The difference between 3% and 14%, which is comparable to difference between the return on stocks and the return on treasury bills, is immense when compounded over 72 years, as highlighted in Figure 1.1.

The gist of the foregoing is that 72 years' worth of data is not enough to measure the risk premium with sufficient precision to satisfy most investors. Although the historical risk premium over treasury bonds is 7.4%, the data are so imprecise that the hypothesis that the true forward-looking risk premium is 3% or 12% cannot be rejected at standard levels of statistical significance. Nonetheless, the difference between a 3% premium and a 12% premium is huge in economic terms.

One immediate implication of this imprecision with which the risk premium can be estimated is that historical estimates will be sensitive to the choice of the sample period. This is illustrated in Table 2.1. Using monthly data, the table presents estimates of the historical risk premium over a variety of subsets of the full 1926-to-1997 period. The table shows that even over extended periods of 30 years or more, estimates of the risk premium can vary from about 3% to over 10%. Over shorter periods, the variation is even greater. For instance, the historical risk premium over the period from the end of July 1929 through the end of June 1932 is –59% over bonds and –57% over bills.

The table also includes data on the behavior of the premium prior to 1926. Schwert (1990) and later Siegel (1998) extended the information on stock, bonds, and bills back to 1802 by piec-

Table 2.1. Average Historical Risk Premiums over Various Sample Periods

Sample Period	Stock Premium over Bonds (%)	Stock Premium over Bills (%)
Full sample: January 1926 to December 1997	7.24	8.67
January 1946 to December 1997	7.54	8.11
January 1946 to December 1972	10.46	9.48
January 1973 to December 1997	4.39	6.64
January 1973 to December 1987	3.13	3.03
August 1929 to June 1932	−59.30	−56.92
January 1990 to December 1997	5.59	11.32
Extended sample period: January 1802 to December 1997	4.00	5.00
Pre-Ibbotson period: January 1802 to December 1925	3.40	3.50

ing together data from a variety of sources. (The data are described in detail in Chapter 3. Table 2.1 shows that during the years between 1802 and 1925, the average risk premium was significantly less than during the later period from 1802 to 1926.

The conclusion that emerges is that the historical averages for the risk premium of approximately 7% over bonds and 9% over bills are at best rough estimates of the appropriate risk premium to use going forward. Even if it is assumed that the future is like the past, the estimates are so imprecise that it is not clear what the risk premium has truly been in the past.

Nonstationarity and Historical Estimates of the Equity Risk Premium

For past averages to be meaningful, the data being averaged have to be drawn from the same population. If this is not the case—if the data come from populations that are different—the data are said to be nonstationary. When data are nonstationary, projecting past averages typically produces nonsensical results. The problem caused by nonstationarity can be illustrated by a simple example. Consider the problem of forecasting what the high temperature will be on New York City on July 10, 2050. One way to do this would be to average the high temperatures for every day during the preceding 10 years. The result, which turns out to be about 55°F, is a ridiculous estimate for the high temperature on July 10. The reason the estimation procedure fails is that with respect to temperature, different days in the year come from different populations. A winter day is fundamentally different from a summer day. Mixing winter and summer days together to compute an average brings to mind the fate of a soldier who drowned in a river that was only 6 inches deep on average.

When historical data are used to estimate the risk premium, the implicit assumption being made is that the past data are stationary. However, there are many reasons for suspecting that the true unobservable risk premium may be changing over time. For example, during the height of the Great Depression, when stocks had fallen over 85%, people viewed the stock market with suspicion at best. Conversely, during the 1990s after nearly a decade of rising stock prices, the popular view of the market was a good deal different. It is not unreasonable to suggest that this change in viewpoints was associated with a change in the risk premium. In addition, the economy has evolved in a number of ways that could have affected the risk premium. The government's role in stabilizing the economy has been greatly expanded, including the Federal Reserve's right to control the money supply. Regulation and oversight of the securities markets has also increased dramatically. All of these changes, and many more, suggest that the historical data used to estimate the risk premium may be nonstationary.

One particularly useful piece of evidence for investigating the possible nonstationarity of stock returns (and the risk premium) is the variability of those returns. Unlike the average return and the average risk premium, the variability of returns can be estimated with a high degree of accuracy. This follows from a basic theorem of statistics. In brief, the theorem, which has enormous implications for the financial analysis, goes like this: Assume that there is a given data set that can be divided into partitions of different fineness. For example, assume that there is a 20-year history of the stock market that can be expressed in terms of annual, monthly, or daily returns. The theorem says that when it comes to estimating the mean, using a finer partition does not help because the accuracy of the estimate is determined almost exclusively by the length of the sample period—in this case, 20 years. It does not matter whether the data are partitioned into 20 annual observations or 240 monthly observations. When it comes to estimating the variability of returns, however, the accuracy depends on the number of observations. Consequently, finely partitioning the data can greatly increase the number of observations and hence the accuracy of the estimates. For instance, modern estimates of market variability often use returns measured at 5-minute intervals. The upshot of the theorem is that it is possible to estimate market variability over short periods of time. As a result, tests of nonstationarity become possible, at least as far as variability of returns is concerned. Such tests reveal statistically significant changes in market variability. Most notably, returns were much more variable prior to World War II than afterward. For instance, the standard deviation of monthly risk premiums over treasury bonds is 9.65% over the period between January 1926 and December 1941 and 4.12% over the period between January 1946 and December 1997. This difference is statistically significant at the 1% level.

The nonstationarity in the variability of returns is important for the level of returns because economic theory implies that for the market as a whole, greater variability should be associated with a larger risk premium.[6] Assuming that the risk–return relation im-

---

[6] The theoretical relationship between risk and return for stocks generally is discussed in detail in Chapter 4.

plied by economic theory holds, it follows that the risk premium should be nonstationary.

Recognition that the risk premium may be nonstationary provides a warning signal regarding the projection of past averages into the future. Unfortunately, this recognition does not solve the problem. For reasonable forward-looking estimates of the risk premium to be constructed, the nature of the nonstationarity must be specified. Consider, again, the problem of estimating the high temperature in New York on July 10, 2050. Once it is realized that the data are nonstationary and that the nonstationarity is caused by seasonal variation, statistical techniques can be employed to solve the problem. The simplest solution is to limit the sample used to calculate the average to stationary data. For instance, an average of the average high temperature on the preceding 20 July 10ths could be computed.

In the case of the risk premium, taking explicit account of nonstationarity requires developing a model of how the premium varies over time or at least specifying variables on which that variation depends. For example, suppose that economic theory implies that the risk premium should be proportional to the standard deviation of returns. Under such circumstances, the constant of proportionality could be estimated from historical data. The future risk premium could then be forecast by multiplying the current standard deviation of returns, which can be estimated using a short sample period, by the constant of proportionality.

Another ground-up empirical approach would be to track variation over time in the risk premium and see with what variables it is correlated. What makes this approach difficult to implement is the imprecision with which mean returns are measured. Fortunately, statistical theory provides a possible solution to this problem. Correlations, like variances, can be estimated more accurately by more finely partitioning the data set. Taking advantage of this property, numerous researchers since the 1970s have attempted to estimate the possible correlation between the risk premium and variables with which various economic theories predict it should be correlated.

Attempts to Model Changes in the Risk Premium

Before a consideration of attempts that have been made to model changes in the risk premium, a particular conceptual issue must be addressed. The issue is most readily illustrated by an example. Assume that the dividend yield is found to be correlated with stock returns and that, on this basis, it is selected as a variable to assess changes in the risk premium. More specifically, assume, as the empirical evidence indicates, that the current dividend yield is positively correlated with the future risk premium. That is, stock prices tend to rise faster, relative to bond returns, when dividends are large. Such a finding can be interpreted two ways. First, the dividend yield can be seen as a variable that explains variation in the ex-ante risk premium. High dividends, for whatever reason, signal that investors required a larger risk premium to hold stocks. This interpretation, which is entirely consistent with market efficiency, allows one to model changes in the risk premium as a function of the dividend yield.

There is, however, a second possible interpretation. Suppose that the market is not perfectly efficient. Instead, there are periods during which the market is significantly under- or overvalued. Under such circumstance, the dividend yield will tend to be correlated with future stock returns. Suppose, for example, that the market is subject to self-limiting waves of optimism and pessimism. When the market is unduly low, perhaps due to a spate of investor pessimism, the dividend yield will be high. (The dividend-to-price ratio [D/P] rises because price [P] falls without reason.) Because the pessimism dissipates over time, the market will eventually return to more normal levels. During the period of readjustment, prices will rise more rapidly than normal and the ex-post risk premium will be observed to be above average. The process is reversed after a wave of optimism. As a result of the ebb and flow of emotion, the dividend yield will be observed to be positively correlated with subsequent observations of the risk premium. However, under this interpretation, the true ex-ante risk premium never changes. Instead, the ex-post premium becomes a poor indicator of the ex-ante premium whenever investor emotions lead to the mispricing of common stocks.

In short, there are two fundamentally different explanations for the correlation between the dividend yield and future risk premium. One is that high dividend yields are associated with a change in market conditions that is rationally associated with higher future stock returns. The other is that the high yields are evidence of artificially depressed stock prices. As stock prices return to normal levels, returns are above average.

This distinction between rational "equilibrium" changes in the risk premiums and changes that are due to market mispricing lies at the core of many debates in finance. One other example is worth mentioning despite the fact that it is not related to the market risk premium. In a widely cited article, Fama and French (1989) reported that the risk premiums for individual stocks were significantly correlated with a company's market capitalization and the ratio of the company's book value to market value. They attributed these risk premiums to be compensation for risk factors correlated with market capitalization and book-to-market ratios. However, other authors, including Lakonishok, Shleifer, and Vishny (1994), have argued that size and book-to-market ratios are better interpreted as indicia of security mispricing. Despite numerous contributions by many leading scholars, this debate remains unresolved.

What makes the two interpretations so difficult to assess is that the true ex-ante risk premiums are unobservable. For that reason, systematic market mispricing and variation in the ex-ante risk premium become indistinguishable. Above-average increases in stock prices may be the result of a higher risk premium or the result of irrational market forces. The American stock market boom of the 1990s provides an illustration of the problem. Should the boom be attributed to a rational decline in the risk premium or is it an example of excessive optimism on the part of investors? A discussion of the question as to which, if either, of these explanations is correct is postponed until Chapter 5, but for now, the point to recognize is that historical correlations alone do not allow the two interpretations to be distinguished.

Models Based on the Variability of Returns

The first attempts to explain possible variation in the risk premium focused on the risk–return relation described above. The literature on the relation between stock returns and the variability of returns includes contributions by Black (1976); Merton (1980); French, Schwert, and Stambaugh (1987); Poterba and Summers (1988); Breen, Glosten, and Jagannathan (1989); Turner, Startz, and Nelson (1989); Nelson (1991); Campbell and Hentschel (1992); and Glosten, Jagannathan, and Runkle (1993). All of these articles document the fact that the variability of returns changes over time. Unfortunately, their authors disagree as to how the changing variability is related to the risk premium. Some present findings that indicate a positive relation, others present findings that indicate a negative relation, and still others find no statistically significant relation at all.

If there is a bottom line, it is that the relation between stock returns and the variability of returns is remarkably weak. It turns out that the economic intuition that periods of high price variability should also be characterized by high stock-market returns is false. In retrospect, Glosten et al. (1993) pointed out why this is not so surprising:

> At first blush, it may appear that rational risk-averse investors would require a relatively larger risk premium during times when the payoff from the security is more risky. A larger risk premium may not be required, however, because time periods which are relatively more risky could coincide with time periods when investors are better able to bear particular types of risk. Further, a larger risk premium many not be required because investors may want to save relatively more during periods when the future is more risky [p. 1790].

Whatever the explanation for the weak relation between the ex-post risk premium and the variability of returns, it means that return variability is not a good variable for modeling possible changes in the risk premium.

Models Based on Dividend and Earnings Yield

In an influential early article, Fama and French (1988a), reported the results of regressions of the ex-post equity premium over treasury bills on the dividend yields. Regressions similar to theirs are reproduced and updated in Table 2.2. The data are limited to the postwar period beginning in 1948. The dependent variable (the ex-post premium) is the difference between the return on the S&P 500 and the return on 1-month treasury bills. The ex-post premium is measured over horizons of 1 year, 2 years and 5 years after the date on which the dividend yield is observed. When the longer horizons are used, the observations are overlapping. In each case, the explanatory variable is the D/P ratio for the S&P 500 measured at the beginning of the observation interval.

Consistent with the findings of Fama and French, the table shows that dividend yields have significant power to predict the ex-post risk premium, particularly at longer horizons. The regression at a 1-year horizon shows that about 10% of the variation in the ex-post premium is explained by the dividend yield at the start of the year. At a 5-year horizon, the variation explained by the div-

Table 2.2. Regressions of the Ex-post Risk Premium
on Dividend Yield: 1948–1997

Horizon (k)	a	$t(a)$	b	$t(b)$	R^2
1 year	−0.086	1.02	4.45	2.22	0.093
2 years	−0.218	−1.79	10.01	3.47	0.204
5 years	−0.79	−3.75	30.59	6.22	0.468

Regression equations are of the form $Ex\text{-}post\ Premium\ (t\ to\ t+k) = a + b\ D(t)/P(t)$.

idend yield rises to almost 50%. What this implies is that a low D/P ratio does portend a period of below-average returns on stocks relative to treasury bill returns and relative to dividend growth. The slower growth in stock prices, relative to dividends, is what brings the D/P ratio back toward its historical average. Because the adjustment occurs slowly over time, however, there are no short-term gains to be made from the relationship. Nonetheless, the 5-year regression implies that when the D/P ratio is near its historical low, the risk premium over the next 5 years will be on the order of 1% per year below its historical average.

The fact that the D/P ratio changes slowly over time casts doubt on the meaning of the 5-year regressions. During the 50-year period from 1948 to 1997, there are only 10 independent observations with a 5-year horizon. Because the D/P ratio varies so slowly, it means that there are even fewer truly informative observations. It turns out that most of the explanatory power comes from three periods. Specifically, the high dividend yields of the 1950s preceded the market boom of the 1960s, the low dividend yields of the mid-1960s preceded the sharp market downturn in the early 1970s, and the high dividend yields in the late 1970s preceded the boom of the 1990s. Is that really sufficient information for using dividend yields to predict future variation in the risk premium?

Although the data are limited, the dividend yield regressions do provide evidence that the risk premium is nonstationary. The implied variation, however, is not large. Movements of yields between historical highs and lows are associated with only a 1% per year change in the risk premium. Nonetheless, the dividend yield regressions serve as a warning against assuming that the risk premium is stationary and naively projecting past averages into the future.

Does Nonstationarity Really Matter for Estimating the Long-Run Risk Premium?

In light of the fact that the ultimate goal is to estimate the long-run future risk premium, it is possible that nonstationarity, even if it exists, is a minor issue. The relation between the premium and dividend yield provides a perfect example. Suppose the regressions in Table 2.2 are taken at their face value and that dividend yield has the power to predict variation in the risk premium. As long as the dividend yield tends to wander around its mean value in the long run, which all available evidence indicates that it does, long-run estimates of the risk premium are largely unaffected by the nonstationarity related to dividend yields. This is because the future, like the past, will be characterized by intervals of high and low dividend yields. However, if there is no permanent change in the process generating dividends and if the sample period used to calculate the average is sufficiently long, the average yield in the future should be near the average yield in the past. This implies that the average risk premium in the future will be close to its past average. Consequently, there is no need to take account of the variation in either the dividend yield or the ex-post risk premium to predict long-run future values. A past average of ex-post risk premiums over a period sufficiently long to include several ups and downs in dividend yields provides a perfectly acceptable estimate of the future premium. The only benefit of modeling the relation between dividend yields and the risk premium explicitly is that it allows an attempt at identifying periods of time when the risk premium will be above or below its long-run average value.

As another illustration of a situation in which variation in the risk premium may not matter, consider possible variation of the risk premium over the business cycle. Fama and French (1989) presented evidence that expected returns are correlated with the business cycle. Specifically, expected returns are greater during recessions than during expansions.[7] Nonetheless, business cycles, by their nature, come and go—that is why they are called cycles. Consequently, although the premium may rise and fall temporarily

---

[7] Fama and French argued that this occurs because the marginal utility of another dollar of consumption is higher during recessions than during booms. Before investors can be induced to forgo consumption, therefore, they must expect a higher rate of return on their investments.

as business conditions change, it is not permanently affected. In an estimation of the long-run risk premium, therefore, ignoring the nonstationarity associated with the business cycle introduces only minor errors as long as the historical data used to estimate the premium cover a number of business cycles.

The same is true of another variable that has been found to have some ability to predict future risk premiums—past stock returns. Fama and French (1988b) reported that stock returns tend to be mean reverting, so that periods of abnormally high returns tend to be followed by periods of below-average returns. This means that past returns on the market can be used to predict the future risk premium. However, these past returns, by their nature, wander above and below the long-run average. There is no evidence that the mean reversion found by Fama and French affects the long-run average itself.

The foregoing arguments apply only when the variable used to explain nonstationarity in the risk premium wanders up and down around its mean value. If the explanatory variable changes in a permanent fashion, then the long-run average future risk premium will be altered. For instance, if dividend yields are expected to be lower on average in the future than they were on average in the past, then the average risk premium would also be permanently lower (assuming that the regressions are correct). It turns out that such permanent changes in the risk premium have an impact on stock prices that complicates the calculation and interpretation of historical averages.

The Impact of Permanent Changes in the Risk Premium on Stock Prices

There is a unique property of stock prices and the risk premium that makes the calculation and interpretation of past averages particularly hazardous when the data are nonstationary. Once again, the problem is best illustrated with an example. The example is based on the fundamental valuation equation, which implies that a permanent drop in the risk premium, and therefore in the discount rate, will lead to a permanent increase in stock prices. This fact has been the subject of a great deal of discussion in the financial press. On March 30, 1998, the *Wall Street Journal* published an article by James Glassman and Kevin Hassett that argued that the high level of stock prices at that time was the result of a permanent drop in the risk premium.

To develop the example and to illustrate Glassman and Hassett's point, consider the following calculation. To begin, assume that the risk-free rate of interest is 5% on treasury bills (close to the number on March 30) and that the equity risk premium is 8% (near the Ibbotson historical estimate). In addition, assume that dividends on common stocks are expected to grow at 5%. This equals 3% growth to compensate for inflation and 2% real growth. The real growth number equals the long-run forecast real growth for the U.S. economy. Next, assume that for some reason the risk premium suddenly drops to 3%. The impact on the level of stock prices can be approximated using the constant-growth version[8] of the fundamental valuation equation. The constant-growth version adds the simplifying assumption that dividends grow at a constant rate. With that simplifying assumption, the fundamental valuation equation reduces to

$$P = \frac{D_1}{k - g} \tag{2.1}$$

When Equation 2.1 is applied to the S&P 500, D_1 is the next year's dividend payout for the stocks in the index, k is the discount rate (equal to the expected return on market), and g is the expected growth rate of dividends. When the risk premium is 8%, the discount rate is 13% (equal to the 5% risk-free rate plus the 8% risk premium). Therefore, Equation 2.1 states that the level of prices is given by

---

[8] A derivation of the constant-growth model can be found in any textbook on corporate finance or investments.

$$P = \frac{D_1}{.13 - .05}$$

When the risk premium drops to 3%, the level of prices rises to

$$P = \frac{D_1}{.08 - .05}$$

Therefore, the ratio of the price level after the drop to before the drop is

$$\text{Ratio of Price Level after to before} = \frac{.13 - .05}{.08 - .05} = 2.67$$

which is independent of the dividend payment. This simple calculation shows that a drop in the risk premium of 500 hundred basis points leads to a 167% increase in stock prices!

The fact that declines in the risk premium are associated with rising stock prices makes it particularly hazardous to use past averages to estimate the forward-looking premium. The potential pitfalls can be illustrated by complicating the example slightly and letting the risk premium fall slowly rather than drop 500 basis points all at once. Specifically, suppose that the financial markets had been in equilibrium for a long period of time with the risk-free rate on treasury securities equal to 5% and the equity risk premium equal to 8% as described above. Under such circumstances, long-run averages of stock returns and the risk premium, during the period of equilibrium, should converge to 13% and 8%, respectively. Next, assume that rather than falling instantaneously, the risk premium declines 1% per year for 5 years, to reach a new equilibrium level of 3%. If underlying corporate earnings and dividends remain constant, stock prices will rise as the equity premium drops. For reasonable levels of earnings and dividends, it can be shown that the returns on the stock market during the 5 years that risk premium is declining would be 31%, 33%, 37%, 45%, and 62%, respectively, assuming that nothing else changed.[9] After the decline, stock returns would settle into a new, lower equilibrium. In the new equilibrium, the average return would converge to 8% and the average risk premium to 3%, *in the long run.*

Under the conditions described above, consider the plight of a market observer who does not know that the true unobservable risk premium has fallen and is instead relying on recent historical data to estimate the premium. As the true unobservable premium falls, the observer's historical estimate, based on recent returns, rises dramatically! As a specific illustration, suppose that the observer uses 20 years' worth of historical data to estimate the risk premium. In the period before the decline in the equity premium, his or her estimates should be approximately equal to the underlying premium of 8% on average. However, if the observer estimates the risk premium after the 5 years of decline, the expected value for the estimate would be 13.5%. This not only vastly overstates the now true risk premium of 3% but also greatly overstates the original risk premium of 8%.

The inverse relation between changes in the risk premium and returns on stock makes nonstationarity a more complex problem for stock returns than for other types of data. As the underlying risk premium changes, stock returns, and therefore the historical estimates of the risk premium, move in the opposite direction. Consequently, when the risk premium falls, it is doubly likely to be overestimated. First, the historical returns before the drop will overstate the now lower premium. Second, the historical returns during the drop will be even greater and will compound the error. (The reverse occurs when the risk premium rises.)

It must be stressed that the foregoing conclusions hold only for permanent changes in the risk premium. In the preceding calculations, when the risk premium changed, it was assumed to change forever. That is why one discount rate, k, could be used to discount all future cash flows. If the risk premium wanders up and down over time, the impact of changes will be much less for two reasons.

---

[9] The underlying calculations are available from the author.

First, investors will become aware of the pattern changes and will adjust their beliefs accordingly. Under such circumstances, the duration of the increase in the discount rate will match the expected duration of the increase in the risk premium. If *k* is affected for only a few periods, the impact on stock prices will be limited. Second, if the discount rate wanders up and down, periods of underestimation and overestimation will tend to cancel one another out. This means that a long-run historical average will be a relatively unbiased estimate of the future long-run risk premium.

The Bottom Line on Nonstationarity

Several fundamental conclusions emerge from the discussion of nonstationarity. First, the expected risk premium is *probably* nonstationary. The uncertainty arises because of the immense error with which expected returns are measured. Nonetheless, variables that are likely to affect the expected risk premium, such as the volatility of stock returns, dividend yields, and business conditions, clearly change over time. Although the jury is still out on the meaning of the relations, researchers have found significant correlations between these variables and the ex-post risk premium. This implies that the unobservable ex-ante premium is also changing.

From the point of view of estimating the future long-run risk premium, the variation in the risk premium associated with changing dividend yields or business conditions is probably not important. Those factors cause the ex-ante premium to wander up and down but not to change in a permanent fashion. Short-term variation in the expected risk premium will have a relatively small impact on stock prices, because it affects the discount rate, *k*, for only a few periods. In addition, it will have almost no impact on long-run future expected returns. Consequently, past averages of the ex-post data that are computed over periods sufficiently long to include several historical ups and downs in the expected premium will still be excellent estimates of the long-run future premium.

The situation in which the past will not be a good guide to the future is one in which there is a fundamental permanent change in the premium. Such a permanent change will cause historical estimates to significantly over- or understate the future premium. It is precisely this type of change that Glassman and Hassett (1998), among others, have argued led to the stock market boom of the 1990s. However, this argument cannot be evaluated adequately on the basis of the historical average alone.

Survival Bias

The Impact

The analysis thus far has been based on the apparently innocuous assumption that it is appropriate to use historical American data to estimate the equity risk premium for the United States. In fact, because U.S. stock-market data are more complete than those for any other country, U.S. data are often used to analyze the equity risk premium generally—but there is a reason that the U.S. data are more complete. Unlike Germany, France, Italy, and Japan, the United States has never been invaded or lost a major war. Unlike Russia, it did not undergo two internal revolutions in the twentieth century. In fact, in the years following 1926, when detailed stock-market data became available, the United States led pretty much a charmed life. Its economy prospered, its military might grew, and it rose in stature to become the dominant nation in the world. As of 1926, it was not clear that the future was going to be so bright.

The problem raised by the United States' charmed life goes by the name of *survival bias* in the statistical literature. U.S. stock-market data are continuous and complete precisely because the United States has avoided the convulsions that devastated the market in other nations. For this reason, U.S. historical data may not be a good guide as to what can be expected in the future, even in the case of the United States.

As an illustration of the potential importance of survival bias when conducting statistical studies, consider the following example, which is based on an early study of the effects of smoking. Assume that two random samples of people age 65 are selected, one from the population of smokers and one from the population of nonsmokers. To assess the impact of smoking, track the health of each group going forward. In particular, determine which group lives longer on average. Surprisingly enough, the early study found that the smokers lived longer on average. This seems to imply that smoking improves one's life expectancy.

The paradoxical conclusion arises because of survival bias. Understanding how survival bias works necessitates starting with the population of all smokers, not just those who are over 65. This distinction is important because many smokers are dead before age 65. Those who do survive tend to have something else going for them: Perhaps they were lucky enough to be born female or have other genetic characteristics that favor longevity. Perhaps other than smoking they live an exemplary life. Among nonsmokers, on the other hand, some overweight men manage to make it to 65 precisely because they do not smoke. In short, the two populations are not comparable, because of survival bias. Smokers who have lived 65 years are on average better genetically endowed and healthier than are nonsmokers of the same age. Were this not the case, they would already be dead.

In a widely cited academic study, Brown, Goetzmann, and Ross (1995) attempted to assess the potential impact of survival bias on estimation of the risk premium. They developed a mathematical model that has a critical price level for stock prices. If stock prices fall to the critical level, the market collapses and trading stops. They then investigated the difference between the average performance of stocks generally and the average performance of stocks in countries that have never fallen to the critical barrier. Not surprisingly, they found that the equity risk premium, conditional on the fact that the market never reached the critical level, is significantly higher than the unconditional premium.

To assess the empirical importance of their results, Brown et al. (1995) parameterized their model using historical U.S. data similar to those presented in Table 1.2. Specifically, they set the model so that the observed equity risk premium, conditional on the market's never having reached the critical level during 80 years of trading, is 8%. Solving the model, they found that an 8% conditional risk premium is consistent with an unconditional risk premium of 4%. This means that using data from successful markets that have not had trading interruptions leads to an upward bias in the estimate of the equity risk premium of approximately 100%.

Survival bias affects estimates of the riskiness of stock as well as the mean returns. The reason is that conditional on survival, it must be the case that "things never got too bad." Otherwise, the critical level would have been reached and the market would have collapsed. This implies that returns for such markets have been less variable because the downside has been limited. In addition, major interruptions are associated not only with lower returns on average but also with highly volatile returns. Consequently, computing the standard deviation from a sample that does not include rare disasters understates the true level of uncertainty. As a result, the confidence intervals for the risk premium calculated earlier, wide as they may be, are probably too narrow, even for the U.S. market.

For the same reason, stock returns in markets that have survived show evidence of mean reversion. This occurs because markets always recover from downturns. If they did not, they would hit the critical barrier. This fact may explain, at least in part, the mean reversion in stock returns found by Fama and French (1988b).

Assessing the overall impact of survival bias, Brown et al. (1995) put the matter this way:

> Looking back over the history of the London or New York stock markets can be extraordinarily comforting to an investor—equities appear to have provided a substantial premium over bonds, and markets appear to have recovered nicely after huge crashes. ... Less comforting is the past history of other major markets: Russia, China, Germany and Japan. Each of these markets has had one or more major interruptions that prevent their inclusion in long term studies [p. 853].

Perhaps an even more cogent summary of the implications of survival bias was offered by Cochrane (1997):

Was it clear to people in 1945 that throughout the period (to the present) that the average return on stocks would be 8 percent greater than that of bonds? If so, one would expect them to have bought more stocks, even considering the risk described by the 17 percent year-to-year variation. But perhaps it was not in fact obvious in 1945, that rather than slipping back into depression, the U.S. would experience a half century of growth never before seen in human history. If so, much of the equity premium was unexpected good luck [p. 7].

Good luck, though, is just that—good luck. By definition, it cannot be expected to recur. If Cochrane was correct, then U.S. history is not a reliable guide for estimating the forward-looking risk premium.

There is another theoretical argument, related to survival bias, that also suggests that the ex-post risk premium is likely to overstate the forward-looking premium. Suppose, for instance, that there is a very small probability, say 0.25%, of a major financial catastrophe in a given year. In that case, one would expect that there would be one catastrophe every 400 years. This means that even with more than 100 years of data, it is more likely than not that a catastrophe will not be observed. If it is not observed, however, the ex-post risk premium will overstate the ex-ante risk premium because the possibility of a catastrophe is not reflected in the historical data. On the other hand, if it is observed, the ex-post risk premium will understate the ex-ante risk premium. In the case of the United States, the catastrophe did not occur during the Ibbotson data period between 1926 and 1997. In other countries, however, it did. This implies that the empirical importance of survival bias can be estimated by examining international data.

To estimate the impact of survival bias, scholars have begun to look more carefully at the long-term performance of common stocks in countries other than the United States. Use of international data allows the sample to be greatly expanded. In addition, including both countries that have had catastrophes and those that have not eliminates—or at least attenuates—survival bias.

To study the importance of survival bias, Siegel (1998) reconstructed return series for the United Kingdom, Germany, and Japan over the period between 1926 and 1997. On the basis of analysis of that data, he reported that the geometric average of real returns on U.S. stocks exceeded the average for German stocks by 60 basis points, for British stocks by 100 basis points, and for Japanese stocks by 380 basis points. The Japanese returns are the lowest because the collapse of the Japanese market during and after World War II was far more extensive than was the case in Germany.

The overall impression conveyed by the Siegel data is that survival bias is a problem but not one as large as the work of Brown et al. (1995) indicates. The German real returns are surprisingly close to U.S. real returns. Even in the case of Japan, which suffered the most complete collapse, the observed difference in returns is less than Brown et al. would have predicted.[10] Despite the collapse during the war, Japanese stocks still outperformed U.S. treasury bonds.

To more fully assess the impact of survival bias, Goetzmann and Jorion (1997) pieced together real returns for 39 markets with histories going as far back as the 1920s. The problem is that for countries other than the United States and the United Kingdom, comprehensive data have been collected only since 1970 for developed countries and since 1980 for emerging markets. To extend the return series back in time, Goetzmann and Jorion turned to data provided by the International Monetary Fund and, before that, by the League of Nations. In this fashion, they were able to construct relatively complete data on the rate of stock-market appreciation back to 1926 for most of the 39 countries. Unfortunately, total returns could not be computed because dividend data were not available for many of the countries. For this reason, Goetzmann and Jorion analyzed exclusively rates of appreciation, net of dividends, for every country.

They found that the U.S. market had by far the highest average rate of real appreciation, at about 5% annually. For the other

---

[10] Remember that the difference Brown, Goetzmann, and Ross (1995) computed is the difference between the equity risk premium conditional on survival and the unconditional risk premium. The difference between the risk premium conditional on survival and the risk premium conditional on collapse is a good deal larger. The German and Japanese data are conditional on the occurrence of a collapse.

countries, both the median rate and the average rate of real appreciation were about 1.5%. On the basis of these findings, the authors concluded that there is

> . . . striking evidence in support of the survival explanation for [the] equity risk premium. . . . The main lesson from our unique long-term data is that global capital markets have been systematically subject to dramatic changes over [the twentieth] century. Major disruptions have afflicted nearly all markets in our sample, with the exception of a few such as the United States. Markets have been closed or suspended due to financial crises, wars, expropriations or political upheaval. No doubt this explains our finding that the 5 percent real capital appreciation return on U.S. stocks is rather exceptional, as other markets typically have returned 3 percent less than U.S. equities. These empirical results provide support for the hypothesis that the equity premium puzzle[11] is due to conditioning estimates upon the best performing market [p. 16].

The empirical findings of Goetzmann and Jorion (1997) provide convincing support for the theoretical work of Brown et al. (1995). The upward bias of approximately 300 to 350 basis points implied by their empirical study is remarkably close to the ballpark estimate of 400 basis points produced by the model of Brown et al.

It is worth nothing that survival bias is not limited to equity. Economic problems, particularly hyperinflation, can also spell disasters for investors in long-term corporate bonds. For instance, investors in Japanese bonds saw the value of their principal fall almost 100-fold when post–World War II inflation led to a devaluation of the yen from 4 to the dollar to 360 to the dollar. The situation was worse in Germany after the first world war. Bond investors were wiped out entirely by the hyperinflation of 1922–23 when prices rose by a factor of 10^{12}. In fact, the United States is one of the few countries that has not experienced inflation of 20% or more for sustained periods in the years since the collapse of the gold standard in 1931.

Another way to assess the importance of survival bias is to use U.S. data from an independent period. In this regard, Schwert

[11] The equity risk premium puzzle is the subject of Chapter 4.

(1990) reconstructed indexes of U.S. stock prices back to 1802. When compared with the experience of other countries, the U.S. experience between 1802 and 1925 is less dominant than that between 1926 and 1997. Most notably, the country suffered through a particularly bloody civil war that all but destroyed commerce in the South. Therefore, it is possible that the pre-1926 data are more representative of the true expected risk premium of American equities.

To construct a long-term index back to 1802, Schwert was forced to splice together various stock indexes developed by prior researchers. In some cases, the sample was relatively sparse. In addition, dividends were often omitted and the averaging techniques varied. Where possible, therefore, Schwert adjusted the data to arrive at a consistent index. More specifically, the Schwert index in the years prior to 1926 was constructed as follows:

- For the period between 1802 and 1815, the index is based on an equally weighted index of seven bank stocks reported by Smith and Cole (1935). The Smith–Cole data did not include dividends, so Schwert added an estimate of dividends to calculate returns.

- For the period between 1815 and 1834, the index is based on an equally weighted index of 14 bank and insurance stocks reported by Smith and Cole. Once again, Schwert added an estimate of dividends.

- For the period between 1834 and 1845, the index is based on two indexes reported by Smith and Cole. The first is an equally weighted index of 7 bank and insurance stocks and the second is an equally weighted index of 27 railroad stocks. Schwert constructed a weighted average of the two indexes with weights proportional to the number of stocks in the index. He then added an estimate of dividends.

- For the period between 1846 and 1862, the Smith–Cole index of railroad stocks is the only one available. Once again, Schwert added estimated dividends.

- For the period between 1863 and 1871, the index is based on Macaulay's value-weighted portfolio (1938) of railroad stocks. Schwert added an estimate of the dividends.

- For the period between 1872 and 1885, the index is based Cowles's value-weighted index (1939) of all NYSE listed stocks whose prices were reported in the *Commercial and Financial Chronicle*. The Cowles data include dividends.
- For the period between 1885 and 1925, the index is based on the Dow Jones (1972) index. This is a price-weighed precursor to the current DJIA. Over the time period, it included between 12 and 50 stocks. The dividends on the Dow stocks are available from Cowles.

The fact that so many different indexes are employed and that the samples are often small means that over short periods of time, measurement error in the market return could be significant. Over the long term, however, these measurement problems should tend to cancel and the Schwert index should provide a reasonable approximation to the return on the market.

Siegel (1998) supplemented Schwert's index with data on inflation and with returns on short-term and long-term government securities to make the data set comparable to that reported in Table 1.2. The results provide further support for the survival-bias hypothesis. Average returns and risk premiums during periods between 1802 and 1871 and between 1871 and 1925 are presented in Table 2.3. For both periods, the risk premiums compute both with respect to short-term and long-term government securities. The table shows that in every case, the premiums are approximately 400 basis points less than the comparable premiums for the period between 1926 and 1997.

Table 2.3 raises two questions. The first is, why are stock returns lower in the pre-1802 periods? There is an easy answer to that—inflation. Table 2.4, which presents geometric averages of real returns, shows that the compound real return on common stocks was essentially constant over all three periods: 1802 to 1870, 1871 to 1925, and 1926 to 1997. As discussed below, that is what one would expect if common stocks were a reasonable long-term hedge against inflation.

If real returns on stocks were relatively constant, then the increase in the risk premium in the final period must be due to a rel-

Table 2.3. Stocks, Bonds, Bills, and Inflation before 1926

Period	Schwert Index Return (%)	Long-Term Government Return (%)	Short-Term Government Return (%)	Inflation (%)	Bond Premium (%)	Bill Premium (%)
1802–1870	8.1	4.9	5.1	0.1	3.2	3.0
1871–1925	8.4	4.4	3.2	0.6	4.0	5.2

Returns are arithmetic averages over the periods shown.

ative decline in the real return on fixed-income securities. Table 2.4 supports this conclusion. The real returns on both bonds and bills declined monotonically from one period to the next. In the case of bills, the drop was drastic, from 5.1% in the first period to only 0.6% in the final period.

It is tempting to blame the decline in real returns on fixed-income securities on unexpected inflation, but inflation cannot be the explanation. First, there was a period of unexpected inflation (mostly from 1965 to 1982), but it was followed by an unexpected drop in the inflation rate. By 1997, the inflation rate was not much higher than it had been in 1926. Second, as noted earlier, the short maturity of treasury bills means that the yields are continually readjusted to reflect a new inflationary environment. Consequently, inflation cannot explain a drop in the real return on bills in any case. Table 2.4 shows that the real return on bills dropped more than the real return on bonds.

Table 2.4. Real Returns on Stocks, Bonds, and Bills over Long-Term Holding Periods

Period	Stocks (%)	Bonds (%)	Bills (%)
1802–1870	7.00	4.80	5.10
1871–1925	6.60	3.70	3.20
1926–1997	7.70	2.40	0.60

Returns are geometric averages of the periods shown.

Another possible explanation is that the panic associated with the Great Depression drove investors out of stock into government securities, thereby bidding the prices of bills and bonds up and forcing yields down. The problem with this explanation is that even though stock prices had bounced back by the 1950s, the real return on treasury securities remained depressed.

It is also possible that government policy might have depressed interest rates during the final period. For example, during World War II and the early postwar years, the Federal Reserve artificially supported the prices of government securities. However, the Federal Reserve abandoned that policy in 1951 and the real return on government securities failed to rise thereafter.

The unfortunate fact is that there is currently no convincing explanation for the decline in real interest rates on fixed-income securities. In fact, it has been referred to by some economists as the "real interest rate puzzle."[12] The focus here, however, is not the real interest puzzle but the equity risk premium. In that regard, the pre-1925 data are remarkably consistent with the international work of Goetzmann and Jorion (1997) and with the theoretical work on survival bias. All three suggest that the risk premium observed during the period between 1926 and 1997 overstates a fair estimate of the expected risk premium by 300 to 400 basis points.

The Bottom Line

Survival bias is a significant problem for estimating the long-run future risk premium. In the period between 1926 and 1997, during which the Ibbotson data were accumulated, the United States led a charmed financial life. There were no market interruptions and no bouts of hyperinflation. As a result, American data during that interval are not representative of the behavior of equities in general in the past and are unlikely to be representative of the behavior of American equity markets in the future.

---

[12] See, for example, Brewer and Kaufman (1994).

The theoretical work of Brown et al. (1995) and the empirical work of Goetzmann and Jorion (1997) on international markets both suggest that the unique experience of the United States leads to an overestimate of the equity risk premium in the range of 300 to 400 basis points. An overestimate of that magnitude is also consistent with U.S. data prior to 1926. During the years between 1802 and 1925, the average premiums over bills and bonds were approximately 400 basis points less than during the years between 1926 and 1997.

To understand how important a drop of 400 basis points in the premium can be, look back to Table 1.2. The table shows that a $1 investment in the S&P 500 in 1926 grew to $1,829.50 by 1997 at a geometric average rate of 11%. Had the geometric average rate been 7% instead, the value of the investment in 1997 would have been only $130. That is less than one fourteenth of what it turned out to be.

Does this mean that in an estimation of the forward-looking risk premium the historical estimates should be reduced by 300 to 400 basis points? An answer to that question is postponed until Chapter 6. Whatever the specific answer, though, it is clear that survival bias cannot be ignored in an analysis of historical U.S. data on stock returns.

Stock and Bond Returns

Over the Long Horizon

A look at the stock and bond returns reported in Table 1.2 makes it clear that stock returns are more variable. This impression is confirmed by the fact that the standard deviation for stock returns is about twice what it is for bond returns. The greater volatility of stock returns is generally offered as one explanation for the equity risk premium. However, if holding periods longer than 1 year are used, a different picture emerges.

Figures 2.2A and 2.2B plot rolling 10-year and 20-year averages, respectively, for the returns on the S&P 500 and 20-year treasury bonds. In Figure 2.2B, notice that there is no 20-year interval in the period beginning January 1926 during which treasury bonds outperformed common stocks. This includes the early years of the Great Depression, when stock prices dropped dramatically and bond prices rose. Although stocks declined approximately 85% from the peak in 1929 to the trough in 1932, they rebounded enough to slightly outperform bonds in the 20-year period between 1929 and 1949. The figure shows that between 1929 and 1949, the average return for both stocks and treasury bonds was 3.9% per year.

Figure 2.2A demonstrates that stocks also outperformed bonds over virtually every 10-year holding period. The only exceptions are the periods including the crash between 1929 and 1932 and the pronounced market drop in 1973–1974.

The reason for these impressive results is the size of the equity risk premium. The premium acts like a current in a river carrying stocks up past bonds. During any one year, the volatility of stock returns is so large that stocks can significantly underperform bonds. As the years accumulate, however, the upward drift provided by the equity premium becomes more and more important relative to self-canceling random fluctuations. By the time a 10-year horizon is reached, the drift has become so important that stocks almost invariably outperform bonds. At a 20-year horizon, stocks outperform bonds in every case.

If these results sound too good to be true, they may be. Interpretation of the findings is complicated by survival bias. The longer the interval, the greater the relative importance of survival bias when stocks are compared with short-run treasury bills. When stocks are compared with long-term bonds, the results are more difficult to interpret because, as noted earlier, survival bias also affects the returns on long-term bonds. Furthermore, the types of economic upheavals that affect stocks and bonds typically differ. Stocks perform particularly poorly during deep recessions. It is during such times that the risk of market collapse is the great-

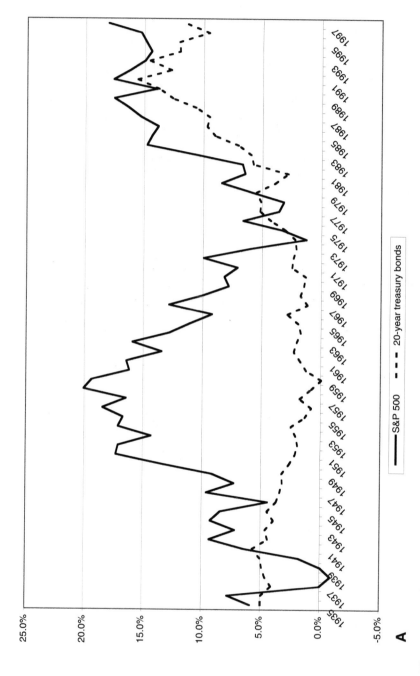

Figure 2.2. (**A**) Ten-year and (**B**) 20-year average returns for Standard & Poor's (S&P) 500 Index and treasury bonds.

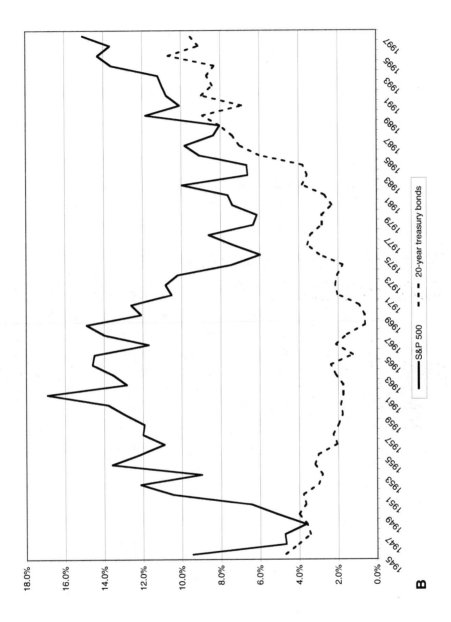

S&P 500 ―――― 20-year treasury bonds - - -

B

est. The Great Depression in the United States is one example. Table 1.3 shows that during the depression, however, the real returns on bonds were near record levels. The greatest risk to bondholders is runaway inflation. Bondholders in countries as varied as Germany, Hungary, Argentina, and Brazil have been wiped out not by recession but by inflation. In the United States, the worst periods for bondholders were when inflation accelerated unexpectedly in both the late 1960s and 1970s. Because of the nature of inflation, the difference between the inflation risk that stockholders and bondholders face tends to grow with the investment horizon. It also critically depends on the resolve of monetary authorities and the role of government in the economy.

The Impact of Inflation

The relation among stock returns, bond returns, and inflation during the years between 1926 and 1997 is complicated further by the fact that the nature of the inflationary process changed during those years. The reason for the change in the nature of inflation was the collapse of the gold standard. The demise of the gold standard began when Great Britain suspended conversion of sterling to gold in September 1931. Next, the United States suspended the conversion of dollars into gold by private citizens in April 1933. The final death knell for the gold standard came in 1971 when President Richard Nixon stated that the United States was no longer willing to allow foreign central banks to convert dollars to gold at the official price of $35 an ounce.

The worldwide collapse of the gold standard opened the door to an new type of economic crisis for investors—high and consistent inflation. As long as currency had to be backed by gold, the rate at which a government could expand the money supply was limited by the rate at which gold could be accumulated. Because accumulation of gold, either by production or by running trade surpluses, was limited by forces beyond governmental control, so was the ability to increase the money supply. These limits on monetary growth placed corresponding limits on the rate of inflation. For example, in the

United States, the average inflation rate between 1802 and 1932 was only 0.003% per year. Putting control of the money supply in the hands of central banks eliminated the constraints imposed by the need to accumulate gold on the rate of monetary growth. In times of recession, central banks were strongly encouraged to increase the money supply to get the economy moving. In boom times, however, there were political pressures to keep central banks from "stealing the punch bowl" by reducing monetary growth and slowing the economy. As a result, the collapse of the gold standard led to a worldwide bias toward higher rates of inflation. In some cases, such as in Hungary after the second world war, monetary growth spiraled to percentages of hundreds per *month*. The results were hyperinflation, which destroyed the value of the currency and any securities whose payments were fixed in nominal terms.

In the United States, the Federal Reserve was established to be independent of the other branches of the government in an effort to overcome the inflationary bias. Although the Fed has been quite successful in this regard, the trend toward greater inflation is still clear. In the years between 1934 and 1997, the average inflation rate was 4.1%, more than 10 times what it had been under the gold standard. Furthermore, in the 8 years after the oil shock of 1973, when inflationary pressure was at its height, the average inflation rate in the United States was nearly 10%.

Given the fact that the rate of inflation is now determined by political forces, not by the ability to accumulate gold, there is clearly an added risk to investing in long-term fixed-income securities. If governments allow the rate of monetary expansion to get out of control, the value of fixed-income securities is destroyed. This new inflationary risk could well alter the equity risk premium, particularly measured with respect to long-term treasury bonds, on both an ex-ante and ex-post basis. Ex-ante, the added risk of investing in long-term fixed-income securities produced by unpredictable inflation should reduce the spread over long-term bonds that investors require to hold stock. Ex-post, if inflation accelerates, bond returns will be below equilibrium levels during the period of unexpected inflation. This will artificially increase historical estimates of the risk premium.

Although its impact cannot be ignored, the change in the inflationary environment does not explain the large historical risk premiums observed in the United States for several reasons. To begin with, inflation can never be a good explanation for changes in the risk premium measured with respect to 1-month treasury bills. As noted previously, yields on treasury bills are reset monthly. At the end of each month, the newly adjusted expected inflation rate gets impounded into the next month's treasury bill rate. Therefore, investors catch up with any unexpected inflation after a month or less. Because the inflation rate tends to change slowly over time, investors in 1-month bills are protected by the monthly resetting of yields. Consequently, inflation does not greatly affect the long-run real returns on treasury bills. In addition, uncertainty as to future inflation is not a great risk, because investors will get their money back at the end of the month and can reinvest it at a new rate that reflects any changes in the inflationary environment. With respect to equities, greater inflation risk, if it does anything at all, is likely to increase required returns. Putting the two pieces together, neither inflation nor inflation uncertainty explains the high premium of stock over treasury bills.

As noted above, the impact of inflation and of uncertainty regarding inflation is much greater for 20-year treasury bonds than for 1-month treasury bills. Because the rate of interest is fixed for 20 years, if inflation accelerates, the price of the bond must fall until the yield on the bond matches current yields available in the high-inflation environment. The drop in bond prices is experienced as negative returns for long-term bond investors. If inflation rises unexpectedly over a prolonged interval, historical returns on long-term bonds will be low or negative during the period. Although the United States did experience a prolonged period of unexpected high inflation between 1973 and 1980, the rate then dropped unexpectedly over the period between 1982 and 1990. The 1998 rate of inflation of between 2% and 3% is approximately equal to the average rate of 3.1% over the full period between 1926 and 1997. This means that although bondholders have experienced both good and bad intervals because of inflation, inflation has had almost no impact over the full period on their average returns. Consequently, inflation cannot explain the large average difference between the historical returns on equity and the historical returns on long-term treasury bonds.

Although it cannot explain the large historical premium, it is still possible that the new inflationary environment has changed the ex-ante equity risk premium of stocks over bonds. To the extent that stocks offer a long-run hedge against serious inflation, they may actually be less risky than long-term fixed-income securities over the long haul. In fact, evidence presented by Siegel (1998) supports this viewpoint. Recall that in the case of Germany and Japan, bondholders suffered even more than stockholders did. In the case of the United States, which has never experienced a hyperinflation or a market collapse, neither stockholders nor bondholders have ever been wiped out. Nonetheless, over very long investment horizons, the real returns on stocks have been less variable than those on bonds. Turn back to Table 2.4, which shows the geometric average real returns on common stocks, long-term bonds, and short-term bills over the three major periods since 1802.[13] The three periods cover markedly different eras with different economic policies and different inflation rates. Nonetheless, the average real return on common stocks remained in the range of 6.60% to 7.70%. The real returns on both bonds and bills were not only lower but more variable.

Going forward, if investors expect inflation to be one of the most—if not the most—important source of long-term investment risk, then stocks could actually be less risky than bonds over the long-term. The implication of that viewpoint is that the ex-ante risk premium over bonds could be close to zero in the years ahead.

A Final Assessment of the Historical Record

The most salient feature of the historical record of stock and bond returns is the huge equity risk premium. The rate at which U.S.

---

[13] The pre-1926 data are from Schwert (1990) and Siegel (1998).

equity investors have compounded their wealth is so much greater than the rate at which fixed-income investments have grown that it makes investors who placed most of their wealth in bonds look foolish. However, a closer look at the historical record reveals some doubts about the extraordinary performance of common stock. First, the returns on stock are so variable that the equity risk premium cannot be measured accurately, even using 72 years' worth of data. Second, there is evidence that the equity premium has been changing over time, so that averaging past data may mix apples and oranges and not provide a good indicator of the future premium. Third, using U.S. data over the period between 1926 and 1997 is likely to produce an overly rosy estimate of the risk premium. The performance of U.S. financial markets was exemplary during that period. Not only is the U.S. experience unrepresentative of what happened to financial markets worldwide but it also may overstate what can be expected of American markets in the future. Fourth, when it comes to comparing the risk of stocks and bonds, the results are highly sensitive to the observation interval. Over short intervals of 1 month or 1 year, stocks are clearly more volatile. However, as the observation interval is lengthened to 10 or 20 years, the risk of stocks relative to bonds falls sharply. Finally, the nature of the inflation process changed dramatically with the collapse of the gold standard. As a result, unexpected inflation has become a significant long-run inflation risk. Because this risk affects long-term bonds far more than it does common stocks, the required returns on stocks compared with bonds might have been affected.

   This chapter suggests that the historical record provides an indication as to what the future risk premium may be, but it is by no means definitive. Problems caused by survival bias and nonstationarity indicate that projecting past averages to estimate future risk premiums is hazardous at best and may be outright misleading. For that reason, additional information must be brought to bear to estimate the forward-looking risk premium. Chapter 3 presents several direct methods for estimating the risk premium that do not rely on historical data.

Appendix 2.1. Monthly Data for Stocks, Bonds, Bills, and Inflation

Date	S&P 500	One-Month Treasury Bill	Twenty-Year Treasury Bond	Inflation Rate
Jan-26	0.00	0.34	1.38	0.00
Feb-26	−3.85	0.27	0.63	−0.37
Mar-26	−5.75	0.30	0.41	−0.56
Apr-26	2.53	0.34	0.76	0.94
May-26	1.79	0.01	0.14	−0.56
Jun-26	4.57	0.35	0.38	−0.75
Jul-26	4.79	0.22	0.04	−0.94
Aug-26	2.48	0.25	0.00	−0.57
Sep-26	2.52	0.23	0.38	0.57
Oct-26	−2.84	0.32	1.02	0.38
Nov-26	3.47	0.31	1.60	0.38
Dec-26	1.96	0.28	0.78	0.00
Jan-27	−1.93	0.25	0.75	−0.76
Feb-27	5.37	0.26	0.88	−0.76
Mar-27	0.87	0.30	2.53	−0.58
Apr-27	2.01	0.25	−0.05	0.00
May-27	6.07	0.30	1.09	0.77
Jun-27	−0.67	0.26	−0.69	0.96
Jul-27	6.70	0.30	0.50	−1.90
Aug-27	5.15	0.28	0.76	−0.58
Sep-27	4.50	0.21	0.18	0.58
Oct-27	−5.02	0.25	0.99	0.58
Nov-27	7.21	0.21	0.97	−0.19
Dec-27	2.79	0.22	0.72	−0.19
Jan-28	−0.40	0.25	−0.36	−0.19
Feb-28	−1.25	0.33	0.61	−0.97
Mar-28	11.01	0.29	0.45	0.00
Apr-28	3.45	0.22	−0.04	0.20
May-28	1.97	0.32	−0.77	0.58
Jun-28	−3.85	0.31	0.41	−0.78
Jul-28	1.41	0.32	−2.17	0.00
Aug-28	8.03	0.32	0.76	0.20
Sep-28	2.59	0.27	−0.41	0.78
Oct-28	1.68	0.41	1.58	−0.19
Nov-28	12.92	0.38	0.03	−0.19
Dec-28	0.49	−0.24	0.04	−0.39

(continues)

Date	S&P 500	One-Month Treasury Bill	Twenty-Year Treasury Bond	Inflation Rate
Jan-29	5.83	0.34	−0.90	−0.19
Feb-29	−0.19	0.36	−1.57	−0.20
Mar-29	−0.12	0.34	−1.44	−0.39
Apr-29	1.76	0.36	2.75	−0.39
May-29	−3.62	0.44	−1.96	0.59
Jun-29	11.40	0.52	1.45	0.39
Jul-29	4.71	0.33	0.00	0.98
Aug-29	10.28	0.40	−0.34	0.39
Sep-29	−4.76	0.35	0.28	−0.19
Oct-29	−19.73	0.46	3.82	0.00
Nov-29	−12.46	0.37	2.36	−0.19
Dec-29	2.82	0.37	−0.89	−0.58
Jan-30	6.39	0.14	−0.57	−0.39
Feb-30	2.59	0.30	1.29	−0.39
Mar-30	8.12	0.35	0.83	−0.59
Apr-30	−0.80	0.21	−0.16	0.59
May-30	−0.96	0.26	1.40	−0.59
Jun-30	−16.25	0.27	0.51	−0.59
Jul-30	3.86	0.20	0.34	−1.39
Aug-30	1.41	0.09	0.13	−0.60
Sep-30	−12.82	0.22	0.74	0.61
Oct-30	−8.55	0.09	0.35	−0.60
Nov-30	−0.89	0.13	0.42	−0.81
Dec-30	−7.06	0.14	−0.70	−1.43
Jan-31	5.02	0.15	−1.21	−1.45
Feb-31	11.93	0.04	0.85	−1.47
Mar-31	−6.75	0.13	1.04	−0.64
Apr-31	−9.35	0.08	0.86	−0.64
May-31	−12.79	0.09	1.45	−1.08
Jun-31	14.21	0.08	0.04	−1.09
Jul-31	−7.22	0.06	−0.42	−0.22
Aug-31	1.82	0.03	0.12	−0.22
Sep-31	−29.73	0.03	−2.81	−0.44
Oct-31	8.96	0.10	−3.30	−0.67
Nov-31	−7.98	0.17	0.27	−1.12
Dec-31	−14.00	0.12	−2.20	−0.91
Jan-32	−2.71	0.23	0.34	−2.06
Feb-32	5.70	0.23	4.13	−1.40
Mar-32	−11.58	0.16	−0.18	−0.47
Apr-32	−19.97	0.11	6.04	−0.71

(continues)

Date	S&P 500	One-Month Treasury Bill	Twenty-Year Treasury Bond	Inflation Rate
May-32	−21.96	0.06	−4.97	−1.44
Jun-32	−0.22	0.02	3.92	−0.73
Jul-32	38.15	0.03	4.81	0.00
Aug-32	38.69	0.03	0.03	−1.23
Sep-32	−3.46	0.03	0.57	−0.50
Oct-32	−13.49	0.02	−0.17	−0.75
Nov-32	−4.17	0.02	0.32	−0.50
Dec-32	5.65	0.01	1.31	−1.01
Jan-33	0.87	0.01	1.48	−1.53
Feb-33	−17.72	−0.03	−2.58	−1.55
Mar-33	3.53	0.04	0.97	−0.79
Apr-33	42.56	0.10	−0.32	−0.27
May-33	16.83	0.04	3.03	0.27
Jun-33	13.38	0.02	0.50	1.06
Jul-33	−8.62	0.02	−0.17	2.89
Aug-33	12.06	0.03	0.44	1.02
Sep-33	−11.18	0.02	0.23	0.00
Oct-33	−8.55	0.01	−0.91	0.00
Nov-33	11.27	0.02	−1.49	0.00
Dec-33	2.53	0.02	−1.13	−0.51
Jan-34	10.69	0.05	2.57	0.51
Feb-34	−3.22	0.02	0.81	0.76
Mar-34	0.00	0.02	1.97	0.00
Apr-34	−2.51	0.01	1.26	−0.25
May-34	−7.36	0.01	1.31	0.25
Jun-34	2.29	0.01	0.67	0.25
Jul-34	−11.31	0.01	0.40	0.00
Aug-34	6.11	0.01	−1.18	0.25
Sep-34	−0.33	0.01	−1.46	1.50
Oct-34	−2.86	0.01	1.82	−0.74
Nov-34	9.42	0.01	0.37	−0.25
Dec-34	−0.10	0.01	1.12	−0.25
Jan-35	−4.11	0.01	1.82	1.49
Feb-35	−3.41	0.02	0.92	0.74
Mar-35	−2.86	0.01	0.41	−0.24
Apr-35	9.80	0.01	0.79	0.98
May-35	4.09	0.01	−0.57	−0.48
Jun-35	6.99	0.01	0.92	−0.24
Jul-35	8.50	0.01	0.46	−0.49
Aug-35	2.80	0.01	−1.33	0.00

(continues)

Date	S&P 500	One-Month Treasury Bill	Twenty-Year Treasury Bond	Inflation Rate
Sep-35	2.56	0.01	0.09	0.49
Oct-35	7.77	0.01	0.61	0.00
Nov-35	4.74	0.02	0.10	0.49
Dec-35	3.94	0.01	0.70	0.24
Jan-36	6.70	0.01	0.55	0.00
Feb-36	2.24	0.01	0.81	−0.48
Mar-36	2.68	0.02	1.06	−0.49
Apr-36	−7.51	0.02	0.35	0.00
May-36	5.45	0.02	0.40	0.00
Jun-36	3.33	0.03	0.21	0.98
Jul-36	7.01	0.01	0.60	0.48
Aug-36	1.51	0.02	1.11	0.72
Sep-36	0.31	0.01	−0.31	0.24
Oct-36	7.75	0.01	0.06	−0.24
Nov-36	1.34	0.02	2.05	0.00
Dec-36	−0.29	0.01	0.38	0.00
Jan-37	3.90	0.01	−0.13	0.72
Feb-37	1.91	0.02	0.86	0.24
Mar-37	−0.77	0.01	−4.12	0.71
Apr-37	−8.09	0.03	0.39	0.47
May-37	−0.24	0.06	0.53	0.47
Jun-37	−5.04	0.03	−0.18	0.23
Jul-37	10.45	0.03	1.38	0.46
Aug-37	−4.83	0.02	−1.04	0.23
Sep-37	−14.03	0.04	0.45	0.92
Oct-37	−9.81	0.02	0.42	−0.46
Nov-37	−8.66	0.02	0.96	−0.69
Dec-37	−4.59	0.00	0.82	−0.23
Jan-38	1.52	0.00	0.57	−1.39
Feb-38	6.74	0.00	0.52	−0.94
Mar-38	−24.87	−0.01	−0.37	0.00
Apr-38	14.47	0.01	2.10	0.47
May-38	−3.30	0.00	0.44	−0.47
Jun-38	25.03	0.00	0.04	0.00
Jul-38	7.44	−0.01	0.43	0.24
Aug-38	−2.26	0.00	0.00	−0.24
Sep-38	1.66	0.02	0.22	0.00
Oct-38	7.76	0.01	0.87	−0.47
Nov-38	−2.73	−0.06	−0.22	−0.24
Dec-38	4.01	0.00	0.80	0.24

(continues)

Date	S&P 500	One-Month Treasury Bill	Twenty-Year Treasury Bond	Inflation Rate
Jan-39	−6.74	−0.01	0.59	−0.48
Feb-39	3.90	0.01	0.80	−0.48
Mar-39	−13.39	−0.01	1.25	−0.24
Apr-39	−0.27	0.00	1.18	−0.24
May-39	7.33	0.01	1.71	0.00
Jun-39	−6.12	0.01	−0.27	0.00
Jul-39	11.05	0.00	1.13	0.00
Aug-39	−6.48	−0.01	−2.01	0.00
Sep-39	16.73	0.01	−5.45	1.93
Oct-39	−1.23	0.00	4.10	−0.47
Nov-39	−3.98	0.00	1.62	0.00
Dec-39	2.70	0.00	1.45	−0.48
Jan-40	−3.36	0.00	−0.17	−0.24
Feb-40	1.33	0.00	0.27	0.72
Mar-40	1.24	0.00	1.77	−0.24
Apr-40	−0.24	0.00	−0.35	0.00
May-40	−22.89	−0.02	−2.99	0.24
Jun-40	8.09	0.00	2.58	0.24
Jul-40	3.41	0.01	0.52	−0.24
Aug-40	3.50	−0.01	0.28	−0.24
Sep-40	1.23	0.00	1.10	0.24
Oct-40	4.22	0.00	0.31	0.00
Nov-40	−3.16	0.00	2.05	0.00
Dec-40	0.09	0.00	0.67	0.48
Jan-41	−4.63	−0.01	−2.01	0.00
Feb-41	−0.60	−0.01	0.20	0.00
Mar-41	0.71	0.01	0.96	0.47
Apr-41	−6.12	−0.01	1.29	0.94
May-41	1.83	0.00	0.27	0.70
Jun-41	5.78	0.00	0.66	1.86
Jul-41	5.79	0.03	0.22	0.46
Aug-41	0.10	0.01	0.18	0.91
Sep-41	−0.68	0.01	−0.12	1.80
Oct-41	−6.57	0.00	1.40	1.10
Nov-41	−2.84	0.00	−0.29	0.87
Dec-41	−4.07	0.01	−1.77	0.22
Jan-42	1.61	0.02	0.69	1.30
Feb-42	−1.59	0.01	0.11	0.85
Mar-42	−6.52	0.01	0.92	1.27
Apr-42	−4.00	0.01	−0.29	0.63

(continues)

Date	S&P 500	One-Month Treasury Bill	Twenty-Year Treasury Bond	Inflation Rate
May-42	7.96	0.03	0.75	1.04
Jun-42	2.21	0.02	0.03	0.21
Jul-42	3.37	0.03	0.18	0.41
Aug-42	1.64	0.03	0.38	0.61
Sep-42	2.90	0.03	0.03	0.20
Oct-42	6.78	0.03	0.24	1.01
Nov-42	−0.21	0.03	−0.35	0.60
Dec-42	5.49	0.03	0.49	0.80
Jan-43	7.37	0.03	0.33	0.00
Feb-43	5.83	0.03	−0.06	0.20
Mar-43	5.45	0.03	0.09	1.58
Apr-43	0.35	0.03	0.48	1.17
May-43	5.52	0.02	0.50	0.77
Jun-43	2.23	0.03	0.18	−0.19
Jul-43	−5.26	0.03	−0.01	−0.76
Aug-43	1.71	0.03	0.21	−0.38
Sep-43	2.63	0.03	0.11	0.39
Oct-43	−1.08	0.03	0.05	0.38
Nov-43	−6.54	0.03	−0.01	−0.19
Dec-43	6.17	0.03	0.18	0.19
Jan-44	1.71	0.03	0.21	−0.19
Feb-44	0.42	0.03	0.32	−0.19
Mar-44	1.95	0.02	0.21	0.00
Apr-44	−1.00	0.03	0.13	0.58
May-44	5.05	0.03	0.28	0.38
Jun-44	5.43	0.03	0.08	0.19
Jul-44	−1.93	0.03	0.36	0.57
Aug-44	1.57	0.03	0.27	0.38
Sep-44	−0.08	0.02	0.14	0.00
Oct-44	0.23	0.03	0.12	0.00
Nov-44	1.33	0.03	0.24	0.00
Dec-44	3.74	0.02	0.42	0.38
Jan-45	1.58	0.03	1.27	0.00
Feb-45	6.83	0.02	0.77	−0.19
Mar-45	−4.41	0.02	0.21	0.00
Apr-45	9.02	0.03	1.60	0.19
May-45	1.95	0.03	0.56	0.75
Jun-45	−0.07	0.02	1.69	0.93
Jul-45	−1.80	0.03	−0.86	0.18
Aug-45	6.41	0.03	0.26	0.00

(continues)

Date	S&P 500	One-Month Treasury Bill	Twenty-Year Treasury Bond	Inflation Rate
Sep-45	4.38	0.03	0.54	−0.37
Oct-45	3.22	0.03	1.04	0.00
Nov-45	3.96	0.02	1.25	0.37
Dec-45	1.16	0.03	1.94	0.37
Jan-46	7.14	0.03	0.25	0.00
Feb-46	−6.41	0.03	0.32	−0.37
Mar-46	4.80	0.03	0.10	0.74
Apr-46	3.93	0.03	−1.35	0.55
May-46	2.88	0.03	−0.12	0.55
Jun-46	−3.70	0.03	0.70	1.08
Jul-46	−2.39	0.03	−0.40	5.90
Aug-46	−6.74	0.03	−1.12	2.20
Sep-46	−9.97	0.03	−0.09	1.16
Oct-46	−0.60	0.03	0.74	1.96
Nov-46	−0.27	0.03	−0.54	2.40
Dec-46	4.57	0.03	1.45	0.78
Jan-47	2.55	0.03	−0.06	0.00
Feb-47	−0.77	0.03	0.21	−0.16
Mar-47	−1.49	0.03	0.20	2.18
Apr-47	−3.63	0.03	−0.37	0.00
May-47	0.14	0.03	0.33	−0.30
Jun-47	5.54	0.03	0.10	0.76
Jul-47	3.81	0.03	0.63	0.91
Aug-47	−2.03	0.03	0.81	1.05
Sep-47	−1.11	0.06	−0.44	2.38
Oct-47	2.38	0.06	−0.37	0.00
Nov-47	−1.75	0.06	−1.74	0.58
Dec-47	2.33	0.08	−1.92	1.30
Jan-48	−3.79	0.07	0.20	1.14
Feb-48	−3.88	0.07	0.46	−0.85
Mar-48	7.93	0.09	0.34	−0.28
Apr-48	2.92	0.08	0.45	1.42
May-48	8.79	0.08	1.41	0.70
Jun-48	0.54	0.09	−0.84	0.70
Jul-48	−5.08	0.08	−0.21	1.25
Aug-48	1.58	0.09	0.01	0.41
Sep-48	−2.76	0.04	0.14	0.00
Oct-48	7.10	0.04	0.07	−0.41
Nov-48	−9.61	0.04	0.76	−0.68
Dec-48	3.46	0.04	0.56	−0.69

(continues)

Date	S&P 500	One-Month Treasury Bill	Twenty-Year Treasury Bond	Inflation Rate
Jan-49	0.39	0.10	0.82	−0.14
Feb-49	−2.96	0.09	0.49	−1.11
Mar-49	3.28	0.10	0.74	0.28
Apr-49	−1.79	0.09	0.11	0.14
May-49	−2.58	0.10	0.19	−0.14
Jun-49	0.14	0.10	1.67	0.14
Jul-49	6.50	0.09	0.33	−0.70
Aug-49	2.19	0.09	1.11	0.28
Sep-49	2.63	0.09	−0.11	0.42
Oct-49	3.40	0.09	0.19	−0.56
Nov-49	1.75	0.08	0.21	0.14
Dec-49	4.86	0.09	0.52	−0.56
Jan-50	1.97	0.09	−0.61	−0.42
Feb-50	1.99	0.09	0.21	−0.28
Mar-50	0.70	0.10	0.08	0.43
Apr-50	4.86	0.09	0.30	0.14
May-50	5.09	0.10	0.33	0.42
Jun-50	−5.48	0.10	−0.25	0.56
Jul-50	1.19	0.10	0.55	0.98
Aug-50	4.43	0.10	0.14	0.83
Sep-50	5.92	0.10	−0.72	0.69
Oct-50	0.93	0.12	−0.48	0.55
Nov-50	1.69	0.11	0.35	0.41
Dec-50	5.13	0.11	0.16	1.35
Jan-51	6.37	0.13	0.58	1.60
Feb-51	1.57	0.10	−0.74	1.18
Mar-51	−1.56	0.11	−1.57	0.39
Apr-51	5.09	0.13	−0.63	0.13
May-51	−2.99	0.12	−0.69	0.39
Jun-51	−2.28	0.12	−0.62	−0.13
Jul-51	7.11	0.13	1.38	0.13
Aug-51	4.78	0.13	0.99	0.00
Sep-51	0.13	0.12	−0.80	0.64
Oct-51	−1.03	0.16	0.10	0.51
Nov-51	0.96	0.11	−1.36	0.51
Dec-51	4.24	0.12	−0.61	0.38
Jan-52	1.81	0.15	0.28	0.00
Feb-52	−2.82	0.12	0.14	−0.63
Mar-52	5.03	0.11	1.11	0.00
Apr-52	−4.02	0.12	1.71	0.38

(continues)

Date	S&P 500	One-Month Treasury Bill	Twenty-Year Treasury Bond	Inflation Rate
May-52	3.43	0.13	−0.34	0.13
Jun-52	4.90	0.15	0.03	0.25
Jul-52	1.96	0.15	−0.20	0.76
Aug-52	−0.71	0.15	−0.70	0.12
Sep-52	−1.76	0.16	−1.30	−0.12
Oct-52	0.20	0.14	1.48	0.12
Nov-52	5.71	0.10	−0.15	0.00
Dec-52	3.82	0.16	−0.86	−0.12
Jan-53	−0.49	0.16	0.12	−0.25
Feb-53	−1.06	0.14	−0.87	−0.50
Mar-53	−2.12	0.18	−0.88	0.25
Apr-53	−2.37	0.16	−1.05	0.13
May-53	0.77	0.17	−1.48	0.25
Jun-53	−1.34	0.18	2.23	0.38
Jul-53	2.73	0.15	0.39	0.25
Aug-53	−5.01	0.17	−0.08	0.25
Sep-53	0.34	0.16	2.99	0.12
Oct-53	5.40	0.13	0.74	0.25
Nov-53	2.04	0.08	−0.49	−0.37
Dec-53	0.53	0.13	2.06	−0.12
Jan-54	5.36	0.11	0.89	0.25
Feb-54	1.11	0.07	2.40	−0.12
Mar-54	3.25	0.08	0.58	−0.12
Apr-54	5.16	0.09	1.04	−0.25
May-54	4.18	0.05	−0.87	0.37
Jun-54	0.31	0.06	1.63	0.12
Jul-54	5.89	0.05	1.34	0.00
Aug-54	−2.75	0.05	−0.36	−0.12
Sep-54	8.51	0.09	−0.10	−0.25
Oct-54	−1.67	0.07	0.06	−0.25
Nov-54	9.09	0.06	−0.25	0.12
Dec-54	5.34	0.08	0.64	−0.25
Jan-55	1.97	0.08	−2.41	0.00
Feb-55	0.98	0.09	−0.78	0.00
Mar-55	−0.30	0.10	0.87	0.00
Apr-55	3.96	0.10	0.01	0.00
May-55	0.55	0.14	0.73	0.00
Jun-55	8.41	0.10	−0.76	0.00
Jul-55	6.21	0.10	−1.02	0.37
Aug-55	−0.25	0.16	0.04	−0.25

(continues)

Date	S&P 500	One-Month Treasury Bill	Twenty-Year Treasury Bond	Inflation Rate
Sep-55	1.30	0.16	0.73	0.37
Oct-55	-2.84	0.18	1.44	0.00
Nov-55	8.27	0.17	-0.45	0.12
Dec-55	0.15	0.18	0.37	-0.25
Jan-56	-3.47	0.22	0.83	-0.12
Feb-56	4.13	0.19	-0.02	0.00
Mar-56	7.10	0.15	-1.49	0.12
Apr-56	-0.04	0.19	-1.13	0.12
May-56	-5.93	0.23	2.25	0.50
Jun-56	4.09	0.20	0.27	0.62
Jul-56	5.30	0.22	-2.09	0.74
Aug-56	-3.28	0.17	-1.86	-0.12
Sep-56	-4.40	0.18	0.50	0.12
Oct-56	0.66	0.25	-0.54	0.61
Nov-56	-0.50	0.20	-0.57	0.00
Dec-56	3.70	0.24	-1.79	0.24
Jan-57	-4.01	0.27	3.46	0.12
Feb-57	-2.64	0.24	0.25	0.36
Mar-57	2.15	0.23	-0.24	0.24
Apr-57	3.88	0.25	-2.22	0.36
May-57	4.37	0.26	-0.23	0.24
Jun-57	0.04	0.24	-1.80	0.60
Jul-57	1.31	0.30	-0.41	0.47
Aug-57	-5.05	0.25	0.02	0.12
Sep-57	-6.02	0.26	0.76	0.12
Oct-57	-3.02	0.29	-0.50	0.00
Nov-57	2.31	0.28	5.33	0.35
Dec-57	-3.95	0.24	3.07	0.00
Jan-58	4.45	0.28	-0.84	0.59
Feb-58	-1.41	0.12	1.00	0.12
Mar-58	3.28	0.09	1.02	0.70
Apr-58	3.37	0.08	1.86	0.23
May-58	2.12	0.11	0.01	0.00
Jun-58	2.79	0.03	-1.60	0.12
Jul-58	4.49	0.07	-2.78	0.12
Aug-58	1.76	0.04	-4.36	-0.12
Sep-58	5.01	0.19	-1.17	0.00
Oct-58	2.70	0.18	1.39	0.00
Nov-58	2.84	0.11	1.20	0.12
Dec-58	5.35	0.22	-1.81	-0.12

(continues)

Date	S&P 500	One-Month Treasury Bill	Twenty-Year Treasury Bond	Inflation Rate
Jan-59	0.53	0.21	−0.80	0.12
Feb-59	0.49	0.19	1.17	−0.12
Mar-59	0.20	0.22	0.17	0.00
Apr-59	4.02	0.20	−1.17	0.12
May-59	2.40	0.22	−0.06	0.12
Jun-59	−0.22	0.24	0.10	0.46
Jul-59	3.63	0.25	0.60	0.23
Aug-59	−1.02	0.19	−0.41	−0.11
Sep-59	−4.43	0.31	−0.57	0.34
Oct-59	1.28	0.30	1.50	0.34
Nov-59	1.86	0.26	−1.19	0.00
Dec-59	2.92	0.34	−1.59	0.00
Jan-60	−7.00	0.33	1.12	−0.11
Feb-60	1.47	0.29	2.04	0.11
Mar-60	−1.23	0.35	2.82	0.00
Apr-60	−1.61	0.19	−1.70	0.57
May-60	3.26	0.27	1.52	0.00
Jun-60	2.11	0.24	1.73	0.23
Jul-60	−2.34	0.13	3.68	0.00
Aug-60	3.17	0.17	−0.67	0.00
Sep-60	−5.90	0.16	0.75	0.11
Oct-60	−0.07	0.22	−0.28	0.45
Nov-60	4.65	0.13	−0.66	0.11
Dec-60	4.79	0.16	2.79	0.00
Jan-61	6.45	0.19	−1.07	0.00
Feb-61	3.19	0.14	2.00	0.00
Mar-61	2.70	0.20	−0.38	0.00
Apr-61	0.51	0.17	1.15	0.00
May-61	2.39	0.18	−0.46	0.00
Jun-61	−2.75	0.20	−0.75	0.11
Jul-61	3.42	0.18	0.35	0.45
Aug-61	2.43	0.14	−0.38	−0.11
Sep-61	−1.84	0.17	1.29	0.22
Oct-61	2.98	0.19	0.71	0.00
Nov-61	4.47	0.15	−0.20	0.00
Dec-61	0.46	0.19	−1.25	0.00
Jan-62	−3.66	0.24	−0.14	0.00
Feb-62	2.09	0.20	1.03	0.22
Mar-62	−0.46	0.20	2.53	0.22
Apr-62	−6.07	0.22	0.82	0.22

(continues)

Date	S&P 500	One-Month Treasury Bill	Twenty-Year Treasury Bond	Inflation Rate
May-62	−8.11	0.24	0.46	0.00
Jun-62	−8.03	0.20	−0.76	0.00
Jul-62	6.52	0.27	−1.09	0.22
Aug-62	2.08	0.23	1.87	0.00
Sep-62	−4.65	0.21	0.61	0.55
Oct-62	0.64	0.25	0.84	−0.11
Nov-62	10.86	0.20	0.21	0.00
Dec-62	1.53	0.23	0.35	−0.11
Jan-63	5.06	0.25	−0.01	0.11
Feb-63	−2.39	0.23	0.08	0.11
Mar-63	3.70	0.23	0.09	0.11
Apr-63	5.00	0.25	−0.12	0.00
May-63	1.93	0.24	0.23	0.00
Jun-63	−1.88	0.23	0.19	0.44
Jul-63	−0.22	0.27	0.31	0.44
Aug-63	5.35	0.25	0.21	0.00
Sep-63	−0.97	0.27	0.04	0.00
Oct-63	3.39	0.29	−0.26	0.11
Nov-63	−0.46	0.27	0.51	0.11
Dec-63	2.62	0.29	−0.06	0.22
Jan-64	2.83	0.30	−0.14	0.11
Feb-64	1.47	0.26	−0.11	−0.11
Mar-64	1.65	0.31	0.37	0.11
Apr-64	0.75	0.29	0.47	0.11
May-64	1.62	0.26	0.50	0.00
Jun-64	1.78	0.30	0.69	0.22
Jul-64	1.95	0.30	0.08	0.22
Aug-64	−1.18	0.28	0.20	−0.11
Sep-64	3.01	0.28	0.50	0.22
Oct-64	0.96	0.29	0.43	0.11
Nov-64	0.05	0.29	0.17	0.21
Dec-64	0.56	0.31	0.30	0.11
Jan-65	3.45	0.28	0.40	0.00
Feb-65	0.31	0.30	0.14	0.00
Mar-65	−1.33	0.36	0.54	0.11
Apr-65	3.56	0.31	0.36	0.32
May-65	−0.30	0.31	0.18	0.21
Jun-65	−4.73	0.35	0.47	0.53
Jul-65	1.47	0.31	0.22	0.11
Aug-65	2.72	0.33	−0.13	−0.21

(continues)

Date	S&P 500	One-Month Treasury Bill	Twenty-Year Treasury Bond	Inflation Rate
Sep-65	3.34	0.31	−0.34	0.21
Oct-65	2.89	0.31	0.27	0.11
Nov-65	−0.31	0.35	−0.62	0.21
Dec-65	1.06	0.33	−0.78	0.32
Jan-66	0.62	0.38	−1.04	0.00
Feb-66	−1.31	0.35	−2.50	0.63
Mar-66	−2.05	0.38	2.96	0.31
Apr-66	2.20	0.34	−0.63	0.42
May-66	−4.92	0.41	−0.59	0.10
Jun-66	−1.46	0.38	−0.16	0.31
Jul-66	−1.20	0.35	−0.37	0.31
Aug-66	−7.25	0.41	−2.06	0.51
Sep-66	−0.53	0.40	3.32	0.20
Oct-66	4.94	0.45	2.28	0.41
Nov-66	0.95	0.40	−1.48	0.00
Dec-66	0.02	0.40	4.13	0.10
Jan-67	7.98	0.43	1.54	0.00
Feb-67	0.72	0.36	−2.21	0.10
Mar-67	4.09	0.39	1.98	0.20
Apr-67	4.37	0.32	−2.91	0.20
May-67	−4.77	0.33	−0.39	0.30
Jun-67	1.90	0.27	−3.12	0.30
Jul-67	4.68	0.31	0.68	0.50
Aug-67	−0.70	0.31	−0.84	0.30
Sep-67	3.42	0.32	−0.05	0.20
Oct-67	−2.76	0.39	−4.00	0.30
Nov-67	0.65	0.36	−1.97	0.30
Dec-67	2.78	0.33	1.92	0.30
Jan-68	−4.25	0.40	3.28	0.39
Feb-68	−2.61	0.39	−0.33	0.29
Mar-68	1.10	0.38	−2.12	0.49
Apr-68	8.34	0.43	2.27	0.29
May-68	1.61	0.45	0.43	0.29
Jun-68	1.05	0.43	2.30	0.58
Jul-68	−1.72	0.48	2.89	0.48
Aug-68	1.64	0.42	−0.03	0.29
Sep-68	4.00	0.43	−1.02	0.29
Oct-68	0.87	0.44	−1.32	0.57
Nov-68	5.31	0.42	−2.69	0.38
Dec-68	−4.02	0.43	−3.63	0.28

(continues)

Date	S&P 500	One-Month Treasury Bill	Twenty-Year Treasury Bond	Inflation Rate
Jan-69	−0.68	0.53	−2.06	0.28
Feb-69	−4.26	0.46	0.42	0.37
Mar-69	3.59	0.46	0.10	0.84
Apr-69	2.29	0.53	4.27	0.65
May-69	0.26	0.48	−4.90	0.28
Jun-69	−5.42	0.51	2.14	0.64
Jul-69	−5.87	0.53	0.79	0.46
Aug-69	4.54	0.50	−0.69	0.45
Sep-69	−2.36	0.62	−5.31	0.45
Oct-69	4.59	0.60	3.65	0.36
Nov-69	−2.97	0.52	−2.43	0.54
Dec-69	−1.77	0.64	−0.68	0.62
Jan-70	−7.43	0.60	−0.21	0.35
Feb-70	5.86	0.62	5.87	0.53
Mar-70	0.30	0.57	−0.68	0.53
Apr-70	−8.89	0.50	−4.13	0.61
May-70	−5.47	0.53	−4.68	0.43
Jun-70	−4.82	0.58	4.86	0.52
Jul-70	7.52	0.52	3.19	0.34
Aug-70	5.09	0.53	−0.19	0.17
Sep-70	3.47	0.54	2.28	0.51
Oct-70	−0.97	0.46	−1.09	0.51
Nov-70	5.36	0.46	7.91	0.34
Dec-70	5.84	0.42	−0.84	0.51
Jan-71	4.19	0.38	5.06	0.08
Feb-71	1.41	0.33	−1.63	0.17
Mar-71	3.82	0.30	5.26	0.34
Apr-71	3.77	0.28	−2.83	0.33
May-71	−3.67	0.29	−0.06	0.50
Jun-71	0.21	0.37	−1.59	0.58
Jul-71	−3.99	0.40	0.30	0.25
Aug-71	4.12	0.47	4.71	0.25
Sep-71	−0.56	0.37	2.04	0.08
Oct-71	−4.04	0.37	1.67	0.16
Nov-71	0.27	0.37	−0.47	0.16
Dec-71	8.77	0.37	0.44	0.41
Jan-72	1.94	0.29	−0.64	0.08
Feb-72	2.99	0.25	0.88	0.49
Mar-72	0.72	0.27	−0.82	0.16
Apr-72	0.57	0.29	0.27	0.24

(continues)

Date	S&P 500	One-Month Treasury Bill	Twenty-Year Treasury Bond	Inflation Rate
May-72	2.19	0.30	2.70	0.32
Jun-72	−2.05	0.29	−0.65	0.24
Jul-72	0.36	0.31	2.16	0.40
Aug-72	3.91	0.29	0.29	0.16
Sep-72	−0.36	0.34	−0.83	0.40
Oct-72	1.07	0.40	2.34	0.32
Nov-72	5.05	0.37	2.26	0.24
Dec-72	1.31	0.37	−2.29	0.32
Jan-73	−1.59	0.44	−3.21	0.31
Feb-73	−3.33	0.41	0.14	0.70
Mar-73	−0.02	0.46	0.82	0.93
Apr-73	−3.95	0.52	0.46	0.69
May-73	−1.39	0.51	−1.05	0.61
Jun-73	−0.51	0.51	−0.21	0.68
Jul-73	3.94	0.64	−4.33	0.23
Aug-73	−3.18	0.70	3.91	1.81
Sep-73	4.15	0.68	3.18	0.30
Oct-73	0.03	0.65	−1.30	0.81
Nov-73	−10.82	0.56	1.61	0.73
Dec-73	1.83	0.64	−0.82	0.65
Jan-74	−0.85	0.63	−0.83	0.87
Feb-74	0.19	0.58	−0.24	1.29
Mar-74	−2.17	0.56	−2.92	1.13
Apr-74	−3.73	0.75	−2.53	0.56
May-74	−2.72	0.75	1.23	1.11
Jun-74	−1.29	0.60	0.45	0.96
Jul-74	−7.59	0.70	−0.29	0.75
Aug-74	−8.28	0.60	−2.32	1.28
Sep-74	−11.70	0.81	2.47	1.20
Oct-74	16.57	0.51	4.89	0.86
Nov-74	−4.48	0.54	2.96	0.85
Dec-74	−1.77	0.70	1.71	0.71
Jan-75	12.51	0.58	2.25	0.45
Feb-75	6.74	0.43	1.31	0.70
Mar-75	2.37	0.41	−2.67	0.38
Apr-75	4.93	0.44	−1.82	0.51
May-75	5.09	0.44	2.12	0.44
Jun-75	4.62	0.41	2.92	0.82
Jul-75	−6.59	0.48	−0.87	1.06
Aug-75	−1.44	0.48	−0.68	0.31

(continues)

Date	S&P 500	One-Month Treasury Bill	Twenty-Year Treasury Bond	Inflation Rate
Sep-75	−3.28	0.53	−0.98	0.49
Oct-75	6.37	0.56	4.75	0.61
Nov-75	3.13	0.41	−1.09	0.61
Dec-75	−0.96	0.48	3.90	0.42
Jan-76	11.99	0.47	0.90	0.24
Feb-76	−0.58	0.34	0.62	0.24
Mar-76	3.26	0.40	1.66	0.24
Apr-76	−0.99	0.42	0.18	0.42
May-76	−0.73	0.37	−1.58	0.59
Jun-76	4.27	0.43	2.08	0.53
Jul-76	−0.68	0.47	0.78	0.59
Aug-76	0.14	0.42	2.11	0.47
Sep-76	2.47	0.44	1.45	0.41
Oct-76	−2.06	0.41	0.84	0.41
Nov-76	−0.09	0.40	3.39	0.29
Dec-76	5.40	0.40	3.27	0.29
Jan-77	−4.89	0.36	−3.88	0.57
Feb-77	−1.51	0.35	−0.44	1.03
Mar-77	−1.19	0.38	0.89	0.62
Apr-77	0.14	0.38	0.73	0.79
May-77	−1.50	0.37	1.21	0.56
Jun-77	4.75	0.40	1.65	0.66
Jul-77	−1.51	0.42	−0.38	0.44
Aug-77	−1.33	0.44	1.63	0.38
Sep-77	0.00	0.43	−0.27	0.38
Oct-77	−4.15	0.49	−0.94	0.27
Nov-77	3.70	0.50	0.95	0.49
Dec-77	0.48	0.49	−1.66	0.38
Jan-78	−5.96	0.49	−0.83	0.54
Feb-78	−1.61	0.46	0.09	0.69
Mar-78	2.76	0.53	−0.23	0.69
Apr-78	8.70	0.54	0.00	0.90
May-78	1.36	0.51	−0.65	0.99
Jun-78	−1.52	0.54	−0.62	1.03
Jul-78	5.60	0.56	1.41	0.72
Aug-78	3.40	0.56	2.16	0.51
Sep-78	−0.48	0.62	−1.02	0.71
Oct-78	−8.91	0.68	−2.03	0.80
Nov-78	2.60	0.70	1.90	0.55
Dec-78	1.72	0.78	−1.27	0.55

(continues)

Date	S&P 500	One-Month Treasury Bill	Twenty-Year Treasury Bond	Inflation Rate
Jan-79	4.21	0.77	1.93	0.89
Feb-79	−2.84	0.73	−1.29	1.17
Mar-79	5.75	0.81	1.30	0.97
Apr-79	0.36	0.80	−1.14	1.15
May-79	−1.68	0.82	2.59	1.23
Jun-79	4.10	0.81	3.14	0.93
Jul-79	1.09	0.77	−0.89	1.30
Aug-79	6.11	0.77	−0.37	1.01
Sep-79	0.25	0.83	−1.15	1.04
Oct-79	−6.56	0.87	−8.46	0.90
Nov-79	5.14	0.99	3.13	0.93
Dec-79	1.92	0.95	0.56	1.05
Jan-80	6.10	0.80	−7.42	1.44
Feb-80	0.31	0.89	−4.63	1.37
Mar-80	−9.87	1.21	−3.17	1.44
Apr-80	4.29	1.26	15.24	1.13
May-80	5.62	0.81	4.20	0.99
Jun-80	2.96	0.61	3.57	1.10
Jul-80	6.76	0.53	−4.78	0.08
Aug-80	1.31	0.64	−4.28	0.65
Sep-80	2.81	0.75	−2.65	0.92
Oct-80	1.86	0.95	−2.64	0.87
Nov-80	10.95	0.96	1.08	0.91
Dec-80	−3.15	1.31	3.44	0.86
Jan-81	−4.38	1.04	−1.13	0.81
Feb-81	2.08	1.07	−4.28	1.04
Mar-81	3.80	1.21	3.78	0.72
Apr-81	−2.13	1.08	−5.17	0.64
May-81	0.62	1.15	6.26	0.82
Jun-81	−0.80	1.35	−1.85	0.86
Jul-81	0.07	1.24	−3.56	1.14
Aug-81	−5.54	1.28	−3.88	0.77
Sep-81	−5.02	1.24	−1.43	1.01
Oct-81	5.28	1.21	8.32	0.21
Nov-81	4.41	1.07	14.09	0.29
Dec-81	−2.65	0.87	−7.14	0.29
Jan-82	−1.63	0.80	0.52	0.36
Feb-82	−5.12	0.92	1.91	0.32
Mar-82	−0.60	0.98	2.20	−0.11
Apr-82	4.14	1.13	3.74	0.42

(continues)

Date	S&P 500	One-Month Treasury Bill	Twenty-Year Treasury Bond	Inflation Rate
May-82	−2.88	1.06	0.42	0.98
Jun-82	−1.74	0.96	−2.33	1.22
Jul-82	−2.15	1.05	5.02	0.55
Aug-82	12.67	0.76	7.75	0.21
Sep-82	1.10	0.51	6.21	0.17
Oct-82	11.26	0.59	6.40	0.27
Nov-82	4.38	0.63	−0.06	−0.17
Dec-82	1.73	0.67	3.11	−0.41
Jan-83	3.48	0.69	−3.10	0.24
Feb-83	2.60	0.62	4.99	0.03
Mar-83	3.65	0.63	−0.96	0.07
Apr-83	7.58	0.71	3.53	0.72
May-83	−0.52	0.69	−3.91	0.54
Jun-83	3.82	0.67	0.40	0.34
Jul-83	−3.13	0.74	−4.83	0.40
Aug-83	1.70	0.76	0.12	0.33
Sep-83	1.36	0.76	5.07	0.50
Oct-83	−1.34	0.76	−1.33	0.27
Nov-83	2.33	0.70	1.86	0.17
Dec-83	−0.61	0.73	−0.57	0.13
Jan-84	−0.65	0.76	2.38	0.56
Feb-84	−3.28	0.71	−1.74	0.46
Mar-84	1.71	0.73	−1.55	0.23
Apr-84	0.69	0.81	−1.08	0.49
May-84	−5.34	0.78	−5.18	0.29
Jun-84	2.21	0.75	1.56	0.32
Jul-84	−1.43	0.82	6.88	0.32
Aug-84	11.25	0.83	2.65	0.42
Sep-84	0.02	0.86	3.51	0.48
Oct-84	0.26	0.95	5.61	0.25
Nov-84	−1.01	0.73	1.19	0.00
Dec-84	2.53	0.64	0.91	0.13
Jan-85	7.68	0.65	3.64	0.19
Feb-85	1.37	0.58	−4.94	0.41
Mar-85	0.18	0.62	3.07	0.44
Apr-85	−0.32	0.72	2.42	0.41
May-85	6.15	0.66	8.96	0.37
Jun-85	1.59	0.55	1.42	0.31
Jul-85	−0.26	0.60	−1.80	0.16
Aug-85	−0.61	0.58	2.59	0.22

(continues)

Date	S&P 500	One-Month Treasury Bill	Twenty-Year Treasury Bond	Inflation Rate
Sep-85	−3.21	0.60	−0.21	0.31
Oct-85	4.48	0.65	3.38	0.31
Nov-85	7.16	0.61	4.01	0.34
Dec-85	4.67	0.65	5.41	0.24
Jan-86	0.44	0.56	−0.25	0.31
Feb-86	7.61	0.53	11.45	−0.27
Mar-86	5.54	0.60	7.70	−0.46
Apr-86	−1.24	0.52	−0.80	−0.21
May-86	5.49	0.49	−5.05	0.31
Jun-86	1.66	0.52	6.07	0.49
Jul-86	−5.69	0.52	−1.08	0.03
Aug-86	7.48	0.46	4.99	0.18
Sep-86	−8.22	0.45	−5.00	0.49
Oct-86	5.56	0.46	2.89	0.09
Nov-86	2.56	0.39	2.67	0.09
Dec-86	−2.64	0.48	−0.18	0.09
Jan-87	13.43	0.42	1.62	0.60
Feb-87	4.13	0.43	2.02	0.39
Mar-87	2.72	0.47	−2.23	0.45
Apr-87	−0.88	0.44	−4.73	0.54
May-87	1.03	0.38	−1.05	0.30
Jun-87	4.99	0.48	0.98	0.41
Jul-87	4.98	0.46	−1.78	0.21
Aug-87	3.85	0.47	−1.65	0.56
Sep-87	−2.20	0.45	−3.69	0.50
Oct-87	−21.52	0.59	6.23	0.26
Nov-87	−8.19	0.35	0.37	0.14
Dec-87	7.38	0.39	1.66	−0.03
Jan-88	4.27	0.29	6.67	0.26
Feb-88	4.70	0.46	0.52	0.26
Mar-88	−3.02	0.46	−3.07	0.43
Apr-88	1.08	0.46	−1.60	0.52
May-88	0.78	0.49	−1.01	0.34
Jun-88	4.64	0.49	3.68	0.43
Jul-88	−0.40	0.51	−1.70	0.42
Aug-88	−3.31	0.59	0.58	0.42
Sep-88	4.24	0.62	3.45	0.67
Oct-88	2.73	0.61	3.08	0.33
Nov-88	−1.42	0.57	−1.97	0.08
Dec-88	1.81	0.63	1.10	0.17

(continues)

Date	S&P 500	One-Month Treasury Bill	Twenty-Year Treasury Bond	Inflation Rate
Jan-89	7.23	0.55	2.03	0.50
Feb-89	-2.49	0.61	-1.79	0.41
Mar-89	2.36	0.67	1.22	0.58
Apr-89	5.16	0.67	1.59	0.65
May-89	4.02	0.79	4.01	0.57
Jun-89	-0.54	0.71	5.50	0.24
Jul-89	8.98	0.70	2.38	0.24
Aug-89	1.93	0.74	-2.59	0.16
Sep-89	-0.39	0.65	0.19	0.32
Oct-89	-2.33	0.68	3.79	0.48
Nov-89	2.08	0.69	0.78	0.24
Dec-89	2.36	0.61	-0.06	0.16
Jan-90	-6.71	0.57	-3.43	1.03
Feb-90	1.29	0.57	-0.25	0.47
Mar-90	2.63	0.64	-0.41	0.55
Apr-90	-2.47	0.67	-2.02	0.16
May-90	9.75	0.68	4.15	0.23
Jun-90	-0.70	0.63	2.30	0.54
Jul-90	-0.32	0.68	1.07	0.38
Aug-90	-9.03	0.66	-4.19	0.92
Sep-90	-4.92	0.60	1.17	0.84
Oct-90	-0.37	0.68	2.15	0.60
Nov-90	6.44	0.57	4.02	0.22
Dec-90	2.74	0.60	1.87	0.00
Jan-91	4.42	0.52	1.30	0.60
Feb-91	7.16	0.48	0.30	0.15
Mar-91	2.38	0.44	0.38	0.15
Apr-91	0.28	0.53	1.40	0.15
May-91	4.28	0.47	0.00	0.30
Jun-91	-4.57	0.42	-0.63	0.29
Jul-91	4.68	0.49	1.57	0.15
Aug-91	2.35	0.46	3.40	0.29
Sep-91	-1.64	0.46	3.03	0.44
Oct-91	1.34	0.42	0.54	0.15
Nov-91	-4.04	0.39	0.82	0.29
Dec-91	11.43	0.38	5.81	0.07
Jan-92	-1.86	0.34	-3.24	0.15
Feb-92	1.28	0.28	0.51	0.36
Mar-92	-1.96	0.34	-0.94	0.51
Apr-92	2.91	0.32	0.16	0.14

(continues)

Date	S&P 500	One-Month Treasury Bill	Twenty-Year Treasury Bond	Inflation Rate
May-92	0.54	0.28	2.43	0.14
Jun-92	−1.45	0.32	2.00	0.36
Jul-92	4.03	0.31	3.98	0.21
Aug-92	−2.02	0.26	1.50	0.28
Sep-92	1.15	0.26	1.85	0.28
Oct-92	0.36	0.23	−1.56	0.35
Nov-92	3.37	0.23	0.10	0.14
Dec-92	1.31	0.28	2.46	0.07
Jan-93	0.73	0.23	2.80	0.49
Feb-93	1.35	0.22	3.54	0.35
Mar-93	2.15	0.25	0.21	0.35
Apr-93	−2.45	0.24	0.72	0.28
May-93	2.70	0.22	0.47	0.14
Jun-93	0.33	0.25	4.49	0.14
Jul-93	−0.47	0.24	1.91	0.00
Aug-93	3.81	0.25	4.32	0.28
Sep-93	−0.74	0.26	0.07	0.21
Oct-93	2.03	0.22	0.96	0.41
Nov-93	−0.94	0.25	−2.59	0.07
Dec-93	1.23	0.23	0.20	0.00
Jan-94	3.35	0.25	2.57	0.27
Feb-94	−2.70	0.21	−4.50	0.34
Mar-94	−4.35	0.27	−3.95	0.34
Apr-94	1.30	0.27	−1.50	0.14
May-94	1.63	0.32	−0.82	0.07
Jun-94	−2.47	0.31	−1.00	0.34
Jul-94	3.31	0.28	3.63	0.27
Aug-94	4.07	0.37	−0.86	0.40
Sep-94	−2.41	0.37	−3.31	0.27
Oct-94	2.29	0.38	−0.25	0.07
Nov-94	−3.67	0.37	0.66	0.13
Dec-94	1.46	0.44	1.61	0.00
Jan-95	2.60	0.42	2.73	0.40
Feb-95	3.88	0.40	2.87	0.40
Mar-95	2.96	0.46	0.92	0.33
Apr-95	2.91	0.44	1.69	0.33
May-95	3.95	0.54	7.90	0.33
Jun-95	2.35	0.47	1.39	0.20
Jul-95	3.33	0.45	−1.68	0.00
Aug-95	0.27	0.47	2.36	0.26

(continues)

Date	S&P 500	One-Month Treasury Bill	Twenty-Year Treasury Bond	Inflation Rate
Sep-95	4.19	0.43	1.75	0.20
Oct-95	−0.35	0.47	2.94	0.33
Nov-95	4.40	0.42	2.49	−0.07
Dec-95	1.85	0.49	2.72	−0.07
Jan-96	3.44	0.43	−0.11	0.59
Feb-96	0.96	0.39	−4.83	0.32
Mar-96	0.96	0.39	−2.10	0.52
Apr-96	1.47	0.46	−1.65	0.39
May-96	2.58	0.42	−0.54	0.19
Jun-96	0.41	0.40	2.03	0.06
Jul-96	−4.45	0.45	0.18	0.19
Aug-96	2.12	0.41	−1.39	0.19
Sep-96	5.62	0.44	2.90	0.32
Oct-96	2.74	0.42	4.04	0.32
Nov-96	7.59	0.41	3.51	0.19
Dec-96	−1.96	0.46	−2.56	0.00
Jan-97	6.21	0.45	−0.79	0.32
Feb-97	0.81	0.39	0.05	0.31
Mar-97	−4.16	0.43	−2.52	0.25
Apr-97	5.97	0.43	2.55	0.12
May-97	6.14	0.49	0.97	−0.06
Jun-97	4.46	0.37	1.95	0.12
Jul-97	7.94	0.43	6.26	0.12
Aug-97	−5.56	0.41	−3.17	0.19
Sep-97	5.48	0.44	3.16	0.25
Oct-97	−3.34	0.42	3.41	0.25
Nov-97	4.63	0.39	1.48	−0.06
Dec-97	1.72	0.48	1.84	−0.12

Chapter 3

Forward-Looking Estimates of the Equity Risk Premium

The amount of attention lavished on the history of the stock market and its implications for the equity risk premium overshadows the fact that there are more direct ways to estimate the premium. These direct methods, furthermore, are free of many of the nonstationarity and survival-bias problems that bedevil historical analysis. The direct approaches are based on the fundamental valuation equation, which states that the value of the market portfolio equals the present value of expected future dividends on the market discounted at the expected return on the market. If future dividends can be forecast, the present value relation can be solved for the expected return. Deducting the current yield on treasury bills or treasury bonds yields a forward-looking estimate of the market risk premium.

To develop and illustrate this approach, this chapter starts with the example of an individual equity. Once the principles have been established, the difficulties involved with applying the approach to the market as a whole can be addressed.

The Discounted Cash Flow Model

The basic forward-looking approach is referred to as the discounted cash flow (DCF) method because it is based on the definition of the long-run expected return as the discount rate that equates the stock price with the stream of expected future dividends. More formally, the expected return, k, is the solution to the equation

$$P = \frac{Div_1}{1+k} + \frac{Div_2}{(1+k)^2} + \frac{Div_3}{(1+k)^3} + \dots \qquad (3.1)$$

where Div_1 is the expected dividend in year 1, Div_2 is the expected dividend in year 2, and so on, and k is the expected return (or equivalently, the cost of equity capital).

Equation 3.1 makes it clear that the key to application of the DCF model is the dividend forecast. This makes it difficult to apply the DCF model to companies that do not have a history of paying dividends. Without a historical record, future dividends are much more difficult to forecast. In addition, if the company is not currently paying a dividend, the initiation date must be forecast as well. For these reasons, Equation 3.1 usually is applied only to companies that are paying reasonable dividends.

Because ongoing companies do not have a defined life, Equation 3.1 potentially involves an infinite number of terms. Clearly, dividends cannot be forecast year by year forever, so at some point an assumption must be made about the time path of future dividends in order to solve the equation for k. That point is usually referred to as the terminal horizon. The idea is that by the terminal horizon, the company will have settled down to an equilibrium so that a simple rule of thumb can be applied to forecast dividends from then on.

Forms of the Model

Constant-Growth Form

One particularly simple assumption that is reasonable to employ in some situations is dividends grow at the constant rate, g, right from the start. This is the constant-growth version of the model presented earlier. For the case of constant growth, Equation 2.1 can be solved for k to yield

$$k = \frac{Div_1}{P} + g \tag{3.2}$$

Equation 3.2 states that the expected return on a stock over the long run equals the current dividend yield, Div_1/P, plus the expected dividend growth rate, g. As an illustration, consider the application of Equation 3.2 to AT&T International as of December 31, 1996. On that date, AT&T closed at $43.375. Assuming that the next year's expected dividend payout equals four times the current quarterly dividend, Div_1 comes to $1.32. Therefore, the dividend yield in Equation 3.2 is 3.04%. At the end of 1996, the IBES (Institutional Brokers' Estimate System) forecast (more about this in the section "Multistage Form") of growth for AT&T was 9.67% per year. Assuming that this growth forecast can be substituted into Equation 3.2, the expected return for AT&T comes to 12.71%.[1]

One area in which the constant-growth form of the DCF equation has found widespread application is in setting fair rates of return for utilities. In two precedent-setting cases, *Bluefield Water Works v. Public Service Commission*, 262 U.S. 679,692 (1923), and *Federal Power Commission v. Hope Natural Gas Company*, 320 U.S. 591,603 (1944), the U.S. Supreme Court held that investors in utilities must earn a rate of return that fairly compensates them for the risk they bear. Consequently, a central aspect of rate setting is determining a fair rate of return on equity. Finance theory teaches that the appropriate fair rate is the expected return given by the solution to Equation 3.1. Faced with the problem of solving Equation 3.1, utility regulators in many states traditionally have turned to the constant-growth model. Because the assumption of constant growth is not unreasonable for many utilities, particularly for more mature companies, application of Equation 3.2 often pro-

---

[1] This is an approximation because dividends are paid quarterly, not annually. If quarterly data are employed, the solution for k is a quarterly rate.

duces estimates of expected returns falling within a range that both ratepayers and utility shareholders are willing to accept.

Although the constant-growth model has a long history, practitioners have come to recognize that its applicability is limited to companies, such as mature utilities, for which the constant-growth assumption is reasonable. As stressed by numerous authors—including Cornell (1993); Copeland, Koller, and Murrin (1994); Damodaran (1994); and Sharpe, Alexander, and Bailey (1995)—constant growth is not an accurate characterization of the future for most companies. Under normal circumstances, a multistage version of the DCF model that more appropriately approximates the expected path of future dividends is required. The practical problem, of course, is deciding how to approximate the time series for future dividends. Before turning to that critical question, there are several details that need to be addressed regarding application of the DCF model.

First, there is a dispute among practitioners as to what stock price should be used when applying the DCF model. Efficient market theory clearly implies that the appropriate stock price is the market price observed at the same time as the dividend forecast—that is, the price that reflects publicly available information about the company's future. Nonetheless, because of the volatility of stock prices, some practitioners use—and some regulatory bodies accept—3- or 6-month averages of stock prices. The problem with using such an average is that it introduces outdated information that can bias the estimate of the cost of equity. The reason that the market price moves is because new information arrives that affects the assessment of value. Averaging in old prices is equivalent to ignoring, or giving inappropriate weight to, the new information. For that reason, and given the growing acceptance of efficient market theory, the current stock price is used here.

Second, there is a question regarding the compounding interval. Because dividends are paid quarterly, k should be estimated as a quarterly rate and converted to an effective annual rate. In many practical situations, however, the cost of capital is computed as an annual rate and then payments based on that rate are made monthly. For instance, regulated utilities earn income monthly at the allowed rate of return. In that case, the effective annual rate computed from quarterly dividends should be decompounded on a monthly basis. In the present case, the DCF model is applied on an annual basis, so no added adjustment for compounding is required.

Finally, there is an issue with respect to flotation costs. Should the stock price in the DCF model be reduced by the costs of issuing new securities? This question has a long history in utility rate cases, and there are theoretical arguments on both sides. However, the debate is of little practical importance in most situations because virtually all the new equity capital raised in the United States comes from retained earnings, not new stock sales. Consider, for instance, the telecommunications industry. Between 1993 and 1998, the industry invested tens of billions of dollars in new infrastructure. Nonetheless, net stock issuances in that same time period were approximately zero. Virtually the entire investment has been financed from retained earnings. Rather than complicate the discussion by including a second-order effect, this discussion excludes flotation costs here.[2]

Returning to the question of estimating the time path of dividends, there is a growing consensus that the best place to start is with security analysts' forecasts. This consensus is based on a substantial academic literature which indicates that analysts' forecasts of earnings take account of all the information provided by more formulaic forecasting rules and incorporate other information as well.[3] Based on these findings, the most common solution is to assume that the dividend payout rate remains effectively constant and to use analyst forecasts of earnings growth as a proxy for the growth rate of dividends.

---

[2] For a more detailed analysis of how to incorporate transactions costs, see Arzac and Marcus (1981).

[3] Studies comparing analyst earnings forecasts with more formulaic forecasting models include Brown and Rozeff (1978); Brown, Hagerman, Griffin, and Zmijewski (1987); Brown and Kim (1991); and VanderWeide and Carleton (1988).

The practical problem raised by relying on analysts forecasts is that such forecasts typically have short horizons. Services that aggregate forecasts, including those by IBES and Zacks Investment Research, do not provide forecasts beyond 5 years. From the standpoint of the DCF model, which extends into perpetuity, this horizon is too short. One possibility is to assume that the forecast growth can be maintained into perpetuity. This amounts to substituting the forecast growth rate into the constant-growth model. If the forecast growth rate is less than that of the aggregate economy, then constant growth is a possibility. However, it is unlikely because it implies that the company will become relatively smaller as time passes. In most cases, the IBES forecasts are greater than the long-run economic growth rate. Such high growth rates clearly cannot be maintained forever. Although it is possible that a company's dividends can grow significantly faster than the general economy for 5 years, if such a growth rate were maintained indefinitely, the company would eventually engulf the entire economy. Accordingly, a transition must occur between the growth rates forecast by analysts for the first 5 years and the company's long-run sustainable growth rate. Developing a model of this transition is a difficult task.

The procedure suggested here is one that the author has found reasonable in a wide variety of consulting assignments. It should be stressed, however, that there are a large number of transition models that can be developed.[4] The critical condition is that long-run company growth eventually falls to the rate of long-run economic growth or less.

Multistage Form

In the model used here, dividends for the first 5 years are assumed to grow at the median 5-year earnings growth rate reported by IBES, a service made available by the firm of Lynch, Jones, and

---

[4] Damodaran (1994) discussed a variety of the multistage discounted cash flow (DCF) model that makes different transition assumptions.

Ryan. To compile the long-term IBES data, Lynch, Jones, and Ryan surveys over 2,000 analysts each month regarding their estimates of 5-year earnings growth rates for a wide variety of major U.S. companies. These analysts represent over 100 different securities firms. The forecasts are tabulated and distributed to subscribers, including most large institutional investors, such as pension funds, banks, and insurance companies. The most widely followed forecasts are the IBES medians.

From year 20 onward, dividends are assumed to grow at the same nominal rate as the national economy. Long-run forecasts for aggregate economic growth are available from most economic forecasting firms. Two well-known firms that provide 25-year forecasts are the WEFA Group and Data Resources Incorporated (DRI). The average of the WEFA and DRI forecasts is employed to estimate the growth rate from year 20 forward. As of December 1996, that average was 6.16% per year.

Finally, during the intervening 15 years, the growth rate is assumed to converge linearly from the IBES forecast to the long-run forecast. Of course, there is nothing sacred about using 15 years. In some cases, it may be more reasonable to assume that convergence takes place over 5, 10, or even 20 years. The choice of convergence rate depends on the nature of the company's business and the discrepancy between the company's growth rate and the growth rate of the aggregate economy. Presumably, the larger the difference, the longer it should take for the two rates to converge. It is also possible to posit nonlinear convergence paths.

As an illustration, apply the multistage DCF model to AT&T. When the growth rate is not constant, there is no analytical solution to Equation 3.1 analogous to that for Equation 3.2. However, Equation 3.1 can be solved quickly using an iterative technique. For AT&T, the following inputs are employed as of December 31, 1996. Recall that at that time, the stock price was $43.375 and the initial dividend was $1.32. From there, the dividends are assumed to grow at the 9.67% IBES rate for the next 5 years. After that, the growth rate drops linearly to 6.16% (the average of the long-run economic growth rates forecast by WEFA and DRI) over the next

15 years. It then remains at 6.16% into perpetuity. With these assumptions, the only unknown remaining in Equation 3.1 is k, the expected return. Solving iteratively for k gives 10.58%.

Notice that the multistage estimate of the expected return, 10.58%, is about 200 basis points below the constant growth estimate of 12.71%. This is because the dividend stream is lower in the multistage model. Whereas the constant-growth model assumes that the IBES growth rate of 9.67% is maintained in perpetuity, the multistage models assumes that it begins to decline in year 6 and converges to the economic growth rate of 6.16% by year 20. In general, the larger the difference between the 5-year growth rate for a company and the sustainable growth rate, the greater will be the difference between the expected return produced by the constant-growth model and that produced by the multistage growth model.[5]

The objective here is not to estimate the expected return for individual companies but to estimate it for the market generally, or at least for a diversified index of companies. There are two ways that the DCF model can be applied to an index like Standard & Poor's (S&P) 500 Index. First, the DCF model can be applied to the index on an aggregate basis. This approach requires an aggregate dividend forecast for the group of companies that comprise the index. Given an aggregate dividend forecast, the index can be treated as if it were an individual company for purposes of applying the DCF model. Second, the DCF approach can be applied on a case-by-case basis to the companies in the index and results can then be aggregated to estimate the cost of capital for stocks generally. Because the S&P 500 is a value-weighted index, value weights should be used when averaging the costs of capital for the individual companies.

The first approach is commonly used by investment banks. For instance, as of December 1996, Goldman Sachs estimated that the market cost of equity capital was approximately 11%. At that time,

---

[5] If the 5-year growth rate is less than the sustainable growth rate, then the multistage model will produce a higher expected return than will the constant-growth model.

yields on 1-month treasury bills and 20-year treasury bonds were 5.49% and 6.73%, respectively. Therefore, Goldman Sach's expected return on the market translates into a risk premium of 5.51% over bills and 4.27% over bonds.

Table 3.1 illustrates the second approach, the company-by-company approach. This approach is complicated by the fact that not all of the companies in the S&P 500 pay dividends. As noted earlier, the DCF calculation becomes speculative when applied to companies that do not currently pay dividends. Consequently, in Table 3.1 the DCF model is applied to only those companies in the S&P 500 for which the dividend yield at the end of 1996 was at least 3%.

It is possible that limiting the sample to companies that pay dividends of 3% or more introduces an element of selection bias. Research by Fama and French (1992), among others, indicates that small companies with lower dividend payout rates tend to have higher costs of capital. If this is true, then eliminating companies that do not pay a dividend from the sample will tend to reduce the estimate of the market cost of capital. In the case of the S&P 500, however, the bias is likely to be small because even the companies that do not pay dividends, like Microsoft, are hardly small.

In computing the cost of equity for each of the individual firms, the same procedure that was applied to AT&T International is employed. (AT&T is one the firms in the sample.) Growth forecasts are taken from IBES and a 15-year convergence assumption is used. The results for each of the individual companies, as of December 31, 1996, and the value-weighted average are shown in Table 3.1.

The results reported in Table 3.1 are largely consistent with those produced by the Goldman Sachs aggregate approach. The value-weighted average cost of capital comes to 11.26%. This represents a premium of 5.77% over bills and 4.53% over bonds. The fact that these estimates are greater than those obtained by the Goldman Sachs aggregate approach indicates that in this case at least, selection bias did not reduce the estimate of expected return.

As another check on the impact of selection, the calculations in Table 3.1 were repeated using 2% yield as the cutoff point. Using

Table 3.1. Calculation of the Expected Return on Market

Company Name	Price per Share (WSJ) as of 12/31/96 ($)	Dividend per WSJ as of 12/31/96 ($)	Dividend Yield (D/P Ratio) (%)	5-Year IBES Growth Forecast (%)	3-Stage DCF Cost of Equity (%)
ALLTEL Corp.	31.375	1.10	3.51	10.43	11.53
American Brands Inc.	49.625	2.00	4.03	10.15	12.13
American Electric Power	41.125	2.40	5.84	2.70	10.74
American General	40.875	1.30	3.18	9.78	10.81
Ameritech	60.625	2.26	3.73	8.86	11.17
Amoco	80.625	2.80	3.47	8.21	10.59
AT&T Corp.	43.375	1.32	3.04	9.67	10.58
Atlantic Richfield	132.500	5.50	4.15	6.55	10.72
Baltimore Gas & Electric	26.750	1.60	5.98	3.43	11.19
Banc One Corp.	43.000	1.36	3.16	11.60	11.53
Bankers Trust N.Y.	86.250	4.00	4.64	9.44	12.60
Bell Atlantic	64.750	2.88	4.45	7.98	11.67
BellSouth	40.500	1.44	3.56	8.41	10.77
Caliber Systems Inc.	19.250	0.72	3.74	10.60	11.94
Carolina Power & Light	36.500	1.88	5.15	3.91	10.64
Central & South West	25.625	1.74	6.79	3.00	11.70
Chevron Corp.	65.000	2.16	3.32	7.76	10.24
Chrysler Corp.	33.000	1.60	4.85	6.90	11.64
CINergy Corp.	33.375	1.80	5.39	4.67	11.20
Consolidated Edison	29.125	2.08	7.14	1.50	11.27
Consolidated Natural Gas	55.250	1.94	3.51	9.07	10.97
CoreStates Financial	51.875	1.88	3.62	9.57	11.33
Cyprus Amax Minerals Co.	23.500	0.80	3.40	11.00	11.63
Dana Corp.	32.625	1.00	3.07	8.78	10.29
Deluxe Corp.	32.750	1.48	4.52	11.00	13.23
Dominion Resources	38.500	2.58	6.70	3.47	11.85
Dow Chemical	78.375	3.00	3.83	8.00	10.94
DTE Energy Co.	32.375	2.06	6.36	2.73	11.20
Duke Power	46.250	2.12	4.58	4.98	10.54
Dun & Bradstreet	23.750	0.88	3.71	7.36	10.54
Eastern Enterprises	35.375	1.60	4.52	7.33	11.47

(continues)

Company Name	Price per Share (WSJ) as of 12/31/96 ($)	Dividend per WSJ as of 12/31/96 ($)	Dividend Yield (D/P Ratio) (%)	5-Year IBES Growth Forecast (%)	3-Stage DCF Cost of Equity (%)
Eastman Chemical	55.250	1.76	3.19	9.18	10.59
Edison International	19.875	1.00	5.03	3.05	10.20
Entergy Corp.	27.625	1.80	6.52	3.97	11.93
Exxon Corp.	98.000	3.16	3.22	6.30	9.63
Ford Motor	32.250	1.54	4.78	6.22	11.26
FPL Group	46.000	1.84	4.00	4.91	9.95
Frontier Corp.	22.625	0.87	3.85	14.90	14.22
General Mills	63.625	2.00	3.14	10.76	11.15
General Motors	55.750	1.60	2.87	7.33	9.56
Genuine Parts	44.500	1.34	3.01	10.00	10.66
GPU Inc.	33.625	1.94	5.77	3.35	10.96
GTE Corp.	45.375	1.88	4.14	9.17	11.83
Houston Industries	22.625	1.50	6.63	3.84	11.97
International Flavors and Fragrances	45.000	1.44	3.20	11.36	11.48
Jostens Inc.	21.125	0.88	4.17	12.00	13.23
KeyCorp	50.500	1.52	3.01	9.59	10.51
Lincoln National	52.500	1.96	3.73	10.58	11.92
Mobil Corp.	122.250	4.00	3.27	8.94	10.61
Moore Corp. Ltd.	20.500	0.94	4.59	12.00	13.85
Morgan (J.P.) & Co.	97.625	3.52	3.61	9.04	11.08
National City Corp.	44.875	1.64	3.65	9.81	11.47
National Service Ind	37.375	1.20	3.21	12.33	11.92
NICOR Inc.	35.750	1.32	3.69	5.94	10.00
Northern States Power	45.875	2.76	6.02	3.27	11.15
Nynex	48.125	2.36	4.90	6.60	11.56
Occidental Petroleum	23.375	1.00	4.28	8.42	11.66
Ohio Edison	22.750	1.50	6.59	2.70	11.38
ONEOK Inc.	30.000	1.20	4.00	7.00	10.73
PP & L Resources	23.000	1.67	7.26	2.60	11.91
Pacific Enterprises	30.375	1.44	4.74	4.75	10.60
Pacific Telesis	36.750	1.26	3.43	3.88	9.09
PacifiCorp	20.500	1.08	5.27	3.87	10.73

(continues)

Table 3.1. Continued

Company Name	Price per Share (WSJ) as of 12/31/96 ($)	Dividend per WSJ as of 12/31/96 ($)	Dividend Yield (D/P Ratio) (%)	5-Year IBES Growth Forecast (%)	3-Stage DCF Cost of Equity (%)
PECO Energy Co.	25.250	1.80	7.13	3.23	12.12
Penney (J.C.)	48.750	2.08	4.27	9.50	12.15
Peoples Energy	33.875	1.84	5.43	3.71	10.82
PG&E Corp.	21.000	1.20	5.71	−0.76	9.33
Philip Morris	113.000	4.80	4.25	16.10	15.60
Phillips Petroleum	44.250	1.28	2.89	11.43	11.04
PNC Bank Corp.	37.625	1.48	3.93	9.90	11.89
Potlatch Corp.	43.000	1.70	3.95	7.33	10.81
Public Serv. Enterprise	27.250	2.16	7.93	2.26	12.31
Quaker Oats	38.125	1.14	2.99	10.38	10.78
SBC Communications Inc.	51.875	1.72	3.32	10.03	11.10
Southern Co.	22.625	1.26	5.57	3.65	10.91
Sun Co., Inc.	24.375	1.00	4.10	8.78	11.61
Supervalu Inc.	28.375	1.00	3.52	8.71	10.85
Tenneco Inc.	45.125	1.20	2.66	12.06	10.92
Texaco Inc.	98.125	3.40	3.46	9.63	11.14
Texas Utilities	40.750	2.10	5.15	6.29	11.69
US West Communications	32.250	2.14	6.64	4.88	12.51
Unicom Corp.	27.125	1.60	5.90	4.66	11.68
Union Camp	47.750	1.80	3.77	7.67	10.73
Union Electric Co.	38.500	2.54	6.60	2.46	11.28
UST Inc.	32.375	1.62	5.00	12.33	14.65
USX-U.S. Steel Group	31.375	1.00	3.19	20.00	15.71
Westvaco Corp.	28.750	0.88	3.06	8.29	10.11
Weyerhaeuser Corp.	47.375	1.60	3.38	8.82	10.70
				Market-weighted average	**11.26**

D/P ratio = dividend-to-price ratio; DCF = discounted cash flow; IBES = International Brokers' Estimate System; WSJ = Wall Street Journal.

this lower cutoff, the estimate of the expected return on the market fell to 11.12%. This is further indication that for the S&P 500 at end of 1996, selection bias did not reduce the estimate of the expected return.

Although the complete data to replicate Table 3.1 as of June 1998 are not available, FinEcon, a financial economic consulting firm, produces a semiannual update using a subset of the S&P 500 that the firm has found to be representative. As of July 1, 1998, the expected return on the market using the FinEcon data was 10.2%. On that date, the yields on 1-month treasury bills and 20-year treasury bonds were 4.71% and 5.71%, respectively. These data, at least, suggest there has been little change in the expected equity risk premium since the end of 1996. Similarly, an aggregate DCF model developed by Merrill Lynch produced an expected return on the market of 10% during July of 1998, which results in approximately the same risk premium.

In addition to providing an estimate of the expected return on the market, Table 3.1 illustrates several features of the DCF model. First, a comparison of the constant-growth form with the multistage form shows that the multistage model is clearly superior. Whereas the constant-growth model produces estimates that are clearly unreasonable, such as a cost of equity less than the treasury bond yield (and one that is even below zero), this is not the case for the multistage model. Second, the multistage model produces estimates that comport with common sense for every company. The minimum cost of equity is 9.09% and the maximum is 15.71%. This tight range of estimates is one of the reason that practitioners, regulators, and the courts feel comfortable with the DCF model.

Comparison of the Discounted Cash Flow and Historical Estimates of the Risk Premium

The results reported in Table 3.1 are markedly different than the historical estimates of the market risk premium. Whereas the historical estimates using the annual Ibbotson Associates data are 9.2% over bills and 7.4% over bonds, the forward-looking estimates are 5.77% over bills and 4.53% over bonds. This difference represents a decline of between 282 and 339 basis points in the risk premium. To appreciate how important this difference can be, consider again the calculation presented in Chapter 2. Using the constant-growth model for a 5% growth rate and a 5% risk-free rate, a drop of 300 basis points in the risk premium translates into an increase in stock prices of 60%:

$$\text{Ratio of Stock Prices before Drop to after Drop} = \frac{.13 - .05}{.10 - .05} = 1.60$$

The Blanchard Extension of the Discounted Cash Flow Approach

In an attempt to estimate the ex-ante market risk premium, Blanchard (1993) extended the basic DCF model. He developed a dynamic time series model that explicitly takes account of variation in interest rates and dividend yields. To implement his model, Blanchard simultaneously estimated the future path of stock and bond returns. After examining the forward-looking estimates, he concluded that as of 1992:

> The equity risk premium has gone steadily down since the early 1950s, although inflation contributed to transitory increases above the trend in the 1970s and transitory decreases below the trend in the 1980s. Today, the premium appears to be around 2–3 percent [p. 115].

If Blanchard's calculations were extrapolated forward to July 1998, they would predict an even lower risk premium. The dividend yield, which is the key driver of his model for the risk premium, declined almost steadily from 1992 through the end of 1997.[6] Substituting data on dividend yield from the end of 1992 through July 1998 into Blanchard's model leads to lower predictions for the equity risk premium—approximately 2%. This is substantially lower than the predictions of the standard DCF model.

The Kaplan–Ruback Study

As noted at the outset, application of the DCF model is critically dependent on the forecasts of future dividends. Kaplan and Ruback (1995) attempted to avoid the dividend forecasting problem by making use of a unique data set. For a sample of 51 highly leveraged transactions completed between 1983 and 1989, the authors were able to obtain not only the price at which the transaction was executed but also the cash-flow forecasts developed by the purchasers.

Kaplan and Ruback worked with a version of Equation 3.1 that contains a terminal value. The terminal value represents the estimated value of all cash flows beyond a specific horizon. Using a terminal value, Equation 3.1 can be written as follows:

$$P = \frac{Div_1}{1 + k} + \frac{Div_2}{(1 + k)^2} + \frac{Div_n}{(1 + k)^n} + \text{Terminal Value at } \frac{n}{(1 + k)^n} \quad (3.3)$$

In place of the future dividends, Kaplan and Ruback substituted the cash flows that buyers expected to receive from their purchase of the company. They also had estimates of the terminal value provided by the buyers. Given these inputs and the observed price of the deal, Kaplan and Ruback solved Equation 3.3 for the discount rate, k, which equates the present value of the future cash flows

---

[6] A plot of the dividend yield is presented in Chapter 5 as Figure 5.1.

with the sale price. This is their estimate of the cost of capital for the firm involved in the deal.

The cost of capital for an individual firm differs from the market cost of equity for two reasons. First, the cost of capital for a company is based on a mixture of debt and equity. Second, the cost of equity for the firm is generally not equal to the overall market cost of equity. Kaplan and Ruback used a two-step procedure to solve for the equity risk premium from an individual firm's cost of capital. The first step is to solve for the cost of equity from the cost of capital. Because the cost of debt and the capital structure are observable, this is straightforward. The second step is to go from an individual company's cost of equity to the equity risk premium. This requires an asset pricing model. In their study, Kaplan and Ruback inverted the capital asset pricing model (CAPM) to solve for the market risk premium from the cost of equity. In this fashion, Kaplan and Ruback arrived at an estimate of the market risk premium for each firm in their sample. To calculate an overall estimate of the equity risk premium, Kaplan and Ruback averaged the individual estimates produced by each firm.

Although the preceding sounds simple, solving for the market risk premium from each individual firm's cost of equity is in fact quite tricky. For that reason, Kaplan and Ruback used a variety of procedures. Although the exact results obtained depend on the procedures used and the assumptions employed, the authors concluded that "The estimated market risk premium of 7.78 percent is remarkably close to the long-term arithmetic average return spread between the S&P 500 index and long-term Treasury bonds" [p. 1088].

The discrepancy between Kaplan and Ruback's results and the results using the DCF model with the IBES forecasts is puzzling. Accordingly, there are some problems with the Kaplan–Ruback data that are worth noting. First, the highly leveraged nature of the transactions, in which 90% debt financing is not uncommon, makes the estimated market risk premium particularly sensitive to the estimate of terminal value, the leverage adjustment, and the estimate of beta. Second, it is possible that the buyers adjusted the cash-flow forecasts to serve strategic purposes, such as securing debt financing. If the cash-flow forecasts were inflated, the estimate of the risk premium would be biased upward. Third, it is possible that deal makers in leveraged buyouts explicitly use higher discount rates to adjust for the illiquidity of the deals. Finally, the Kaplan–Ruback study is not forward looking from the standpoint of 1998. It is based on expectations of corporate leveraged buyers between 1983 and 1989. Those were heady years for leveraged buyouts. The market was booming, fueled in large part by the explosion in high-yield financing made available by Drexel, Burnham, Lambert. In addition, economic performance was robust. Coming out of the recession of 1982–1983, real economic growth was rapid and inflation was low. Consequently, one would expect that forecasts of leverage buyers during those years would be optimistic. If so, estimates of expected stock-market returns based on those forecasts would be upward biased.

The Fama–French Aggregate Internal Rate of Return Analysis

Whereas Kaplan and Ruback's work was limited to a relatively small sample of highly leveraged transactions, Fama and French (unpublished working paper, 1999) used a similar approach in an attempt to estimate the cost of capital for the entire nonfinancial corporate sector. The Fama–French study covers the period from 1950 to 1996. It includes all nonfinancial firms available in the Compustat database. Compustat, a division of Standard & Poor's, maintains an extensive database that includes quarterly financial information on a growing sample of firms. The number of firms used in the Fama and French study rose from 319 in 1950 to 4,442 in 1996.

Fama and French treated the entire sample as if it were one giant firm. They estimated the cost of capital for this giant firm by using Equation 3.3 in the same fashion that Kaplan and Ruback did. The difficulty was in specifying all the cash flows for the giant corporation. In that regard, Fama and French proceeded as follows: Outflows were defined to include (1) the initial market value of all firms in the sample (analogous to the initial investment in standard internal rate of return [IRR] analysis), (2) the market value of all firms that enter the sample between 1950 and 1996 (analogous to maintenance investments in standard IRR analysis), and (3) investment expenditures made by the firms in the sample each year (analogous to maintenance investments). Inflows included (1) the aggregate cash earnings of all the firms in the sample each year (analogous to the cash produced by an investment project in standard IRR analysis) and (2) the 1996 terminal value of all firms in the sample (analogous to the terminal value of the investment).

As might be expected, Fama and French faced a number of empirical hurdles in estimating all of the necessary cash flows. For example, the Compustat database does not include the market value of debt securities, so the value of the firm, which equals the sum of the value of the debt, equity, and preferred stock, is measured with error. There is also measurement error due to the way that mergers work their way through the calculations. Nonetheless, given the huge magnitude of the underlying cash flows, Fama and French argued that the impact of the measurement error is minor.

Fama and French found that over the entire period from 1950 to 1996, the discount rate, k, which equates the present values of the inflows and outflows, is 10.72%. This is their estimate of the nominal cost of capital for the entire corporate nonfinancial sector. Because this is an estimate of the cost of capital, not the cost of equity, it is necessary to solve for the equity risk premium using a procedure similar to that employed by Kaplan and Ruback.

The procedure used here is as follows. The starting point is the formula for the weighted average cost of capital (WACC). The familiar textbook formula for the WACC is

$$\text{WACC} = k_d(1 - t_c)\, w_d + k_s \cdot w_s \tag{3.4}$$

where k_d is the cost of debt capital, t_c is the corporate tax rate, w_d is the fraction of debt in the capital structure, k_s is the cost of common stock, and w_s is the fraction of equity in the capital structure. Equation 3.4 ignores preferred stock by lumping it in with debt. This is done for simplicity because the amount of preferred stock issued by nonfinancial companies is minimal.

To solve for the cost of equity, it is necessary to invert the formula for the after-tax WACC. With respect to the capital structure weights, Fama and French reported that the average capital structure of the firms in their sample is 72.8% equity, 24.5% debt, and 2.7% preferred stock. To work backward to the cost of equity, an assumption must be made about the cost of debt. As a reasonable approximation, assume that the average cost of debt (including preferred stock) was 150 basis points over the average return on long-term treasury securities during the sample period.[7] From Table 1.2, the average yield on treasury securities over the period 1950 to 1996 is 6.3%. This implies a before-tax cost of debt of 7.8%. Adopting Fama and French's assumption that the average corporate tax rate is 35% gives an after-tax cost of debt of 5.1%.

Substituting 10.72% for the WACC, 5.1% for the cost of debt, 35% for the corporate tax rate, 27.2% for the fraction of debt in the capital structure, and 72.8% for the fraction of equity in the capital structure, it is possible to solve for the cost of equity. The resulting estimate for the cost of equity is 12.8%. This is a nominal estimate. It is not necessary to invert the CAPM because this is already a marketwide estimate. Consequently, all that need be done to calculate the equity risk premium is deduct the average return on treasury bonds. As noted above, that figure is 6.3%. This yields an estimate of the market risk premium of 6.5%.

---

[7] Assuming that debt and preferred stock have the same yield is reasonable, but it ignores the fact that preferred-stock dividends are not deductible. Accounting for this tax effect would increase the estimated cost of equity derived from solving the WACC formula by 1 or 2 basis points, given the amount of preferred stock issued by nonfinancial companies in the Fama and French sample. This is well within rounding error.

Fama and French recognized that the high cost of capital they found might itself be an artifact of the high stock prices that prevailed in late 1996. They observed that by far, the largest cash flow in their IRR calculation was the terminal value of the stocks in the sample in 1996. Consequently, if stock prices were inflated at that time, perhaps for some emotional reason, the estimated cost of capital would also be inflated. To test the empirical significance of this concern, Fama and French reestimated the cost of capital using terminal dates from 1961 onward. They found that from 1979 to 1996, the estimated cost of capital increased by less than 1 percentage point. Consequently, they concluded that while the run-up in stock prices in the 1990s did increase their estimate of the cost of capital, its economic impact was not large.

Although the estimate of the market risk premium produced by the Fama–French analysis is less than both the historical Ibbotson estimate and the estimate produced by the Kaplan–Ruback study, it is still a good deal higher than the other forward-looking estimates. One possible explanation for this discrepancy is survival bias in the Compustat database. Compustat began constructing the database in 1965. To provide a longer historical record, Compustat backfilled the data to include financial information on companies dating back to 1950. In doing so, however, they included only companies that existed as of 1965. Consequently, companies that ceased doing business between 1950 and 1965 were systematically excluded from the data. This tends to create an upward bias in measures of financial performance because firms that cease doing business, on average, do so because they performed poorly. Consequently, prior to 1965, the average performance of firms in the Compustat database is likely to overstate the performance of nonfinancial firms generally.

Another possible explanation for the discrepancy is the fact that the Fama–French analysis is not forward looking. Although they computed an IRR, Fama and French relied on historical data to do so. If the historical data are unduly sanguine because American economic performance during the sample period was not representative, then their estimate would overstate the forward-looking cost of capital just as the historical average does. In fact, the Fama–French study is best characterized as an alternative to averaging stock returns for computing the ex-post cost of equity. Because corporate cash flow is the ultimate source of equity value, the IRR computed by Fama and French should be approximately equal to the historical average stock returns over sufficiently long periods of time. This is borne out by the data. The average monthly return (times 12) on the S&P 500 during the Fama and French sample period was 13%. This is nearly equal to the average equity return implied by the Fama–French analysis of 12.8%. Thus, virtually all of the 100–basis point difference between the Fama–French estimate of the risk premium and the Ibbotson average risk premium is due to the use of a different sample period. When used in a computation involving the same time period, the Fama–French approach yields results consistent with averaging stock returns, as one would expect.

An Earnings Yield Approach to Estimating the Market Risk Premium

Siegel (1998) argued that earnings yield, defined as earnings per share divided by share price (the inverse of the P/E ratio [price-to-earnings ratio]), is the key determinant of long-run real returns on common stock. The long-run data are consistent with this viewpoint. A look back at Table 2.2 reveals that the average compounded real return on common stock over the period from 1926 to 1997 was 7.7%. The median earnings yield over the comparable period was 7.2%. Siegel observed that the relation holds over even longer periods. He reported that over the period from 1871 to 1996, the average compounded real return on stocks was 6.8% and the median earnings yield was 7.3%.[8]

---

[8]Siegel (1998), p. 79.

A long-run relation between earnings yield and real stock returns is consistent with basic economic theory. Earnings, whether paid out as dividends or retained for investment, are the ultimate source of value for shareholders. That is why a decline in dividend yield is not necessarily bad news for investors. As long as cash not paid out as dividends can be invested in projects that earn returns in excess of the cost of capital, a drop in yields should be good news. In addition, because corporate earnings are derived from real assets, they tend to rise and fall with inflation. For that reason, both real stock returns and the earnings yield should be shielded against the impact of inflation in the long run.

From the perspective of earnings yield, future stock returns and future risk premiums should be less than they were in the past. In 1998, the earnings yield on the S&P 500 fell below 4% for the first time in postwar history. Extrapolating Siegel's observation that the real return on common stocks approximately equals the earnings yield forward implies that the geometric average real return on common stocks should be about 4% over the long run. This is 370 basis points below the geometric average for the period 1926 to 1997. If the earnings yield approach is correct, estimates of the risk premiums should be reduced by a commensurate amount.[9] In terms of arithmetic means, this implies estimates of approximately 5.5% over treasury bills and 3.75% over long-term treasury bonds. These numbers are consistent with the standard DCF approach.

The Welch Survey

Perhaps the most direct way to estimate ex-ante equity risk premium is to survey experts in the field. Because the risk premium is a critical input into much of the academic research on stock re-

---

[9]Actually, the arithmetic average risk premiums should be reduced slightly more because of the effect of compounding.

turns, Welch (1998) surveyed leading professors of financial economics regarding their views on the long-term forward-looking risk premium. On the basis of responses from 112 professors, Welch reported that the mean estimate of the future risk premium of stocks over long-term treasury bonds is approximately 6%. This is 150 basis points less than the Ibbotson long-run arithmetic average and approximately equal to the geometric average.

Welch then went on to argue that this premium is "too big." Although the equity premium puzzle is not discussed in this book until Chapter 4, Welch's calculation provides an insightful introduction. The calculation goes as follows:

- As of April 1998, interest rates on treasury bonds with any maturity greater than 10 years were approximately 6%. At that time, virtually all forecasting services were predicting long-run inflation rates of 3% or less. Consequently, 3.5% is a reasonable estimate for the long-run real return on treasury bonds.
- Given a real return on treasury bonds of 3.5%, a 6% risk premium implies that real returns on stock will be 9.5% (slightly less than the Ibbotson long-run average).
- Because not all of the dividends on stock are reinvested, the value of stocks generally does not grow by 9.5%. Welch estimated the maximum leakage at no more than 3% per year. Consequently, the minimum growth in stock-market value implied by a 6% risk premium is $(1.095/1.03) - 1 = 6.3\%$ per year.
- The highest long-run growth forecasts for real gross national product (GNP) are on the order of 2.5% per year. Accordingly, the growth in the value of stocks will outpace GNP growth by $(1.06/1.025) - 1 = 3.7\%$ per year.
- As of April 1998, the ratio of the value of stocks to gross domestic product (GDP) was 1.8. At a growth rate of 3.7% the ratio will grow to more than 10 within 50 years.
- That means that 50 years from now, the expected annual return on common stock will equal the total U.S. real GNP. In "good" years, it will be even higher.

Table 3.2. Risk Premiums Produced by Competing Approaches

Author(s)	Type of Analysis	Premium over Bills	Premium over Bonds
Ibbotson and Associates (1998)	Historical arithmetic average: 1926–1997	9.20%	7.40%
Cornell application of the standard DCF model	Combination of IBES forecasts for company and long-run forecasts for the economy as of December 1996	5.51%	4.27%
Blanchard (1993) DCF	Extension of standard DCF	NA	~2%
Kaplan–Ruback (1995) analysis of highly leveraged transactions	Internal rate of return using buyers forecasts: 1983–1989	NA	7.50%
Fama–French analysis of the return on corporate capital	Internal rate of return using historical data for nonfinancial corporate sector: 1950–1996	NA	Slightly less than Ibbotson average primarily due to different sample period
Siegel (1998) analysis of earning yield	Projection based on earnings yield at the end of 1997	~370 basis points less than Ibbotson average	~370 basis points less than Ibbotson average
Welch (1998) survey	1998 survey of finance professors	NA	6.00%
Welch (1998) calculation	Calculation based on projection of ratio of market value to GDP	NA	< 6%
Brown, Goetzmann, and Ross (1995)	Theoretical analysis of survival bias	~50% of Ibbotson average	~50% of Ibbotson average
Goetzmann and Jorion (1997)	International analysis of the rate of appreciation of stock prices in 39 countries	~350 basis points less than Ibbotson average	~350 basis points less than Ibbotson average

DCF = discounted cash flow; GDP = gross domestic product; IBES = International Brokers' Estimate System; NA = not applicable.

As Welch observed, the foregoing scenario is hard to accept. How could the return on the stock market in 2050 exceed the total GDP? Nonetheless, all of the assumptions on which the scenario is based are conservative, with the exception of the 6% risk premium. Welch concluded, therefore, that a 6% risk premium is too big.

Summary of the Risk Premium Estimates Produced by Competing Approaches

A summary of the risk premium estimates produced by the competing approaches is presented in Table 3.2. The results show that most of the estimates fall into one of two groups. The first group consists of historical estimators. This includes the work of Ibbotson Associates (1998), Kaplan and Ruback (1995), and Fama and French (1998). All of these studies produced estimates of the risk premium of about 7% to 7.5% over treasury bonds. The second group consists of the forward-looking estimates based on application of the DCF model or projection of earnings yield and the work on survival bias. This includes the work of Cornell (this book), Blanchard (1993), and Siegel (1998) as well as of Brown et al. (1995) and of Goetzmann and Jorion (1997). These approaches produce estimates that are approximately 300 basis points lower than the historical data, or about 4% over treasury bonds. The one study that does not fall into either group is Welch's survey (1998), which produced an estimate of the forward-looking premium of 6% over treasury bonds. However, Welch presented a convincing calculation that indicates that this premium is too big.

The net result is that there is significant dispute in the current literature as to whether the future risk premium will equal its past historical average. Chapter 4 examines the extent to which economic theory can be applied to help resolve the debate.

Chapter 4

Risk Aversion and the Risk Premium Puzzle

Chapter 3 ended with a note of skepticism regarding equity risk premiums of 6% or more going forward. This chapter investigates the extent to which that skepticism can be supported by economic theory. From a theoretical perspective, the equity risk premium is not a fundamental economic parameter but a reflection of two fundamental parameters: the risk aversion of investors and the risk of equity relative to other assets. By analyzing how these more fundamental parameters affect returns in a competitive financial market, it is possible to draw theoretical conclusions regarding reasonable levels of the equity risk premium. These theoretical conclusions can then be used both to assess the historical data and to gain insight into what the risk premium might be going forward.

The Economic Theory of Risk Aversion

The economic theory of risk aversion is based on two basic propositions. First, investors prefer more wealth (or consumption) to less.[1] Second, the pleasure, or in economic terminology, utility, derived from an added dollar of wealth decreases as the level of an investor's wealth rises. Put more bluntly, another dollar means more to a homeless person than to Bill Gates.

To analyze the implications of these two propositions, it is convenient to employ a two-period model in which an investor invests today and then consumes all the wealth from the investment tomorrow. Using the two propositions, one can prove that the utility of next period's consumption (or wealth) must look something like the graph shown in Figure 4.1. Utility rises smoothly as consumption grows, but at an ever-decreasing rate.

Figure 4.1 can be used to understand the source of risk aversion. Consider an individual whose current wealth is equal to 10 units of consumption. Suppose that the individual is offered a fair bet. A coin will be flipped. If it lands heads up, the individual wins 4 units of consumption. If it lands tails up, he or she loses 4 units of consumption. If the individual's utility of consumption is as shown in Figure 4.1, the individual will not take this bet, or any fair bet. The reason is that the decline in utility associated with losing the bet is always greater than the gain in utility from winning. In the figure, for example, utility drops approximately 0.20 "utils" if the bet is lost but rises only 0.12 utils if the bet is won. Therefore, the investor's expected utility would fall if the bet were taken.

More specifically, the expected utility equals the probability of winning the bet times the utility achieved if the bet is won plus the probability of losing the bet times the utility achieved if the bet is lost. In the example, the expected utility associated with the bet is equal to 0.67 ($[\frac{1}{2} \cdot 0.82] + [\frac{1}{2} \cdot 0.52]$), compared with a utility of 0.71 if the bet is avoided. Assuming, as economists typically do,

---

[1] In the first part of this chapter, the terms *wealth* and *consumption* are used interchangeably. This is correct only if the investor must consume all his or her wealth immediately. In reality, investors draw down their wealth slowly over the course of a lifetime. This distinction, however, greatly complicates the analysis while adding little to the basic explanation of risk aversion and greatly complicates the calculations. For simplicity, therefore, it is assumed that the investor invests today and consumes the fruits of the investment tomorrow.

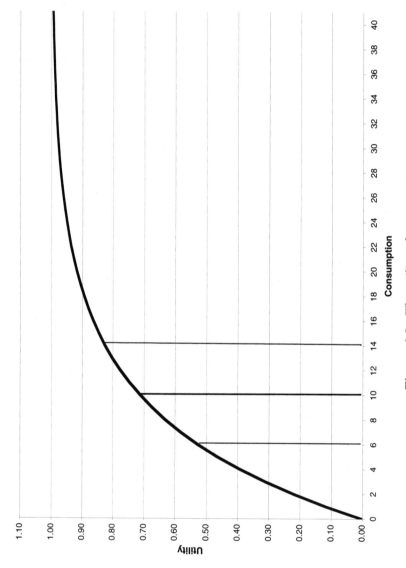

Figure 4.1. The utility of consumption.

that the goal of the investor is to maximize expected utility, the individual in the coin-flipping scenario would not accept this bet. More generally, it can be shown that if the utility curve has the properties shown in Figure 4.1, investors attempting to maximize expected utility will never accept fair bets.[2]

Investors who will not accept fair bets are called risk averse. The risk aversion arises because of the fact that the slope of the utility curve is decreasing. The decrease in the slope is referred to by economists as declining marginal utility. Referring to declining marginal utility is basically just another way of saying the utility conveyed by another dollar of consumption drops as the level of consumption rises.

The preceding example can be used to estimate the risk premium associated with the gamble for the investor with the utility curve shown in Figure 4.1. The question to ask is this: How many units of consumption would the investor have to win if the coin lands heads up to be willing to accept the bet? The condition for just accepting the bet is that expected utility remains constant. According to the figure, consumption would have to rise to approximately 19 units for utility to increase 0.20 utils. Therefore, the investor would have to be offered 9 units if he or she won to accept the coin-flip bet that would cost the investor 4 units if he or she lost. If such a bet were available, the expected payoff would be

$$\text{Expected Payoff} = (\tfrac{1}{2} \cdot -4) + (\tfrac{1}{2} \cdot 9)$$
$$= 2\tfrac{1}{2} \text{ consumption units}$$

This expected payoff is the premium over a fair bet (on which the expected payoff is zero by definition) that the investor requires to bear the risk. Consequently, the risk premium necessary to induce the hypothetical investor to accept the coin flip is $2\tfrac{1}{2}$ units of consumption.

At first blush, it may seem that the economic theory of risk aversion has to be wrong. The theory predicts that investors will

---

[2] A fair bet is one for which the expected return is zero.

not take fair bets, let alone bets where the expected payoff is less than zero. Nonetheless, casino gambling (with a negative expected payoff) is a booming business and state lotteries (also with negative expected payoffs) have been a huge success nationwide. There are two explanations for these deviations from the theory. The first is that gambling has two aspects—an investment component and an entertainment component. People are willing to pay for the entertainment component in the same fashion that they pay to attend a concert or spend a weekend at the beach. In the case of gambling, the "payment" for the entertainment is the expected loss. Second, the theory may simply be too simplistic to account for the vagaries of human behavior when small stakes and small probabilities are involved.

Even if the theory is oversimplified, it still works remarkably well when large stakes are involved. Were it not for risk aversion, one would expect to see investors bet their entire pension fund on a Sunday football game as soon as they believed that the odds swung marginally in their favor. This virtually never happens. When it comes to investing the funds that people will need to finance their future livelihood, the evidence of risk aversion is overwhelming. The strongest evidence is the equity premium itself. If investors were willing to bear risk without reward, they would have long ago bid up the prices of common stock to the level where average stock returns would be equal to the returns on short-term treasury bills.[3]

What Types of Risk Are Rewarded: A Brief Review of Portfolio Theory

One apparent implication of the economic theory of risk aversion is that the more the risk investors are asked to bear, the greater the

---

[3] In fact, without risk aversion, all financial assets would have to have expected returns equal to the rate on short-term treasury bills. As soon as the expected return on any asset rose above this level, there would be an investment stampede to buy it, which would bid prices up and cause expected returns to fall.

premium they require for bearing it. Aggregating this proposition to investors as a whole leads to the famous risk–return tradeoff. The more risk an investment entails, the greater the expected return associated with the investment. Despite its fame, this risk–return tradeoff is misleading. In fact, it is incorrect, unless risk is precisely and properly defined.

The problems with sloppy definitions of risk are twofold. First, market risk premiums will not arise for idiosyncratic risks that members of society do not have to bear in the aggregate. Consider, for instance, a bet on a football game between the Washington Redskins and the New York Giants. For simplicity, assume that the teams are judged to be of equal skill so that the chance of either team's winning the game is 50%. Suppose that two men, Mr. A and Mr. B, have decided to bet on the game. Assuming that the gamble is a fair one, the bet is analogous to the coin flip analyzed earlier. Will there be a risk premium associated with the risk of losing the bet? If so, a paradox arises. For Mr. A to receive a premium, Mr. B would have to pay it, but if Mr. B is risk averse as well, why would he pay a premium? From the standpoint of the football betting market as a whole, would the people who bet on the Redskins or Giants be expected to earn a premium? Why would one group be favored over the other?

The answer to that paradox is that there would be no risk premium in market equilibrium. The "risk" that one team or the other will win is one that society can avoid, with no economic costs, by having everyone "just say no" to the gambling on football games. There is no need for anyone to bet on the game. Thus, although Mr. A and Mr. B will both perceive the bet to be risky, neither can expect to receive a risk premium.[4]

The same conclusion holds for any type of side bet that is not related to fundamental economic activity, including casino gam-

---

[4] This raises the question of why there is so much betting on football games. There are two answers. One is that people enjoy the action, so that both A and B receive a premium in terms of the pleasure provided by the gamble. The other is that A and B do not view the bet as a fair gamble. Each feels that he is smarter than the other and thereby concludes that the odds are in his favor.

bling and state lotteries. However, it does not apply to investments in common stock. The reason is that society cannot avoid these risks. For a company such as IBM to raise equity, investors must be willing to bear the risk associated with holding IBM stock. To induce them to pay that risk, the stock must be priced so that it offers expected returns in excess of the yield on treasury bills.

Second, saying that there is a risk–return tradeoff is meaningless, unless risk is defined precisely. To understand the problem of defining risk, consider an investment in the equity of a start-up biotechnology company that has one product—a new drug designed to halt the metastasis of breast cancer. This is clearly a risky investment in the sense that the future stock price is highly uncertain. It is also a risk that society must bear if people want the potential benefits of the new drug. Unlike the bet between Mr. A and Mr. B, the risk that the drug will fail cannot be avoided by just saying no. Enough investors must be willing to hold the stock to allow the company to raise sufficient funds to conduct its research. It seems to follow, therefore, that those investors must be rewarded with an expected premium for bearing the risk, but how is risk to be measured and how large should the risk premium be?

Prior to the path-breaking work of Markowitz (1952), the risk of such investments as purchasing the stock of the start-up biotechnology company were evaluated on a stand-alone basis. Because drug research projects have a huge dispersion of possible outcomes, from outright failure to billion-dollar bonanzas, the purchase of the stock of a one-drug biotechnology company is extraordinarily risky when considered in isolation. The insight of Markowitz was that there is no need to hold such investments on a stand-alone basis. In the same fashion that insurance companies diversify risks by writing a large number of policies, investors can diversify risks by holding a large number of securities. Therefore, when considering an individual security, investors will ask how much risk this individual security adds to a diversified portfolio. Markowitz showed that if investors hold well-diversified portfolios, as they should do to minimize bearing unnecessary risk, then the risk of individual securities depends more on the correlation of those possible outcomes with the return on the market portfolio than on the dispersion of individual outcomes.

A direct offshoot of Markowitz's work was articulation of the distinction between systematic and nonsystematic risks. To understand the difference between systematic and nonsystematic risk, consider a hypothetical investment in Apple Computer. The risks associated with this investment can be seen as arising from two sources. First, there are risks that are unique to Apple. Will Apple design competitive products? Will computer users accept Apple's new operating system? Second, there are risks that affect all common stocks. Will the economy enter a recession? Will war break out in the Middle East?

The risks that are unique to Apple can be eliminated by diversification. An investor who invests only in Apple will suffer significant losses if Apple's new products are a failure, but an investor who holds Apple along with hundreds of other securities will hardly notice the impact on the value of his or her portfolio if Apple's new products fail. Therefore, risks that are unique to Apple are said to be nonsystematic or diversifiable.

On the other hand, marketwide risks cannot be eliminated by diversification. If the economy enters a recession and stock prices fall across the board, investors holding hundreds of securities fare no better than investors who put all their money in Apple Computer. Thus, economywide risks are systematic or nondiversifiable.

Building off Markowitz's insights, Sharpe (1964) and Lintner (1965) developed a specific risk measure, beta, that took account of the distinction between systematic and nonsystematic risk. They showed that the market would pay a risk premium only for those risks that could not be eliminated by diversification. The explicit mathematical relation they derived is the now-famous capital asset pricing model (CAPM), shown in Equation 4.1.

$$[E(R_s] - R_f = (\text{the Security's Beta}) \cdot [E(R_m) - R_f] \quad (4.1)$$

The CAPM states that the risk premium for a security—which by definition equals the expected return on the security, $E(R_s)$, minus the risk-free rate, R_f—is equal to the security's beta times the market risk premium.

From Equation 4.1 it is clear that the CAPM is a relative asset pricing model. It tells not what the risk premium is for an individual security but what that security's risk premium is relative to the market portfolio. If a security's beta is 1.0, meaning that its nondiversifiable risk is the same as that of the market, then its risk premium equals that of the market portfolio. More generally, the risk premium for an individual security is proportional to the risk premium on the market with a proportionality constant equal to beta.

The fact that Equation 4.1 is a relative model raises the question of why it is necessary in the first place. Application of Equation 4.1 requires two inputs, the security's beta and the market risk premium, both of which are difficult to estimate. Why not estimate the risk premium for the security directly? The answer to that question is multifaceted.

First, recall the statistical theorem mentioned earlier: Partitioning sample data more finely allows variances and covariances, but not means, to be estimated more accurately. A security's beta is the ratio of a covariance to a variance. Therefore, the beta can be estimated more accurately using a relatively short sample period than can the average risk premium for either the market or an individual security.

Second, as variable as the returns on the market are, the returns on individual securities are typically much more variable. Therefore, as hard as it is to measure the market risk premium, it is even more difficult to measure the premium for an individual security.

Third, whereas nonstationarity is probably a relatively minor problem when it comes to estimating the market risk premium, it is almost certainly a major problem when it comes to estimating the risk premium for individual securities. Given the extraordinary variability of stock returns, 10 years is a very short period of time for estimating a risk premium. Nonetheless, between 1982 and 1992, Microsoft went from being a minor start-up company to being an industrial powerhouse. It is almost certain that this had an impact on its expected return. If the task is to estimate the risk premium for Yahoo, then the problem is worse because when this book was written, the company had been in existence for only 3 years. Three years is much too short a period for estimating mean returns, but betas can be estimated over periods of 1 year or less.

The upshot of all this is that asset pricing models, despite their weaknesses, produce more accurate estimates of the risk premium for individual securities than do direct estimates. This means that every company that wants to estimate its equity capital by a means other than the discounted cash flow (DCF) has to estimate the risk premium for the market.

More sophisticated asset pricing models have been developed, including both conditional versions of the CAPM and arbitrage pricing models.[5] Like the CAPM, however, these are relative pricing models. The models give the cost of equity for an individual firm in terms of the risk premiums associated with underlying risk factors. In virtually every model, the market itself is one of the most important risk factors. This means that the risk premium on the market remains a key determinant of a company's cost of capital.

The Market Risk Premium and the Cost of Equity Capital

To illustrate the importance of the market risk premium in estimating the cost of equity capital for a corporation and in making corporate financial decisions, it is worth presenting a real-world example. The example arises in the context of the telecommunications industry. In August 1996, the Federal Communications Commission (FCC) issued a path-breaking order designed to promote competition in the local telecommunications market.[6] In the

---

[5] See, for example, Ross (1976) and Jagannathan and Wang (1996).

[6] *Implementation of the Local Competition Provisions in the Telecommunications Act of 1996,* CC Dkt. No. 96-98, First Report & Order, FCC 96-325 (rel. August 8, 1996).

order, the commission recognized that incumbent local telephone companies had a substantial first-mover advantage in providing local telephone service, at least in the short run, owing to the fact that they had in place large, costly networks that would take years and tens of billions of dollars to replicate. Consequently, the FCC argued that for competition to develop, potential competitors must be allowed to lease telephone network elements from the incumbent local companies at total element long-run incremental cost, or TELRIC. Because one element of the TELRIC is a fair return on invested capital, the FCC order initiated hearings throughout the United States designed to address the question of an appropriate cost of equity for the business of leasing the telephone network elements at the wholesale level.

In those hearings, the only asset pricing model that was employed was the CAPM.[7] Although there was debate regarding the appropriate choice of beta, most state commissions that conducted the hearings operated under the assumption that the appropriate beta was in the range of 0.80 to 1.0. There was, however, a good deal of dispute regarding the market risk premium that was measured relative to long-term treasury bonds. The maximum estimates used were those derived from the annual Ibbotson Associates data—7.4% over treasury bonds. The minimum used were those derived from an aggregate version of the DCF model—3.0% over treasury bonds.

Given the massive investment in telephone network elements—over $100 billion—the difference of 435 basis points in the estimates of the market risk premium amounts to over $4.3 billion dollars per year in fees for companies that would lease unbundled network elements.

For most companies, of course, estimates of the market risk premium do not have an impact approaching $4 billion a year. Nonetheless, they can have a significant effect on corporate capital

---

[7] The discounted cash flow (DCF) approach, which does not rely on an asset pricing model, was the preferred method for estimating the cost of equity in most states.

expenditure decision making. A change in the discount rate of 435 basis points is often enough to swing the net present value of a proposed project from positive to negative, or vice versa. Consequently, developing reasonable estimates of the forward-looking equity risk premium is an important aspect of corporate capital budgeting. This is particularly true in industries in which investment projects have long lives, such as biotechnology, electricity generation, railroading, and shipping.

Risk Aversion and the Historical Equity Risk Premium: The Risk Premium Puzzle

Because the CAPM and most well-known asset pricing models give the risk premium of individual assets in terms of the market risk premium, they do not allow assessment of the market risk premium itself. That requires a more basic model that relates risk to the ultimate source of benefit provided by investment—future consumption. At a fundamental level, what any investment does is move consumption forward in time. Stated differently, investing means forgoing consumption today in order to have the opportunity to consume more tomorrow. Consequently, the appropriate way to measure the risk of investing in a class of assets, such as equities, is to assess the impact of that investment on the riskiness of future consumption. Combining this insight with Markowitz's insight (1952) regarding diversification leads to the recognition that the key to investment risk is correlation with consumption. As explained below, assets whose returns are highly correlated with consumption are more risky because they pay off a lot when consumption is already high and pay off little when consumption is low. Conversely, assets that pay off more in bad times, when consumption is low, and less in good times have lower or even negative risk.

The realization that the ultimate source of the investment risk, and therefore the determinant of risk premiums, is the correlation of asset returns with consumption, forms the foundation of a large and growing literature in financial economics. Because most of the research is highly technical, it is not reviewed here.[8] Fortunately, the basic message of the research can be summarized in one relatively simple equation[9] that has come to be known as consumption-based asset pricing. The model states that

$$\text{Risk Premium for an Asset} = \gamma \, \text{cov}(\Delta c, \text{Asset Return})$$

In Equation 4.2, Δc represents the percentage change in aggregate per capita consumption over the observation interval, γ is a measure of the average investor's risk aversion, and *cov* refers to the covariance operator.[10] By definition, the covariance operator equals the correlation between two random variables times the standard deviation of each of them, so that Equation 4.2 can also be written as follows:

$$\text{Risk Premium for an Asset} =$$
$$\gamma \cdot \sigma(\Delta c) \cdot \sigma(\text{Asset Return}) \cdot \text{corr}(\Delta c, \text{Asset Return}) \quad (4.3)$$

The intuition behind Equation 4.3 is straightforward. First, the larger γ—that is, the more risk averse investors are—the larger the risk premium. Second, the larger $\sigma(r)$—that is, the greater the variability of asset returns—the larger the risk premium. This corresponds to the notion that the risk of an asset is related to the dispersion of its possible returns. Finally, the larger *corr*(Δc,*asset class return*), that is the more highly correlated the asset returns are with changes in consumption, the greater the risk premium. The final term requires some added explanation. Why should the

---

[8] An excellent review of the literature can be found in Cochrane (1997).

[9] Cochrane (1997) presented a derivation of this equation.

[10] The term *average investor* is a little misleading. The derivation of Equation 4.2 is based on the assumption that all investors can be characterized by a representative investor. That representative investor has a risk-aversion coefficient of γ.

risk premium depend on the correlation of an asset's return with consumption? The key, once again, is Figure 4.1. The figure implies that another dollar of consumption is more valuable when consumption is low than when it is high. Thus, risk-averse investors would prefer securities that paid off more when times were bad and less when times were good. In fact, they would pay a premium to acquire such securities. That motivation provides the foundation for the insurance industry. Insurance, by definition, is a security that pays off when a bad event occurs. Unfortunately, most marketable securities, including virtually all equities, do not have this property. Stocks tend to go up when the economy is doing well and fall when the economy drops. This means that they pay off a lot when times are good and less when times are bad. The stronger this procyclical pattern, the greater the risk to investors that when times turn bad not only will their consumable income from other sources fall but their investments will head south as well. This risk is captured by the correlation between the percent change in consumption and the return on the asset. Notice that if there is no such risk—that is, if the correlation is zero—then the risk premium will be zero no matter what the other terms in Equation 4.3 are.

Equation 4.2 can also be interpreted as a generalization of the CAPM. In the CAPM, the ultimate source of nondiversifiable risk is covariance with the return on the market, which determines beta. However, the CAPM was developed in the context of a limited model that considers only the returns on securities. Ultimately, investors are concerned about security returns only to the extent that they affect consumption. Therefore, a more general model must take account of the forces that affect consumption. In this context, the nondiversifiable risk of a security depends not on the covariance between the security returns and the return on the market but between the security return and the "return," or percentage change, in consumption as given by Equation 4.2.

The key to Equations 4.2 and 4.3 for assessing the market risk premium is that they do not include the expected return on the market as an explanatory variable. Therefore, the equations can be applied to any asset, including the market portfolio. This makes it possible to estimate what the risk premium should be, given various assumptions about the level of risk aversion, γ.

The most direct way to assess the equity risk premium is to divide Equation 4.3 through by σ *(asset return)* so that the left side of the equation becomes the ratio of the risk premium for the asset to the standard deviation of the asset return. This ratio is commonly referred to as the Sharpe ratio.

$$\text{Sharpe Ratio} = \frac{\text{Asset Risk Premium}}{\sigma(\text{Asset Return})} \tag{4.4}$$

$$= \gamma \cdot \sigma(\Delta c) \cdot \text{corr}(\Delta c, \text{Asset Return})$$

The Sharpe ratio for the stock market can be calculated directly from Table 1.2. In computing the Sharpe ratio, the risk-free return typically is taken to be the treasury bill rate because investments in long-term treasury bonds are risky in terms of future consumption. Table 1.2 shows that the risk premium over treasury bills for the market is on the order of 9% and the standard deviation of return for the market is on the order of 18%, so the Sharpe ratio is approximately 0.5. Furthermore, the estimate of the Sharpe ratio is relatively independent of the sample period. If only postwar data are used, the ratio is still about 0.5.

The problem is that 0.5 is more than 10 times greater than what any reasonable application of Equation 4.3 implies that the Sharpe ratio should be. Specifically, during the postwar years, the standard deviation of aggregate consumption growth, $\sigma(\Delta c)$, has about 1% per year, or 0.01. This estimate is relatively insensitive to the sample period. The correlation of consumption growth with stock returns is more difficult to estimate because it depends on the timing of the observations and the observation interval. Nonetheless, on the basis of his review of the empirical literature, Cochrane (1997) reported that 0.2 is a pretty generous number. With respect to the coefficient of risk aversion, γ, 1 to 2 is the standard range used in most economic models. Putting the three pieces together, the consumption based asset pricing model implies that the Sharpe ratio should be approximately

$$\text{Theoretical Sharpe Ratio} = 2 \cdot 0.01 \cdot 0.20 = 0.004$$

This value is less than 1% of the observed ratio. To translate the theoretical Sharpe ratio into an estimate of the equity risk premium, recall that standard deviation of stock returns from Table 1.2 is about 20%. A standard deviation of .20 and a Sharpe ratio of 0.004 implies that the risk premium should be *0.004 · 0.2 = .0008*, or *.08%* per year rather than 9.2% per year!

Part of the discrepancy may be due to the use of overly conservative estimates. Marshall and Daniel (1997) reported that the correlation between consumption and stock returns rises to 0.4 when longer observation intervals are employed. Furthermore, some economists argue that the coefficient of risk aversion may be as large as 10. Substituting these numbers into Equation 4.4, the theoretical Sharpe ratio rises to *10 · 0.01 · 0.4 = 0.04*. A Sharpe ratio of 0.04 implies a risk premium of only 0.8% per year, less than one tenth of its observed value.

It is the foregoing massive discrepancy between the consumption-based asset pricing model and empirical estimates of the Sharpe ratio that Mehra and Prescott (1985) originally termed the risk premium puzzle. Since their pathbreaking article, a cottage industry has developed with the goal of explaining the risk premium puzzle.

Explanations for the Risk Premium Puzzle

The Puzzle Is an Illusion: The Empirical Data Are Wrong

One explanation for the puzzle is that it is premised on faulty data. The problem lies not with the consumption-based asset pricing model but with the empirical estimates of the Sharpe ratio.

Because of survival bias or just pure luck, the historical data overstate the true risk premium.

Although survival bias may explain part of the puzzle, it cannot explain the whole thing. Straightforward application of the consumption-based asset pricing model, even using what are generally considered to be generous assumptions, produces estimates of the equity risk premium of less than 1% per year. This is not only much less than the historical average for the United States but is less than the worldwide historical average reported by Goetzmann and Jorion (1997). Similarly, although the theoretical work of Brown, Goetzmann, and Ross (1995) implies that survival bias will lead to overestimation of the true risk premium, the maximum reasonable error is approximately a factor of 2. If the consumption-based asset pricing model is right, the observed risk premium is 10 times too big. It is clear, therefore, that there is more to the puzzle than survival bias.

High Risk Aversion

One simple explanation for the risk premium puzzle is that investors are much more risk averse than economists believe. If the coefficient of risk aversion is 100, the risk premium puzzle disappears. Unfortunately, this solution runs afoul of other economic facts. Remember that risk aversion comes from the declining marginal utility of consumption—the property that the utility lost by a drop in consumption exceeds the utility gained by an equal increase. The ratio of the utility lost to the utility gained is related to the coefficient of risk aversion, γ. A γ of 100 implies that consumers are incredibly unwilling to give up consumption now to get consumption in the future because utility falls so quickly as consumption drops. This means that variation in consumption growth must be accompanied by huge variation in real (net of inflation) interest rates. Without huge variation in interest rates, consumers would smooth consumption. The problem is that with a γ of 100, the required variation in real interest rates necessary to explain the observed variation in consumption growth is much larger than has ever been observed. For instance, assuming that the 1% standard deviation of consumption used in the calculation of the theoretical Sharpe ratio is correct, real interest rates would have to range from about −100% to +100% per year.

The assumption of a γ of 100 is also inconsistent with the level of interest rates. A theoretical companion to Equation 4.1 for the risk-free asset is given by the relation

$$R_f = \rho + \gamma \cdot E_t(\Delta c) \qquad (4.5)$$

In Equation 4.5, R_f is the real return on the risk-free asset, usually interpreted as short-term treasury bills. The next variable, ρ, is a measure of the rate of time preference. Time preference quantifies the utility of current compared to future consumption. Because a great deal of evidence supports the notion that people prefer consumption today to consumption tomorrow, time preference is built into virtually every economic model. The standard way to do this is to divide time into a number of periods denoted by t. Each period, the investors' utility depends on consumption during that period as given by the utility function, $u(C_t)$. Total lifetime utility is computed by calculating a weighted average of the utility for each period. The weights used in the average are of the form $e^{-\rho t}$. Therefore, future consumption is "discounted" by the rate of time preference. Mathematically, the function for lifetime utility is taken to be of the form

$$U = E\{\textstyle\sum_{t=0}^{T} e^{-\rho t} u(C_t)\} \qquad (4.6)$$

The expectation operator is added because future consumption is uncertain, since it depends on how well the consumer's investments perform, among other things.

Equation 4.6 says that the utility derived from consumption during period t, $u(C_t)$, is discounted by the factor $e^{-\rho t}$. The larger ρ, the greater the rate at which the utility of future consumption is discounted. Consequently, in economic equilibrium, higher values of ρ are associated with higher interest rates because the more heavily future consumption is discounted, the greater the interest that must be earned to induce investors to defer consumption. That is the reason that the rate of time preference is an important determinant of the real interest rate in Equation 4.5.

In addition to time preference, Equation 4.5 shows that the interest rate also depends on the rate at which society is expected to produce added consumption, $E_t(\Delta c)$. The higher the rate of expected consumption growth, the less willing consumers will be to forgo current consumption for future consumption because more will be available in the future. Therefore, to balance current and future consumption, the interest rate must be higher. The magnitude of the impact of expected consumption growth on interest rates depends on the willingness of consumers to forgo current consumption for future consumption. As noted previously, that depends on γ.

Some simple arithmetic shows that Equation 4.5 does not comport with reality when γ equals 100. Consumption growth per capita, an estimate of $E_t(\Delta c)$, is on the order of 1% per year. Thus, if γ equals 100, the second term is approximately 100% per year. In fact, real risk-free interest rates in major industrial countries have averaged about 1% per year. Real rates greater than 5% are almost never observed for any extended period of time. Table 1.2 shows that in the United States, the average real interest rates on treasury bills over the period from 1926 to 1997 is about 0.6% per year. Consequently, for Equation 4.5 to be consistent with the data, ρ must be −99% per year—but a negative ρ implies that people prefer future consumption to present consumption. A ρ of −99% implies that people will forgo huge amounts of consumption today to get minimal amounts of consumption in the future. This is the reverse of what is universally observed. Most empirical studies of consumption behavior indicate that ρ is on the order of 1% to 2% per year. Notice that if it is assumed that γ and ρ equal 1, their "reasonable" values, then Equation 4.5 predicts that the risk-free real interest rate should be about 2%, a number not far from its historical average.

The most direct way to assess the reasonableness of the high γ explanation for the risk premium is to return to the foundation on which risk aversion is based. Recall from the initial discussion in this chapter that risk-averse investors will avoid fair gambles because the utility lost from losing a bet exceeds the utility gained from winning the bet. Accordingly, investors will pay premiums to avoid fair gambles. This fact is the basis for insurance. Rather than bear the risk that his or her home will burn down, the homeowner pays an insurance company to assume the risk. The more risk-averse an investor, the more he or she will pay to avoid a gamble. Thus, one way to measure the magnitude of risk aversion is to ask how much an investor will pay to insure against the risk of a gamble.

To assess what a γ of 100 means in this context, consider a family that annually consumes $50,000 and that faces a fair gamble. A coin will be flipped. If it lands heads, the family wins $10,000; if it lands tails, the family pays $10,000. The amount that the family will pay to avoid this bet is a measure of their risk aversion. The stunning fact is that a γ of 100 implies that the family would pay approximately $9,700 to avoid the bet! This is almost equivalent to losing the bet for sure. In comparison, a family with a γ of 2 would pay about $2,000 to avoid the bet. This is still a healthy insurance premium, but it is not 97% of the money at risk.

In summary, assuming high risk aversion alone is not a reasonable solution to the equity risk premium puzzle. The level of risk aversion that must be assumed is so immense that it not only flies in the face of economic data on the behavior of interest rates but also is inconsistent with common sense and everyday behavior. Nonetheless, high risk aversion might explain a fraction of the puzzle. For instance, increasing γ to 10, a not totally unsupportable level, reduces the discrepancy between the theoretical and empirical Sharpe ratios. An understanding of the entire historical premium, however, requires other explanations.

Nonstandard Utility Functions

Another approach that researchers have taken to rationalize the observed equity premium is to alter the form of the utility function. The standard consumption-based asset pricing model is built on the assumption that each period, utility depends only on the amount of consumption that period, as given by Equation 4.6. The idea is that this is an oversimplification. For example, people may become accustomed to a standard of living. In that case, the utility derived from consumption this period depends on the level of consumption in previous periods. Alternatively, a "keeping up with the Joneses" effect may operate so that the utility of consumption depends on what other people are consuming. By making alterations of these types in the form of the utility function, it is possible to explain the equity premium.

Before there is a discussion of some of the specific alterations that have been suggested, there must be a word of caution. Economists are rightly reticent to alter the standard utility function. The problem is that it becomes too simple to explain too much. For instance, ethnic discrimination can be explained by adding a preference for similar people to the utility function. Doing so, however, may lead to a failure to examine other, perhaps more insightful, theories of discrimination. In finance, departing from the basic assumption that utility each period is determined by the level of consumption that period opens the door to misleadingly direct explanations of investment behavior and asset pricing that may mask the true workings of financial markets.

Although many possible alterations to utility function have been suggested, only a few offer the possibility of explaining the behavior of interest rates and the observed equity premium. The first class of models is based on the assumption that the utility of consumption depends on the force of habit. Specifically, an investor's satisfaction with a given level of consumption depends on his or her standard of living. The motivation for such utility functions is based on such observations as noting that the level of consumption that seemed quite satisfactory when the investor was a college student becomes insufficient when the investor is a middle-aged executive. Campbell and Cochrane (1997) developed this hypothesis by suggesting a utility function of the form

$$U(C_t) = (C_t - X)^{(1-h)} \qquad (4.7)$$

where X represents the accustomed standard of living, which depends on past consumption.

The unique aspect of utility functions such as Equation 4.7 is that the effective risk aversion depends on how far current consumption is from the habitual level. More specifically

$$\gamma = \frac{n \cdot C_t}{C_t - X} \tag{4.8}$$

Equation 4.8 implies that as consumption drops toward X, the accustomed standard of living, people become much more risk averse because they are less willing to accept further declines in consumption. This implies a higher equity risk premium.

Unlike the assumption of high γ at all levels of consumption, however, the habitat model does not make extreme predictions about the behavior of interest rates. The reason is that during bad times, when people are falling below their accustomed standard of living, investors become very reticent to borrow because of the risk associated with increase in leverage. Therefore, large swings in interest rates are not required to explain observed variation in consumption growth. However, the habitat model does contradict other well-known economic facts. Specifically, the percentage growth rate in consumption is highly unpredictable in that the standard deviation is equal to the mean. Unfortunately, the habitat model predicts that consumption growth should be highly predictable because people adjust their consumption slowly as they become accustomed to a new standard of living.

The other main alteration of the utility function that has been suggested to explain the risk premium puzzle is to drop the assumption of separability. Separability relates to the manner in which uncertainty is treated in the utility function. The standard utility function is based on the assumption that the utility of consumption in one state does not affect the utility of consumption in another. For example, if the two states are rain and shine, separability implies that the utility of consumption assuming it rains is unaffected by the utility of consumption assuming it is sunny. Introducing nonseparability allows for the interaction between the states. Unfortunately, this makes these utility functions highly cumbersome to handle. Although nonseparable utility functions have found a variety of applications in financial economics, to date they have not been very successful in explaining the equity risk premium.

Overall, the use of nonstandard utility functions does not adequately explain the equity risk premium. As Cochrane (1997) concluded, "There is currently no model with low risk aversion that is consistent with the equity risk premium, the stability of real interest rates and nearly unpredictable consumption growth" (p. 22).

There is one stronger step that can be taken. Rather than making minor modifications, an alternative is to dispense with the idea of expected utility maximization altogether. This is the approach taken by Benartzi and Thaler (1995), who applied a version of Tversky and Kahneman's prospect theory (1992) to investing. In a nutshell, prospect theory assumes that investors' utility functions depend on *changes* in the value of their portfolios rather than the value of the portfolio. Put another way, utility comes from returns, not from the value of assets. In standard applications of prospect theory, investors display what Benartzi and Thaler called "loss aversion." Loss aversion arises because losses are particularly painful when the utility function is defined in terms of returns.

When investors exhibit loss aversion, their attitude toward risk depends on the time horizon over which returns are evaluated. That is because the key is to avoid losses. An investor who evaluates his or her portfolio every day faces a 50% probability of losing money because stock prices are almost as likely to fall as to rise on a daily basis. As a result, an investor who was trying to avoid losses would shun equities and therefore appear to be highly risk averse. However, this "loss" can be avoided by simply not evaluating the portfolio. Consequently, an investor who evaluates his or her portfolio on a 10-year basis would exhibit little risk aversion because the probability of losing money over such a long interval is close to zero. Assuming that the probability distribution of stock-market returns matches the historical distribution of the Ibbotson Associates data, Benartzi and Thaler showed that a 13-month evaluation period makes investors indifferent between holding stocks and bonds. If they evaluate more frequently, then the risk premium would have to be even larger. If they evaluate less frequently, a smaller risk premium is implied. Benartzi and Thaler argue that their findings make sense because tax returns are filed and portfolio evaluations are reported on an annual basis. Consequently, it seems reasonable to assume that the representative investor has a 12-month evaluation period.

What is not so reasonable is the basic premise on which prospect theory is based. Utility comes from consumption, which depends on the value of assets, not on returns. Prospect theory assumes that in an activity as critical to people as investing for retirement, investors cannot overcome irrational predispositions about risk and furthermore do not hire professionals who act rationally on their behalf. In this respect, prospect theory contradicts the research findings on the valuation of derivative securities. In the case of derivative securities, such as options and futures contracts, there is clear evidence that mathematical models based on standard assumptions of rationality are able to price the securities with great precision.

Finally, the notion of a fixed evaluation period is also suspicious. Professional investment firms monitor the value of their portfolio on an ongoing basis within each trading day. They stand ready to switch course if something unexpected happens, such as a market crash. Many sophisticated individual investors act similarly. What sense does it make to say that they have a 12-month evaluation period?

Autocorrelation in Returns

If returns are autocorrelated, the usual measures of risk, such as the standard deviation of annual returns, will mischaracterize long-term risk. For instance, if returns are mean reverting, then long-term risk will be substantially less than would be predicted by assuming that each year's return was an independent drawing. Siegel (1992) examined whether such autocorrelation of returns can explain the risk premium puzzle.

Unfortunately, Siegel's empirical work serves only to deepen the mystery. Like others before him, Siegel found that stock returns are negatively correlated. Several bad years are more likely to be followed by a good one. This decreases the risk of holding stock over the long term. The same is not true of bonds. If anything, the returns on bonds tend to be positively correlated. Consequently, as the holding period is increased, the risk of holding stocks relative to bonds falls. Such a decline in the relative risk of holding stocks means that the risk premium should be less than analysis of the short-term data predicts. Therefore, Siegel's work provides no solution to the equity premium puzzle.

Time Varying Expected Returns

If stock returns are nonstationary, two types of risk have to be distinguished. The first is the uncertainty regarding the returns on equities this period. This is the standard type of uncertainty addressed in all two-period investment models, including the CAPM. When multiple periods are introduced, a second source of risk arises because expected returns themselves may change as time passes. As an illustration, suppose that as of time zero, the expected return for period 3, two periods from now, is 10%. At time zero, investors face the risk that by the end of the period the expected return for period 3 will change. For instance, it may drop to 9%. Because investors will require compensation for bearing the risk of changes in expected returns, it is conceptually possible that variation in expected returns can explain the equity risk premium.

The explanation of the equity risk premium is this: expected returns must change in a way that makes stocks significantly less attractive to investors and thereby increases the return they require for holding common stocks. For that to be the case, bad news for common stocks—that is, negative returns—must be *heightened* by declines in future expected returns. Such a compounding of risk would make stock less attractive and thereby produce a higher risk premium.

This would be a great theory were it not for the facts. The difficulty is not with the assumption that expected returns vary—which research by Fama and French (1989), among others, indicates that they do—but with the fashion in which they move and by how much. First, the work by Fama and French and many others demonstrates that the variation in expected returns is much smaller than the variation in actual returns. This, in and of itself, does not kill the theory, because the change in expected returns could be long lived. The risk associated with a permanent decline in the expected return on common stocks is much greater than the risk associated with a temporary 1-year decline of the same magnitude.

Second, and more devastating, the evidence indicates that to the extent that expected returns change, the variation is risk reducing, not risk increasing. Consider, for example, an event that leads to a sudden drop in future expected returns. By definition, this will produce a decline in the rate at which corporate earnings are discounted. (Remember that *expected returns* and *discount rate* are two terms for the same thing.) This means that if nothing else changes, current stock prices will rise because of the decline in the discount rate. The positive current return will offset, to an extent, the drop in future expected returns.

The foregoing example is quite general. Stocks act as a hedge against future changes in expected returns. When future expected returns drop, current returns rise. When future expected returns rise, current returns drop. This consideration makes stocks less risky, and more desirable, than they are from the standpoint of two-period models that look only at the history of current returns. As a result, adding variation in expected returns leads to the prediction of a lower, not higher, equity risk premium.

Heterogeneous Investors

Until recently, models of the equity risk premium have relied almost exclusively on the assumption of a representative investor. That is, either investors are identical in their beliefs regarding the probability distribution of future security returns and their utility functions or the market is such that prices are set as if investors were identical. One of the more active areas of research is exploring the implications for the risk premium of meaningful differences among investors. This assumption is clearly more realistic and makes it possible to understand phenomena, such as the huge volume of trading, that representative investor models cannot explain.

Although heterogeneity is necessary to understand market phenomena like the volume of trading, it is less clear that it provides insight into the equity risk premium. What heterogeneity makes possible are unique risks associated with the unique circumstances of individual investors. The problem, as Cochrane (1997) showed, is that these unique risks do not affect the risk premium under most circumstances. This occurs because unique risks, by definition, are not correlated with aggregate per capita consumption—but it is aggregate consumption that determines systematic risk and therefore the risk premium. The unique risks that individual investors face are effectively diversifiable.

In attempting to get around the diversification problem, models that relax the assumption of a representative investor quickly become highly complex. One major roadblock is aggregating the demand for securities across individual investors to arrive at market prices. It is also difficult to decide on what dimensions investors differ and by how much. Nonetheless, the starting point in most models is the role played by human capital. For a majority of investors, their most valuable asset is human capital. Labor income is the return on that capital. That income stream is clearly risky, because an employee may be fired. Furthermore, human capital is difficult to buy or sell, so investors are in some sense "stuck with the risk." Can the idiosyncratic risk factors associated with human capital explain the equity risk premium? The answer is "not easily."

First, it must be assumed that there is no mechanism by which workers can insure against the risks associated with their human capital. For instance, all forms of unemployment insurance must be ruled out. Otherwise, human-capital risk has no impact on the pricing of financial assets. Second, the risk of variation in labor income cannot be correlated with the market return, or investors could hedge the risk in the equity market. For example, an employee whose wages depended on the success of a software company could hedge by taking short positions on software stocks. Third, there must be impediments to self-insurance. Individuals can self-insure by borrowing against their future income when times are bad and saving when times are good. It is reasonable to rule out borrowing against future income because it is difficult for most people to obtain unsecured loans. However, it is hard to imagine why investors could not self-insure by saving. Nonetheless, *assuming* that there are such impediments, Heaton and Lucas (1996) showed that the risks associated with labor income can explain up to half of the observed equity risk premium. However, this explanation comes at a price. The Heaton–Lucas model also predicts that interest rates will be as volatile as stock returns. This is clearly inconsistent with the historical record.

Constantinides and Duffie (1996) developed a model that potentially can explain the observed risk premium by introducing idiosyncratic risk in a new fashion. As noted above, it is not sufficient that investors face the risk of being fired. If that risk is correlated with the returns on stock, they can hedge it. As an alternative, Constantinides and Duffie assumed that it is the variance of the idiosyncratic risk is correlated with the market. Specifically, during bad times, when the market falls, the idiosyncratic risk associated with labor income rises. The authors showed that this increase in variance cannot be hedged by trading stock.

The increase in variance gives consumers another reason for fearing declines in the stock market. Market drops are associated not only with a decline in the value of one's portfolio but also with periods of greater idiosyncratic risk. Because of this double whammy, people are less inclined to hold stock. Inducing them to hold the equities that companies issue requires that a larger risk premium be offered.

The critical question for the Constantinides–Duffie model is whether the proposed relation between the level of the stock market and the amount of idiosyncratic risk is sufficiently strong to explain the equity risk premium. To date, there has been little empirical work on the subject. However, the research that has been completed indicates that the relation is quite weak. Assuming that this is borne out by future studies, it appears that the Constantinidies–Duffie model does not offer a complete solution to the equity risk premium puzzle.

What about a Stew?

Taken alone, none of the theories reviewed in this section convincingly explains the observed equity risk premium on its own. The problem is that the observed premium is so large that the models have to be stretched to the breaking point to explain the data. An easy way to solve the problem is to cook up a stew of explanations. For example, consider the following brew. First, because of survival bias, the observed risk premium overstates the true expected premium. Second, risk aversion is greater than most economists believe. Third, people take account of their habitual standard of living when assessing the utility of consumption. Finally, the inability to hedge idiosyncratic risks makes investing in stocks less desirable. If all these factors interact, none of the models has to be stretched unreasonably to explain the observed premium.

Of course, the fact that a stew *can* explain the equity risk premium does not mean that it is the right explanation. Since the work of Mehra and Prescott (1985), dozens of the best economic minds in the world have been working on the problem of explaining the equity risk premium. It is not surprising that they have come up with some *possible* solutions.

What Explanations of the Equity Risk Premium Say about the Future

In a consideration of what the explanations of the risk premium puzzle say about the future, there is a clear distinction between the survival bias story and all the other theories. The survival-bias explanation is that the past is misleading. There is no puzzle, or at least not as big a puzzle as the historical data indicate. As discussed extensively in Chapter 2, this immediately implies that the future will not be like the past. The future expected premium is by definition less than the historical risk premium if the historical estimate is biased.

All the other explanations are premised on the assumption that the historical average is a good estimate of the true risk premium. The goal is to modify the standard consumption-based asset pricing model to make it consistent with the historical market risk premium. This is done by tinkering with the model in fundamental ways, such as changing the utility function or adding special types of idiosyncratic risk. These alterations are permanent changes to the model; they do not vary from year to year. For instance, Campbell and Cochrane (1997) did not suggest that in 1998 the utility function suddenly began to depend on one's standard of living. They presumed that this has been the case for the past 72 years and that it will be the case in the future. After all, a person's utility function, like his or her eye color, is not something that is supposed to change. Furthermore, even if some individual utility functions did change—perhaps as people aged—the average utility function for the representative investor would still be largely constant. Consequently, the Campbell–Cochrane model and all the other models discussed in this chapter imply, by construction, that the future expected equity risk premium will equal the past historical average. That is the whole point—to explain the puzzle by reconciling the observed data with basic economic theory.

In this respect, there is one other aspect of the solutions to the puzzle that is worth noting. With exception of the work by Benartzi and Thaler (1995), all of the solutions are based on rational models. That is, they all assume that investors accurately assess the risk–return tradeoff offered by common stock and invest accordingly. This implies that stocks are never mispriced. In addition, it implies that the equity risk premium is always fair. For instance, it rules out the possibility that the risk premium rose to unreasonable heights because of the emotional shock caused by the collapse of stock prices at the start of the Great Depression. Some readers may believe that this obsession with rational models reflects a naive bias on the part of economists, but there is a reason for the obsession. Once the door is opened to irrationality, there is no apparent limit on the types of explanations that can be derived for movements in stock prices. An analyst who wants to explain a drop in the market can appeal to fear, or a "panic." Another who wants to explain a jump in the market can appeal to greed. By positing the right psychology, virtually any market movement can be rationalized.

It is worth reiterating, in this regard, that there are no behavioral theories regarding the pricing of options, futures, and other derivative contracts. Rational mathematical models predict market prices with amazing accuracy. If investors are mathematical to the third decimal point when pricing derivatives, why should they suddenly become driven by emotion when attempting to value common stock?

To be fair, behavioral economists have answers to both criticisms. As Thaler (1993) observed, the fact that it is easy to construct bad behavioral theories does not mean that all behavioral theories are bad. Furthermore, the option example is unfair. If investors can observe an arbitrage relation, they will exploit it. Where mathematics works, investors will accept mathematical models. There is, for example, no behavioral theory of physics. When it comes to pricing equities, however, there is no precise mathematical model. The dividend discount model is the best model available for valuing equity. However, that model depends on forecasts of dividends into the indefinite future. When the pricing model is this vague, arbitrage between securities perceived to be under- and overpriced becomes highly risky. The arbitrageur faces a constant doubt: "What if my model is wrong?" The doubt is well founded. As Summers (1986) demonstrated, the observed history of stock returns, including the Ibbotson data, is consistent with the hypothesis that there are large and frequent deviations from rational prices. Given all the noise documented in Chapter 2, investors simply cannot tell if the price of a given stock, or the level of the market generally, is consistent with rational pricing. In light of this imprecision, it is not unreasonable to suggest that emotions come to play an important role in the pricing of equities and that those emotions can affect both expected returns and the level of stock prices.

The fact that the theoretical solutions to the equity premium puzzle rely on rational models that depend on relatively fixed economic parameters limits them in meaningful ways. Most importantly, the models are also incapable of explaining significant changes in the risk premium over relatively short periods of time (10 years or less). Recall, for instance, that Glassman and Hassett (1998) argued that the stock market boom of the 1990s was caused by a sharply falling risk premium. Such a drop is inconsistent with the rational models unless the underlying parameters change dramatically. However, there is no evidence that the risk of stocks changed markedly in the 1990s and there is no reason to believe that risk preferences changed, either. Therefore, the relation models are not good candidates for explaining a sharp drop in the equity premium in the 1990s, if it occurred. Even survival bias does not work in this regard. Survival bias implies that the historical estimate overstates the true expected future value by a given amount. However, the overstatement does not change over time. The only way that survival bias can explain a sudden drop in the risk premium is if investors suddenly become aware of the impact of survival bias where they were not before. This seems unlikely to have occurred in the 1990s in light of the fact that statisticians have been aware of survival bias for over half a century.

In a sense, then, there are two puzzles. The first, addressed in this chapter, is why the observed equity risk premium is so large. The second, which is the subject of Chapter 5, is why stock prices rose so sharply in the 1990s. Can the increase be explained by rational changes in the risk premium or is it possible that "undue exuberance," or some other irrational force, pushed prices too high?

Chapter 5

The Risk Premium and the Stock-Market Boom of the 1990s

One of the fortuitous developments of the 1990s was the remarkable run-up in stock prices. Following the crash of 1987, the Dow Jones Industrial Average (DJIA) stood at approximately 1,550. By July 1998, it had risen to more than 9,000. Furthermore, this dramatic increase understates true investment performance because it excludes dividends. Between October 1987 and July 1998, a dollar invested in the stocks of any one of the companies listed in Standard & Poor's (S&P) 500 Index grew by a factor of seven times.

By the spring of 1998, the American market had risen so much that it became an issue of concern in some quarters. *The Economist* went so far as to publish a cover story entitled "America's Bubble Economy."[1] In the article, the editors argued that

> The American economy is showing dangerous signs of excess. . . . Evidence of speculative excesses is widespread. There are four main symp-

[1] America's Bubble Economy, *The Economist,* April 18, 1998.

toms: overvalued share prices, merger mania, rising property prices and a rapid growth in the money supply. . . . Some of the rise in share prices reflects improved performance. Corporate earnings have set record after record. But even all this does not justify current prices [p.4].

In response to views such as these, the *Wall Street Journal* took a dissenting perspective. In the editorial-page article discussed in Chapter 2, Glassman and Hassett (1998) argued that the increase in share prices in the 1990s was not irrational. Instead, the rising market was a rational response to a decline in the equity risk premium.

The discussion regarding whether the market was "too high" was not limited to a debate among journalists. When asked about the record level of prices, famed investor Warren Buffett claimed that prices were not too high as long as earnings growth could be sustained. Federal Reserve Chairman Alan Greenspan took the opposite view and criticized what he saw as the market's "irrational exuberance." Stock-market analysts at leading investment banks spoke out on both sides of the issue.

Addressing the question in a scientific fashion first necessitates defining what it means to say that stock prices are too high. Because stock prices must be expected to rise continuously to induce investors to hold equities, prices today will always tend to be higher in dollar terms than they were in previous times. For instance, stock prices at the end of 1928 are commonly referred to as high even though the S&P 500 at that time was only 24.3 compared to over 1,200 in July 1998. The example makes it clear that stock prices cannot be said to be high or low without employing a benchmark for comparison.

Determining Whether Stock Prices Are High or Low

The most widely employed benchmarks for assessing the level of stock prices are the earnings of the underlying companies and the dividends that they pay to investors. This makes perfect sense. Because the ultimate value of common stock is derived from earnings and dividends, stock prices must, in some sense, be tied to those indicators. Consequently, stock prices are said to be high when the price paid to receive $1 of dividends or earnings is high. Figure 5.1 and 5.2 illustrate how the level of stock prices, relative to dividends and earnings, have varied over the postwar years from 1946 through the middle of 1998.

Figure 5.1 shows that the dividend yield for the S&P 500 averaged approximately $0.04 on the dollar throughout the entire 52-year period. It has varied from a high of about 7% in 1950 to a low of 1.5% by the middle of 1998. Furthermore, the figure shows that the yield was never below 2% prior to the mid-1990s. By this measure, therefore, stock prices were clearly at record levels by July 1998.

Figure 5.2 shows that the price-to-earnings (P/E) ratio averaged approximately 15 during the sample period. It dropped below 7 during the recession following World War II and during the stock market collapse of 1973–1974. The highest level of the P/E ratio, prior to the 1990s was 22.4. From 1992 through 1997, the average was 22.4. The mid-1998 level of approximately 25 is a postwar record. By this measure as well, stock prices were at record levels during the summer of 1998.

It is also worth noting that the data are somewhat ambiguous with respect to the claim that stock prices were high in 1928. Although not shown in the figures, the dividend yield on the S&P 500 at the end of 1928 was 3.4%, which is below the postwar average of 4.0. On this score, therefore, stocks were slightly overpriced. On the other hand, the P/E ratio was 14, which is below the postwar average of approximately 16. Taken together, the two measures indicate that prices were about right at the end of 1928. They were well below the records reached in the summer of 1998.

There is one caveat that needs to be considered when using dividend yield and P/E data to assess the level of stock prices. The dividend-to-price (D/P) and P/E ratios presented in Figures 5.1 and 5.2 are stated on a per-share basis and therefore can be influenced by share repurchases. If a company diverts funds from pay-

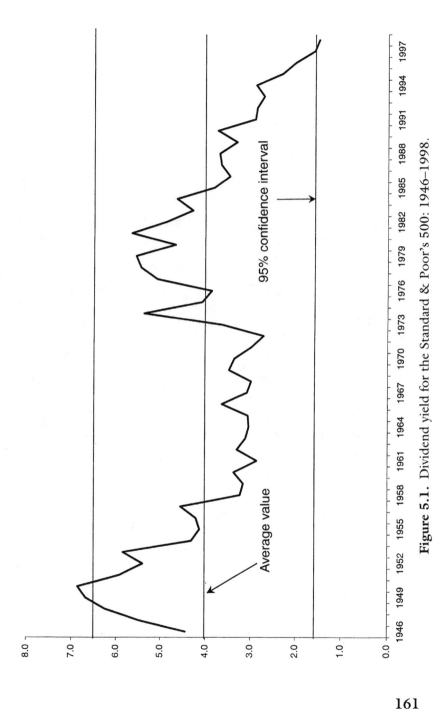

Figure 5.1. Dividend yield for the Standard & Poor's 500: 1946–1998.

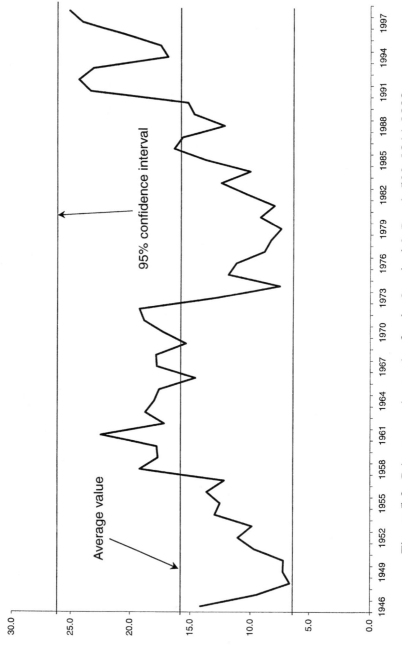

Figure 5.2. Price-to-earnings ratios for the Standard & Poor's 500: 1946–1998.

162

ing dividends to repurchasing shares, without changing anything else, the number of shares outstanding will fall relative to earnings and dividends. As a result, the dividend yield will drop and the P/E will rise. However, shareholders will not be worse off because the negative impact of the repurchase on D/P and P/E ratios is offset by the cash that investors receive from the repurchases. Cole, Helwege, and Laster (1996) argued that repurchases accelerated in the 1990s. Consequently, adjusting for repurchases would significantly increase the dividend yield and reduce the P/E ratio observed during those years, thereby making the 1990s look much less anomalous. However, Shulman, Brown, and Narayanan (1997) presented evidence that suggests the work by Cole et al. is misleading. That work, they noted, was based on the assumptions that both repurchases and issuances of shares take place at the market price. In fact, many companies issue shares below the market price as part of their stock option plans. As a result, they may issue more shares than they repurchase even if more dollars are spent on repurchases than are raised in sales. If this is true, then the dividend yield is *overstated* and P/E ratios are *understated*, not the reverse. Therefore, adjusting for repurchases would make the 1990s look even more anomalous. In light of this finding, it seems fair to conclude that adjusting the dividend and P/E ratios for repurchases would not remove the mystery of the 1990s.

Although dividends and earnings are by far the most common benchmarks used to assess the level of stock prices, they are not the only ones. Two other indicators that economists follow are Tobin's Q and the ratio of stock-market value to gross domestic product (GDP).

Tobin's Q, developed by Nobel laureate James Tobin, measures the ratio of the stock-market value of corporate assets to their replacement cost. Tobin reasoned that if the stock market valued corporate assets at more than it cost to replace them, companies would invest in more assets. Similarly, if the market value was less than replacement cost, firms would postpone investment. As a result, Tobin argued that the Q ratio should tend toward one.

In practice, Tobin's Q is difficult to estimate because there is no unambiguous way to measure the replacement cost of corporate assets. Clearly, historical cost is misleading because of inflation alone, but adjustment for inflation alone does not solve the problem, because the value of corporate assets changes for a host of other reasons.[2] For assessing the relative level of the market, however, measurement error in the Q ratio may not be a critical problem. Although measurement problems make it difficult to estimate the *level* of Tobin's Q, analysis of the *change* in the Q ratio will still provide a useful indicator of the relative ups and downs of stock prices as long as the measurement error is consistent over time. Applying this principal, Siegel (1998) reported that over the period from 1926 to 1997, the average level of Tobin's Q was 0.72. Ninety percent of the Q ratios observed during this period are between 0.40 and 1.35. By comparison, by the end of 1997, the Q ratio was at a record high of over 1.60.

Because GDP can be interpreted as a return on corporate capital, the ratio of the market value of equity to GDP is another way to assess the level of stock prices. Over the period from 1926 to 1996, the average level of this ratio was 0.54. Until 1998, it had exceeded 1.0 only once—in 1929. As Welch (1998) noted in his calculation, described in this book in Chapter 3, by April 1998 the ratio of the value of stocks to GDP had risen to 1.8.

The fact that by the spring of 1998 the level of stock prices was extraordinary relative to all the benchmarks explains the intense interest of investors in the debate about whether the market was too high. The fundamental question on everyone's mind was: What does the current level of stock price augur for stock returns going forward? The answer to that question depends on understanding why prices were so high in the first place.

Explanations for the High Level of Stock Prices

The best place to begin an analysis of the level of stock prices is with the fundamental valuation equation. Recall that the valuation

---

[2] See Lewellen and Badrinath (1997).

equation states that the level of stock prices, *P*, equals the present value at the discount rate, *k*, of all future expected dividends, *D*, or

$$P = \frac{\text{Div}_1}{1 + k} + \frac{\text{Div}_2}{(1 + k)^2} + \frac{\text{Div}_3}{(1 + k)^3} + \ldots \qquad (5.1)$$

Equation 5.1 makes it clear that there are only three distinct types of explanations for an increase in the level of stock prices. First, the discount rate (the equity risk premium) can fall. Second, the dividend stream, and the underlying earnings stream on which dividends depend, can be expected to rise. Finally, stock valuations may depart from the basic valuation model because of speculative excess of one type or another. Given that stock prices as of July 1998 were historically high, to what extent can that be attributed to each of the three foregoing explanations?

A Decline in the Discount Rate Due to a Drop in the Equity Risk Premium

The discount rate, *k*, in Equation 5.1 is composed of two elements: the interest rate and the equity risk premium. Of the two elements, only the risk premium is likely to account for permanent long-run changes in the level of stock prices. The reasons for this are twofold. First, as discussed before, the impact of the inflation component of the interest rate tends to cancel out. Purely inflationary changes in interest tend to be offset by similar changes in the rate of dividend growth, at least in the long run. Second, changes in the real interest rate tend to be limited in magnitude and to be self-correcting. (That is, there is no evidence of a long-run trend in the real interest rate.) For that reason, they do not have permanent effects on the discount rate.

The foregoing implies that if changes in the discount rate are to explain a dramatic increase in stock prices on the order of magnitude of that observed in the 1990s, it must be due to a drop in the equity risk premium. The impact of changes in the risk premium on the level of stock prices measured either by the dividend yield or the P/E ratio can be seen by using the constant-growth version of Equation 5.1. Recall that the constant-growth formula is given by the equation

$$k = \frac{Div_1}{P + g} \tag{5.2}$$

where Div_1 is next period's expected dividend and g is the expected growth rate of future dividends. If it assumed that the dividend payout rate is given by the constant b, Equation 5.2 can also be written as

$$k = \frac{b \cdot E_1}{P + g} \tag{5.3}$$

where E_1 represents next period's expected earnings.

By definition, the discount rate, k, equals the risk-free rate, R_f, plus the equity risk premium. Substituting for k, Equations 5.1 and 5.2 can be written for the dividend yield and the P/E ratio, respectively, in terms of the equity risk premium as follows:

$$\frac{Div_1}{P} = \text{Equity Risk Premium} + (R_f - g) \tag{5.4}$$

$$\frac{P}{E_1} = \frac{b}{\text{Equity Risk Premium} + (R_f - g)} \tag{5.5}$$

Equations 5.4 and 5.5 can be used to calculate how much the equity risk premium must decline to rationalize the changes in the dividend yield and P/E ratio observed in the 1990s. For purposes of comparison, postwar historical averages of the dividend yield and the P/E ratio are assumed to represent "normal" levels. Figure 5.1 shows that the average dividend yield for the S&P 500 over the period from January 1946 to June 1998 was 4%, whereas the dividend yield was 1.5% during June 1998. Assuming that the difference between R_f and g remains relatively constant over time,

Equation 5.3 implies that every percentage-point drop in the equity risk premium will be associated with an equivalent drop in the dividend yield.[3] Consequently, for there to be a decline of 250 basis points in the dividend yield, the equity risk premium must drop by 250 basis points. For example, if the premium over treasury bills started at the long-run average of about 9%, it would have to fall to approximately 6.5%. Such a decline is by no means unreasonable on its face, so a drop in the risk premium *could* explain the fall in dividend yield.

The P/E ratio is a little more difficult to analyze because it depends on the payout rate, *b*. However, the absolute level of *b* does not matter if the sole goal is to determine the approximate amount by which the risk premium must drop to explain a rise in the P/E ratio from 15 to 25. As an example using some reasonable parameters, an equity risk premium of 9%, a 1-month treasury bill rate of 4%, a growth rate of 8.5%, and a payout rate of 65% produce a P/E ratio of approximately 14.5. If the equity risk premium drops 200 basis points, the P/E ratio rises to more than 25. Once again, then, a reasonable drop in the equity premium can potentially explain the high level of stock prices.

The foregoing calculations highlight the question of whether the risk premium has declined. This is a different question than the one considered in Chapter 4—Why has the risk premium been so large?—and it requires a different answer. As noted at the end of Chapter 4, the rational models developed to explain the high level of the risk premium are not candidates to explain its decline because they depend on long-run variables that change too slowly

---

[3] It is reasonable to assume that the difference between R_f and g remains constant for several reasons. First, the most important determinant, over the long run, of nominal growth in dividends and short-term interest rates is the rate of inflation. Because the rate of inflation affects both terms approximately equally, it will leave the difference unchanged. Second, fluctuations in real activity tend to affect the real component of R_f and g in a similar fashion. When times are good, real growth is high and so are real interest rates. Consequently, the difference between R_f and g remains relatively constant.

over time. Similarly, as stressed in Chapter 2, historical data cannot be used to answer the question because the risk premium cannot be estimated with sufficient precision. As a result, it is necessary to employ indirect procedures. One indirect procedure is to determine whether the risk of common stock has declined. Unlike means, standard deviations and correlations can be measured more accurately by dividing the sample period into finer intervals. Therefore, it is possible to measure quite accurately whether the risk of common stock declined markedly in the 1990s. If it did, that provides support for the hypothesis that the risk premium has dropped as well.

Changing Stock-Market Risk

Recall that the consumption-based asset pricing model given by Equation 4.4 states that stock-market risk is determined by two components: the variability of stock returns and the correlation of stock returns with consumption. Of the two, the variability of stock prices has been examined far more thoroughly because the consumption model is relatively new.

To determine whether a decline in the variability of stock prices could explain the bull market of the 1990s, Figure 5.3 plots the standard deviation of returns for the S&P 500 computed using monthly data over rolling 5-year periods from January 1926 through December 1997. So that it is complete, the standard deviation is computed using both real and nominal returns. The figure underscores the point made earlier that when it comes to measuring monthly variability, the distinction between real and nominal is insignificant. The lines for the two types of returns virtually fall on top of each other, demonstrating that essentially all of the short-term variation in stock returns is attributable to factors other than inflation.

Figure 5.3 shows that there was a significant decline in the volatility of stock prices, but the timing is wrong for explaining the 1990s jump in the level of stock prices. The drop in volatility

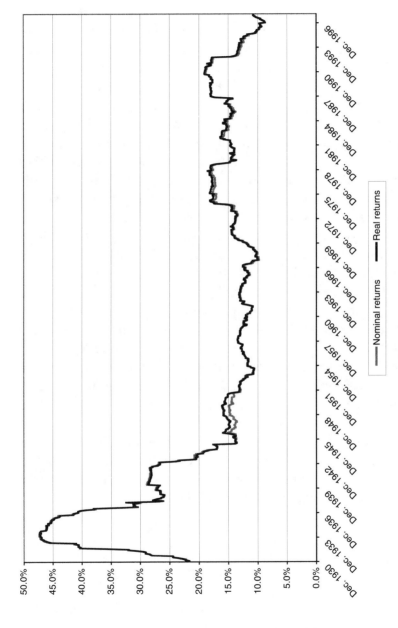

Figure 5.3. Five-year rolling standard deviation for returns on the Standard & Poor's 500: 1926–1997.

— Nominal returns   — Real returns

169

occurred from the depths of the Great Depression to the end of World War II. From then on, however, volatility bounced up and down without any clear trend. More importantly, comparison of Figure 5.3 with Figures 5.1 and 5.2 reveals that there is no tendency for prices to be high relative to dividends or earnings when volatility is low. For instance, dividend yields are low and P/E ratios were high in the early 1990s when the rolling volatility was close to its postwar peak.

To the extent that there is a relation between stock prices and volatility, research indicates that it runs more strongly from prices to volatility, rather than vice versa. Specifically, Black (1976) showed that when equity prices fall, companies become effectively more leveraged, and this increases volatility. However, numerous studies have found that the greater volatility, induced by falling prices, is not correlated with higher expected returns (i.e., with a larger risk premium). As noted earlier, detailed analyses have failed to detect any consistent relation between changes in market volatility and changes in expected returns.

Correlation with consumption does not work much better. First, as noted in Chapter 4, the correlation is too low to explain a market risk premium of any reasonable level. Second, there is no evidence that the correlation was lower during the periods that market prices were relatively high. In fact, the correlation of consumption growth with stock-market returns has remained relatively constant at around 0.20.

Overall, therefore, it does not appear that reduced risk, at least as measured by the volatility of market returns or the correlation of those returns with consumption, can be used to explain why stock prices rose so sharply in the 1990s.

Changing Investors and Changing Investor Demographics

Changes in the nature of investors can also explain the rise in stock prices. One obvious possibility is that investors have become less risk averse. The drawback with this hypothesis is that there is no hard evidence to suggest that it is true. Although it is easy to speculate about how people have changed, hard data on unobservable characteristics such as risk aversion are unavailable. Furthermore, a careful thought experiment suggests it is almost inconceivable that the risk aversion of the representative investor changes markedly from decade to decade. Remember, risk aversion measures the way in which people respond to risk, not the way they assess it. Presumably, a characteristic as fundamental as this is determined by some complex interaction of childhood experience and genetics. Each generation would have a wide dispersion of risk aversion among its members. Some people are test pilots; others are afraid to drive. Nonetheless, on average, over the entire population, there is no reason why the risk aversion of one generation would differ from that of the previous generation. Significant variation in risk aversion over periods less than a decade would be even more unlikely. For this reason, the changing risk aversion hypothesis is not considered further.

Unlike average risk aversion, the information available to investors, and consequently investors' *assessments of risk,* can change dramatically in one generation.[4] The generation that matured in the period during and following the Great Depression had fresh in its minds the devastating 85% drop in stock prices. Furthermore, they were besieged by warnings about the riskiness of common stock. For instance, investment banker Lawrence Chamberlain made the oft-quoted statement that "common stocks, as such, are not superior to bonds as long-term investments, because they are not investments at all. They are speculations" [Chamberlain and Hay, 1931, p. 55].

In the years immediately following the crash, there were no long-run studies of common-stock returns to offset the recent

---

[4] It is easy to confuse changing beliefs about risk with changing risk aversion because both have the same impact on investment behavior. A decline in risk aversion and a decrease in beliefs regarding the risk of common stock will both cause an investor to hold a larger fraction of equity in his or her portfolio.

horrors and repeated warnings from experts like Chamberlain. Although stocks had performed well in the 1920s, there was no convincing evidence to show that over the long run, stocks commonly recovered from disasters like the Great Depression and outperformed fixed-income securities.

As the Depression generation aged and firsthand experience of the market crash receded, information available to investors changed in two important fashions. First, the market recovered from the Depression and rose to record high after record high. The firsthand stock-market experience of young investors who had not lived through the Depression was much different from that of their parents.

Second, comprehensive long-run studies of stock price behavior began to appear. In 1939, Cowles published a detailed account of the behavior of stock prices from 1871 to 1938 based on a value-weighted index that he meticulously constructed. Given the horrid performance of the stock market during the early 1930s, however, the Cowles study did not make stocks appear particularly inviting. Along the same lines, Eiteman and Smith (1962) published a study of the returns on actively traded common stocks that showed that from 1936 through 1960, common-stock investments significantly outperformed investments in long-term bonds. However, this work was criticized for excluding the disastrous years at the start of the Depression.

Studies of the behavior of stock prices kicked into high gear with the establishment of the Center for Research in Security Prices (CRSP) at the University of Chicago. Coincident with the founding of the center, its first director, James Lorie, published an article with Lawrence Fisher (1964) analyzing the return on common stock from 1926 to 1962. The Lorie–Fisher work quickly became a classic and appeared in book form in 1965. Using the CRSP data, Ibbotson and Sinquefield (1976) extended the work of Lorie and Fisher in their article entitled "Stocks, Bonds, Bills and Inflation: Year-by-Year Historical Returns (1926–74)." The article was so well received that Ibbotson formed a consulting company designed to monitor long-run stock-market performance. That company, Ibbotson and Associates, annually publishes a book entitled *Stocks, Bonds, Bills and Inflation* that updates and extends the original Ibbotson–Sinquefield study. Virtually all major institutional investors and their larger clients purchase historical stock-market data from Ibbotson and Associates. (Henceforth, these data will simply be called the Ibbotson data.) Because of the success of the publication and the widespread use of the Ibbotson data at business schools across the country, the historical averages reported in Chapter 2 are common knowledge to essentially all sophisticated investors. Finally, Siegel (1998), in his best-selling book based on work by Schwert (1990), reconstructed the historical data on stock returns backward to 1802. As reported earlier, he found that although it was not as large as during the Ibbotson period, the equity risk premium was still on the order of 4% over the period from 1802 to 1925.

The widespread acceptance of the Ibbotson data has led to a view of common stocks quite different from that expressed by Chamberlain and Hay (1931). The data show that rather than being wildly speculative, long-run investment in common stocks is highly rational and not particularly risky. The basic message conveyed by the Ibbotson data is that over extended periods of time, stocks consistently and significantly outperform both short-term and long-term fixed-income securities. To a remarkable degree, that message has replaced the harrowing experience of the Great Depression as the accepted wisdom on the performance of the stock market. It is not surprising, therefore, that most investors in the 1990s apparently agree with Siegel's advice (1998) that "stock should constitute the overwhelming proportion of all long-term financial portfolios. . . . Based on the historical evidence, even the most conservative investors should place most of their financial wealth in common stocks" [p. 283].

The degree to which Siegel's conclusion has been accepted by investors is illustrated by surveys I have taken of students in MBA investment and finance classes at the University of California, Los Angeles (UCLA). The survey grew out of my own experience. When I began my employment as a professor at UCLA in 1979, the university had two pension funds—a fixed-income fund and a common-stock fund. University employees were allowed to determine how their contributions would be allocated between the two funds. The choices were 0%, 25%, 50%, 75%, or 100% in common stocks. On the basis of the Ibbotson data, I chose 100% in common stocks. At the time, this decision was seen as so anomalous that members of the central administration thought I had made a mistake filling out the form. When I assured them that I wanted 100% in stock, I was questioned repeatedly as to whether I knew what I was doing. Only after I assured them that my conclusion was based on research I had studied as a finance scholar were they convinced that I was not making a speculative mistake.

I found this experience to be so interesting that I began asking students what choice they would have made. In 1979, only 1 of 55 students in my investment classes agreed with the 100% stock allocation. Only another 6 of 55 would have put even 75% in common stock. Part of this reticence, no doubt, reflects the fact that many of these students remembered the oil crisis years of 1973 and 1974 when stock prices declined more than 50% adjusted for inflation. Over the years, as the Ibbotson data were drummed into the heads of students and stock prices continued to climb, views changed. By the start of the 1990s, almost half of the students were choosing 100% common stock. In the most recent survey, conducted in the spring of 1998, enthusiasm for stocks reached record levels. Of 60 students, 42, or about 70% of the class, selected 100% stock. The other 18 students chose 75% stock. Not 1 student in the class wanted to put even 50% of his or her retirement fund in fixed-income securities. When asked why they chose to put such a high fraction in common stock, the students universally cited the Ibbotson data on the long-run performance of stock compared with bonds.

Given the widespread distribution and acceptance of the Ibbotson data, it is not unreasonable to assume that today's investors have significantly different beliefs than their Depression-age predecessors regarding the long-run risk–return tradeoff offered by common stocks and competing fixed-income assets. Because this change in views would increase the relative demand for stocks compared to bonds, it would also cause the risk premium to drop. Assuming that the full impact of the new view was not felt until the 1990s, it follows that the risk premium would have declined then.

In addition to the Ibbotson data, economic developments may well have altered investor perceptions about the relative risks of inflation and recession. During and following the Great Depression, declines in real activity and the associated drop in stock prices were universally seen as the predominant investment risk. If the risk is recession, then high-grade fixed-income securities are ideal investments for avoiding risk. Not only are the payments investors receive fixed without regard to the health of the economy, but the real returns on the securities will rise if inflation drops unexpectedly because of a recession. As noted in Chapter 2, the relative investment risk of inflation and recession began to change with the collapse of the gold standard. Separating growth of the money supply from accumulation of gold had two critical economic effects. First, it made it much more feasible for central banks to fight recession by increasing monetary growth. This lessened the risk of deep recessions such as the one experienced in the 1930s. Second, it introduced a general bias toward inflation and opened the door to serious inflation if governments became profligate. The combined impact was to reduce the investment risk of recession and increase the investment risk of inflation.

The possibility of unexpected acceleration in long-term inflation added a significant new risk for investors. Suddenly, long-term securities whose payouts were fixed in nominal terms became potentially highly risky. In such major industrial countries as Germany and Japan, bondholders were wiped out by inflation. Common stock, on the other hand, proved relatively immune from the ravages of inflation, at least over the long run.

Recognition on the part of investors that inflation rather than recession was now the major investment risk would serve to increase the demand for stock, at least at the expense of long-term fixed-income securities. In fact, the new information about inflation is not unrelated to the long-term holding period results reported in Table 1.2. One reason that common stocks have consistently outperformed bonds as long-term investments is because over the long haul, stocks have proved to be a better inflation hedge than have bonds.

The hypothesis that changing investor beliefs regarding the risk–return tradeoff offered by common stocks in comparison with fixed-income assets is consistent with the data on the stock holdings of American citizens. On the eve of the 1929 crash, only 3% of American households held common stock, either directly or indirectly. By the summer of 1987, that figure had risen to 25%. At the end of 1997, nearly half of all American households held common stock in one form or another.[5] Although part of this increase is no doubt due to the marketing efforts of mutual funds and other institutional investors, such efforts would not have been successful if American citizens viewed common stock with the suspicion that Chamberlain and Hay expressed in 1931.

As appealing as it sounds, the hypothesis of changing investor beliefs suffers from a timing problem. The Ibbotson–Sinquefield article was published in 1976. The Ibbotson data were widely distributed by 1985. By 1985, American investors had also experienced a prolonged bout of significant inflation. Why, then, did they wait until 1988 to start changing their beliefs about common stock, and why did that process continue well into the 1990s? In an efficient market, investors are supposed to respond quickly and completely to new information. One possible explanation is that investors had to live through the 1987 crash. The crash provided dramatic confirmation of the view that stocks could recover quickly from a major correction and move to new highs. That experience underscored the implication of the Ibbotson data that stocks were a safe investment over the long run, despite significant fluctuations in the short run. Unfortunately, this explanation does not fully resolve the timing problem. By 1988, stocks had more than fully recovered from the crash. In an efficient market, prices should quickly reflect whatever investors learned during the crash. What new information could investors have received in 1994 to

[5] Data on shareholding is from *The Economist,* August 8, 1998, p. 15.

further alter their beliefs and to explain a doubling of stock prices over the next 2.5 years?

Whereas the hypothesis that changing investor beliefs led to a drop in the equity risk premium must be based on the inference that beliefs changed, there is direct evidence that investor demographics have been altered. As far as financial assets are concerned, the maximum "investment years" are those between 40 and 60. During those years, earnings are at a peak, the expenses of child rearing are declining, home mortgages are often paid off, and funds are being husbanded in anticipation of future retirement. In 1986, the first of the baby boomers, people born between 1946 and 1964, reached these maximum investment years and began pouring funds into financial assets. Many analysts have suggested that this huge influx of money drove up the prices of financial assets generally, particularly in the 1990s. This makes the impact on the equity risk premium, measured with respect to long-term treasury bonds, somewhat ambiguous. On the one hand, higher prices and lower expected returns on common stocks imply a lower risk premium. On the other hand, higher bond prices imply lower interest rates and a larger equity risk premium.

Empirical research on the impact of baby boomer investing indicates that the impact on expected stock returns has been greater than the impact on bond yields. For instance, Bakshi and Chen (1994) presented evidence in support of the hypothesis that much of the run-up in stock prices following the crash of 1987 can be attributed to the influx of baby boomer investment. However, that article was published in 1994 (and written earlier). In the following 3 years, stock prices jumped more than 100% despite a slowdown in the number of baby boomers reaching their prime earning years. This timing discrepancy is difficult to reconcile with the theory.

It is worth stressing that changes in both investor beliefs and investor demographics will be experienced as a drop in the equity risk premium. In terms of the fundamental valuation equation, saying that baby boomer investments bid up stock prices is equivalent to saying that baby boomers were willing to pay higher prices for securities with a given expected dividend payout. This is equivalent to discounting the expected dividend stream at a lower rate. Consequently, the mechanism by which added investment demand is translated into higher stock prices is through a decline in the equity risk premium. The same is true of changing beliefs. The mechanism by which a more favorable interpretation of the risk–return tradeoff gets translated into higher equity prices is through a decline in the equity risk premium and therefore in the discount rate. As a result, theories that attribute higher stock prices to changing investor beliefs or changing investor demographics are in fact a subset of the theories that attribute higher prices to a lower equity risk premium. What the theories on investor beliefs and investor demographics add is an explanation for the decline in the risk premium.

There is one important distinction between the investor beliefs and investor demographics theories. A change in investor beliefs can be permanent. A drop in the risk premium caused by a new interpretation of the risk–return tradeoff offered by stocks need not be self-limiting. By contrast, the silver lining of the baby boomer investment bonanza is not without its gray cloud. At some point, baby boomers will want to liquidate their financial assets. Shoven and Scheiber (1993) reported that throughout American history each new (and larger) generation has had sufficient purchasing power to buy the financial assets that their parents are selling to fund retirement. The problem is that there are not enough Generation Xers to purchase the assets that the baby boomers will be selling. Consequently, Shoven and Scheiber predict both a real decline in both stock and bond prices beginning around 2010 when baby boomers start selling their financial assets in larger amounts. This decline, by definition, will be associated with an increase in the equity risk premium.

The New Economic Paradigm: Higher Earnings and Dividend Growth

Higher growth in earnings, and thereby dividends, has effectively the same consequences for stock prices as a drop in the discount rate. This is easy to see in the context of the constant-growth model, which states that

$$P = \frac{D_1}{k - g} \qquad (5.6)$$

Because only the difference between the discount rate and the cost of equity enters the denominator, a drop in the discount rate is equivalent to an increase in the growth rate. In more complex models with variable growth rates, the offset is not perfect, but changes in the discount rate and the growth rate remain symmetrical with different signs.

It follows that if a drop in the discount rate of 200 to 250 basis points could explain the increase in stock prices in the 1990s, an increase in the long-term growth rate of earnings of about that magnitude would have the same effect. It is important to stress that the long-term growth rate referred to here is the *long-term* growth rate—that is, the growth rate that can be achieved in perpetuity. Owing to business cycle variation, the growth of corporate profits varies over time. However, that short-term variation is not what is at issue here. The growth rate that enters Equation 5.6 is the long-run average growth rate achievable over a number of business cycles. This is best estimated by the rate of growth in potential economic output.

In Chapter 3, it was pointed out that over the long run, the growth rate in corporate earnings per share must be closely tied to the growth rate of the aggregate economy.[6] The earnings explanation for a rise in aggregate stock prices therefore boils down to the question of whether there as been a permanent increase in the long-term ability of the U.S. economy to grow in real terms.

It is worth stressing that the increased growth rate must be in real terms, not just nominal terms. As noted previously, growth in

---

[6] Once again, this ignores the impact of share buybacks. As noted earlier, the net effect of share buybacks and issuances appears to be close to zero. Consequently, the same conclusions hold on both an aggregate and a per-share basis.

economic activity or corporate earnings that is due solely to inflation will have a minimal impact on value. Because the higher inflation affects both the discount rate and the growth rate in opposite directions, the net effect is close to zero. To the extent that inflationary growth has any impact, it is through such effects as the tax distortions and policy uncertainties that typically accompany high inflation. These effects, however, are second order.

When it comes to explaining the bull market of the 1990s, the fundamental question is this. Is it reasonable to assume that the real long-term economic growth potential of the U.S. economy increased markedly in the 1990s? There are many commentators who think so. The new view, espoused by an enthusiastic cadre of business leaders, journalists, and supply-side economists, is that the American economy of the 1990s is characterized by a new paradigm. The basic idea of the new paradigm is that increased application of information technology and the increased volume of international trade and investment has altered the fundamental capacity of the economy to grow in an noninflationary way. In an effort to summarize the new paradigm thinking, Fleming (1997) wrote:

> Rapid technological change means very basic restructuring of business processes and thus more rapid capacity expansion to meet the demands of a more rapidly growing economy. Improved inventory management systems have enhanced the ability of firms to balance supply and demand better. In addition, growing international trade and investment permits the introduction of global capacity into markets straining to meet demand in cross-global geographies. Further, even in the face of tightened markets, increased global competition severely limits the ability of firms to respond with increased prices and of workers and managers to demand increased salaries and wages [p. 36].

The problem with the new paradigm is that it flies in the face of the most basic economic statistics. The indisputable fact is that long-run real economic growth is determined by two factors: growth in the labor force and increases in output per worker. With regard to these two factors, the facts, as conveyed by Krugman (1997), are these:

First, the U.S. labor force is no longer growing as fast as it did in the years when the baby boomers were growing up and women were moving into paid employment. In the 1990s, the number of people working or looking for work has grown at an annual rate of only about 1%. Second, according to the official numbers, productivity—output per worker—has grown at a sluggish annual rate of only about 1%. The sum of these two numbers is 2%: the growth in the economy's productive potential [p. 37].

Such basic statistics are so contrary to their hypothesis that proponents of the new paradigm have been forced to claim that the data are incorrect. There is not much that can be said about population growth or labor-force participation, so adherents of the new paradigm have focused on productivity. They "feel" productivity must be growing faster than the data show because of the digital revolutionizing of the economy. Such thinking does not give enough credit to past innovations. There is nothing unique about the computer revolution. Numerous other technological innovations have had a huge impact on productivity. Consider, for example, the steam engine, the railroad, the assembly line, electrification, telecommunications, the automobile, and the national highway system. In fact, Krugman argued that these previous innovations had a greater impact on productivity than did digital technology. Furthermore, even if the data do mismeasure productivity, those errors presumably existed in the past as well. Therefore, the impact of earlier innovations should be understated by approximately the same amount as that of current innovations.

In short, the new paradigm is a misguided explanation for what has been a particularly robust but entirely unsustainable burst of real economic growth in the 1990s. Real output was able to grow at a rate significantly greater than the long-run rate of 2% to 3% percent because the economy exploited slack resources. Unemployment fell from over 10% to 4.3% and capacity use rose commensurately—but slack can be exploited only once. When the economy is operating at full capacity, its future growth rate is limited by the growth rate in productive potential. Because productive potential cannot grow faster than the sum of labor force growth and productivity growth, the speed limit for the economy over the long run is the 2% to 3% rate described by Krugman.

Another way to test the new-paradigm hypothesis is to compare its predictions with the forecasts of large-scale economic models. As discussed in Chapter 3, both WEFA Group and Data Resources Incorporated (DRI) produce 25-year forecasts of real economic growth based on econometric models of the U.S. economy. The WEFA and DRI forecasts are largely consistent with Krugman's speed limit. Throughout the 1990s, the average of the 25-year forecasts for real growth in GDP provided by the two companies has hovered around 2%. As of December 1997, the average was 2.1%. This is slightly less than the average real growth achieved between 1950 and 1980. In short, the econometric models do not support the hypothesis of a new paradigm. Of course, proponents of the new paradigm are likely to attribute this to the failure of the econometric models to take proper account of the innovations that they stress.

The implication of the foregoing is that permanently higher growth in earnings is not a reasonable explanation for the level of stock prices observed as of mid-1998. There is no solid economic evidence to support the view that the rate of growth in productive potential is any higher today than it has been throughout the period from 1926 to 1997.

In this respect, it is worth noting that the new-paradigm story is not a new one. Whenever times are good, theories that project those good times forward tend to become fashionable. For example, in June 1929, 4 months before the stock-market crash, *Forbes* magazine opined: "For the last five years we have been in a new industrial era in this country. We are making progress industrially and economically not even by leaps and bounds, but on a perfectly heroic scale." Similarly, in October 1968, just before the onset of a slump that knocked share prices down 60% in real terms, *Forbes* was again cheerful: "As the result of all that has been happening in the economy during the last decade, we are in a different—if not a new—era and traditional thinking, the standard approach to the market, is no longer in synchronization with the real world."[7] It seems that new paradigms, like the greatest game of all time, keep coming back.

Irrational Exuberance: The Market Is Overvalued

A final possibility, of course, is that the high valuation as of July 1998 was simply a mistake. As noted earlier in this chapter, even Federal Reserve Chairman Alan Greenspan, who most often steadfastly refuses to comment on the state of financial markets, referred to the stock market, in his summer 1997 report to Congress, as irrationally exuberant. The following year, the market rose another 30%. Nonetheless, Greenspan returned to Congress in the summer of 1998 and repeated his warning.

In terms of the fundamental valuation equation (Equation 5.1), overvaluation occurs when the stock market reaches levels that cannot be rationalized as the present value of future dividends. But how could this occur? If stock prices reached such a level, then sophisticated investors should begin to sell stocks short to drive prices back into line with Equation 5.1. There is, however, a problem with this strategy. In the fall of 1992, I taught a course at UCLA with famous (infamous?) high-yield bond entrepreneur Michael Milken. As part of a classroom discussion of the similarities and differences between common stocks and high-yield bonds, Milken made the following comments:

> The reason I always favored investing in high-yield bonds as opposed to equities is that for you to earn extraordinary returns in equities, the market has to learn that you are right. If I find a stock that I believe is vastly overvalued and sell it short, I will not make any money; in fact, I will probably lose money until the market accepts my judgment. On the other hand, if I find a high-yield bond that I believe is cheap, I start earning the high yield as soon as I buy the security whether or not anyone else thinks it is a wise investment. Furthermore, I will earn that

[7] Both quotes are from the story "America Bubbles Over," published by *The Economist*, May 9, 1998, page 5.

high yield until the day the bond matures, even if the market never accepts my wisdom. With stock, I don't win until the market agrees that I am right—and who knows when that will occur?

The problem to which Milken referred can be seen mathematically by going back to the definition of the holding-period return. Remember that the holding-period return is defined as follows:

$$\text{Holding Period Return} = \frac{(P_1 - P_0 + D)}{P_0} \qquad (5.7)$$

Because today's price, P_0, is known and any cash payouts during the upcoming period (say, a month or a quarter) are largely known, the predominant source of uncertainty in the holding-period return is next period's price, P_1. Even if stocks are greatly overvalued, an investor who sells them short will lose substantial sums if they become more overvalued next period—that is, if P_1 rises. Furthermore, there is nothing to prevent the same thing from occurring in the subsequent period. This implies that the key to short-term investing is not being able to discern the true value of a security but being able to predict where P_1 will be next period. Of course, that prediction in turn depends on the investor's perception of what investors will expect P_2 to be at the end of period 1. In a famous quote, John Maynard Keynes (1936) summarized the issue this way:

> Most of these [professional investors] are, in fact, largely concerned not with making superior long-term forecasts of the probable yield of an investment over its whole life [applying Equation 5.1] but with foreseeing changes in the conventional basis of valuation a short time ahead of the public. They are concerned not with what an investment is really worth to a man who buys it "for keeps" but with what the market will value it at under the influence of mass psychology, three months or a year hence [p. 155].

Keynes went on to analogize investing to a peculiar beauty contest in which the goal was to pick the winner, not necessarily the prettiest woman:

It is not a case of choosing those which, to the best of one's judgment, are really the prettiest, nor even those which average opinion genuinely thinks the prettiest. . . . We devote our intelligences to anticipating what average opinion expects the average opinion to be [p. 278].

Mathematical economists have shown that the type of thinking to which Keynes refers can lead to self-reinforcing cycles, or "bubbles."[8] Investors buy a stock today not because they believe that it is undervalued—and not even because they believe that other investors believe it is undervalued—but because they believe that the average investor will value it even more highly at the end of the month. As long as this belief is self-sustaining—that is, as long as P_1 turns out to be bigger than P_0—investors continue to buy the stock even though they believe that it is well above its fundamental value.

A bubble, however, is inherently unstable. Because it is not based on fundamental valuation, all that keeps a bubble going is the expectation of higher prices next period. As soon as that expectation changes, prices can drop dramatically. Despite the instability of bubbles, there is evidence that they have arisen in a variety of financial markets. The most famous account of apparent financial bubbles are recorded in the oft-reprinted book by MacKay (1852), *Extraordinary Popular Delusions & the Madness of Crowds*. In the book, MacKay described the Mississippi Scheme, the South Sea Bubble, and the Dutch Tulipomania. Of the three, the tulipomania is perhaps the most famous example of a financial bubble. During the seventeenth century in Holland, the Dutch fascination with tulips turned into a full-scale mania. As MacKay described it:

In 1634, the rage among Dutch to possess them was so great that the ordinary industry of the country was neglected, and the population, even to its lowest dregs, embarked in the tulip trade. So anxious were the speculators to obtain them, that one person offered the fee simple of twelve acres of building-ground for the Haarem tulip [p. 94].

---

[8] See, for example, Behzad and Grossman (1988).

That person was not unique. Another individual traded virtually all of his worldly possessions for one Viceroy tulip. Nonetheless, the mania could not go on forever. As time passed, people began to fear that they could no longer sell bulbs at higher prices. In 1636, the bubble burst. As MacKay recounted:

> At last, however, the more prudent began to see that this folly could not last forever. Rich people no longer bought the flowers to keep them in their gardens, but to sell them again at a cent per cent profit. It was seen that somebody must lose fearfully in the end. As this conviction spread, prices fell, and never rose again. Confidence was destroyed, and a universal panic seized upon the dealers [p. 98].

Is the experience of Holland in the seventeenth century relevant for analyzing the level of stock prices in major industrial countries on the cusp of the twenty-first century approaches? The recent experience of Japan suggests that the answer may well be yes. The experience of Japan is sufficiently dramatic that the possibility of a bubble cannot be ruled out. Even if it was not a true bubble, as mathematical economists would define it, the rise and fall of Japanese stock prices is worth investigating because it raises serious questions about rational pricing, questions that may be applicable to the U.S. market.

To illustrate the Japanese experience, Figure 5.4A compares the growth of $1 invested in Japanese stocks and the S&P 500 during the period from January 1970 to December 1997. The Japanese data are based on the Morgan Stanley Capital International Index. Monthly data on major stock indices from the United States, United Kingdom, Germany, and Japan are presented in Appendix 5.1. This index is used rather than the more well known Nikkei Index because it is value weighted. Like the DJIA, the Nikkei Index is a price-weighted index that does not reflect the investment performance of an actual portfolio. The Morgan Stanley Index, on the other hand, is comparable to the S&P 500 and therefore is a more appropriate choice. From a practical standpoint, however, the two Japanese indexes perform almost identically.

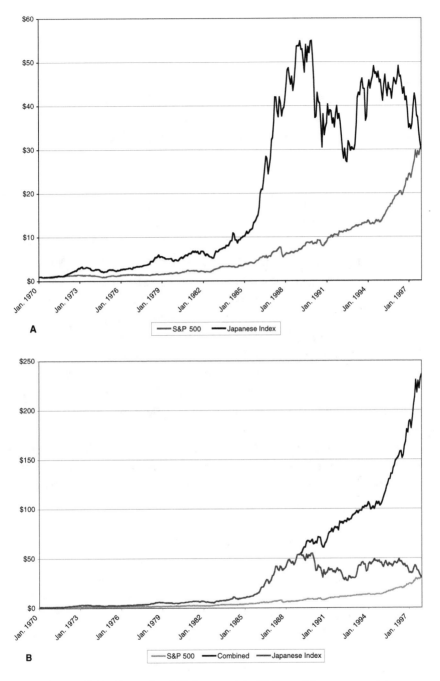

Figure 5.4. Growth of $1 invested in U.S. and Japanese stocks between January 1970 and January 1997: (**A**) indexes contrasted; (**B**) indexes combined. S&P 500 = Standard & Poor's 500 Index.

The returns used to produce Figure 5.4A for Japanese stocks are dollar returns. This means that they are determined by two factors. The first factor is the holding-period return on the Japanese stocks that comprise the index in terms of yen. The second factor is the change in the exchange rate between the dollar and the yen. More specifically, dollar holding-period returns on Japanese stocks are given by the relation

$$\text{Dollar Return} = ([1 + \text{Yen Return}] \times [1 + \% \text{ Change in Exchange Rate}]) - 1$$

The reason for working with dollar returns on Japanese stocks is to allow for direct comparisons, from the point of view of a U.S. investor, of the performance of the markets in the United States and Japan. However, the point to be made about the Japanese market is not a result of movements in the exchange rate. The collapse of the Japanese stock market was so pronounced that it is clearly evident when measured in terms of both dollars and yen.

Figure 5.4A shows that despite the historically high equity risk premium for U.S. stocks documented in Chapter 2, investment in Japanese equities dominated investment in U.S. equities from January 1970 until December 1988. Whereas $1 invested in U.S. equities grew to $6.65 by December 1988, the same $1 invested in Japanese securities would have grown to almost $54.00. Japanese security prices rose so much that during 1989, the aggregate value of the Japanese market surpassed the aggregate value of the U.S. market despite the much greater size of the U.S. economy. By December 1989, Nippon Telegraph & Telephone had become the most valuable company in the world in terms of market value of equity.

In terms of benchmarks based on earnings and dividends, the Japanese market reached dizzying heights. The P/E ratio for the Nikkei as a whole rose to 70.[9] Price-to-earnings ratios for leading

---

[9] Japanese companies use accounting conventions for reporting earnings different from those used by U.S. firms. French and Poterba (1991) showed that the differences tend to make Japanese P/E ratios higher than those for U.S. firms. Nonetheless, a P/E of 70 for the Nikkei Index is extraordinary.

Japanese growth companies in many cases surpassed 100. The dividend yield on the Nikkei dropped to less than 1%.

In 1989, the dramatic growth in Japanese stock prices stopped. Perhaps for this reason, people lost confidence that rising prices would continue to provide extraordinary holding-period returns and began to liquidate their positions. Whatever the explanation, the bubble burst in 1990. During that year, Japanese stock prices lost almost 50% in terms of both yen and dollars. Unlike the U.S. stock market after the crash of October 1987, however, the Japanese market failed to recover. Prices became choppy, but the general trend was down. Even *including* reinvested dividends, as Figure 5.4A does, $1 invested in Japanese stocks *after* the crash of 1990 was worth only approximately $0.85 in December 1997 *without* adjusting for inflation. Overall, the level of stock prices, excluding dividends, fell approximately 65% during the 9-year period from December 1988 to December 1997. The only experience in U.S. history that is remotely comparable to such a prolonged and deep slump is the collapse of prices from the 1929 peak to mid-1938. However, even that comparison is misleading. By the end of 1933, American stock prices were on the way up. By mid-1938, they were well above the level of 1933. By contrast, Japanese stock prices had yet to recover, by 1998, any of their losses from the 1989 crash.

The collapse of the Japanese market erased the all gains that had been achieved relative to U.S. equities since 1970. Figure 5.4A shows that by December 1997, the S&P 500 had caught the Japanese Index. One dollar invested in January 1970 grew to approximately $30 in December 1997 whether it was invested in U.S. or Japanese equities.

Another way to appreciate the depth and length of the slump in the Japanese stock market is to assume that in December 1988, before the Japanese crash, an investor had been wise enough to switch from Japanese stocks to the S&P 500. Figure 5.4B shows that such an investor who started with a $1 investment in Japanese equities from January 1970 until December 1988 and then switched to U.S. securities in December 1988 would have a portfolio worth $236 by December 1998. This is almost eight times the amount resulting from investment in Japanese or American equities alone.

It is hard to explain the Japanese experience without appealing, at least in part, to the notion of irrational pricing. If the prices were rational in 1988, why were they 50% lower 1989? Why have they failed to recover as of this writing? If today's prices are reasonable, how did the Japanese market reach such dizzying heights at the end of the 1980s? In a comprehensive study, French and Poterba (1991) attempted to answer these questions. Using Equation 5.1, they asked if either expectations of future earnings dropped enough or the cost of capital rose enough to explain the rapid rise of Japanese stock price in the late 1980s and the collapse in 1989 and 1990. Although they uncovered some evidence that suggests that growth expectations and the cost of capital did change, the magnitude of the changes is far too small to explain the massive movements of stock prices in either direction. Consequently, French and Poterba (1991) concluded: "We are unable to isolate changes in required stock returns or growth expectations that are large enough to explain recent Japanese stock price movements" [p. 337].

U.S. history is also replete with such unexplainable movements in stock prices. The best example, of course, is the crash of 1987. In a speech at the Atlanta Federal Reserve Bank on February 27, 1998, Federal Reserve Chairman Alan Greenspan said, attempting to explain the crash:

> The United States experienced such a sudden change with the decline in stock prices of more than 20 percent on October 19, 1987. There is no credible scenario that can readily explain so abrupt a change in the fundamentals of long-term valuation on that one day. Such market panic does not appear to reflect a simple continuum from the immediately previous period. The abrupt onset of such implosions suggests the possibility that there is a marked dividing line for confidence. When [it is] crossed, prices slip into free fall—perhaps overshooting the long-term equilibrium—before markets will stabilize.

In light of the Greenspan quote, it is important to be clear about what French and Poterba meant when they said that changes in expected returns are not large enough to explain movements in Japanese stock prices. A look back at Equation 5.1 shows that any change in prices can be explained by variation in the discount rate if *k* moves enough. It is simply a matter of substitution. For a given price level and expected future dividend stream, it is always possible to solve for a *k* that makes Equation 5.1 work. French and Poterba were aware that Equation 5.1 can always be solved for *k*, but they were talking about something else. The changes in required returns that they are speaking of are required returns as derived from a rational economic model—that is, changes that can be attributable either to variation in interest rates or variation in the riskiness of common stock (which would lead to changes in the equity risk premium). They conclude that neither interest rates nor the risk of common stock varied enough. Nonetheless, there are two *k*'s for which Equation 5.1 holds both before and after the collapse in Japanese stock prices. Furthermore, the difference between the low *k*, before the collapse, and the high *k*, after the collapse, can be interpreted as the result of an increase in the equity risk premium. What French and Poterba were saying is that the increase is not consistent with rational economic theory. Some emotional factor must be at play to explain the huge movement in *k* over a short period of time. Because of those emotions, *k* was either too low before the collapse, too high afterward, or both.

This is what makes the debate regarding the equity risk premium and the level of stock prices so maddeningly ambiguous. There is always a change in the premium that can be put forth as an explanation for any move in stock prices. The trick is in explaining why the premium moved. The problem is that there are a host of candidates for the explanation. If finance theory fails to explain the change, as French and Poterba argued in the case of Japan, there are other alternatives. For example, in this chapter, changes in investor beliefs and investor demographics were offered as explanations for a drop in the risk premium in the United States. In addition, a shift in investor emotions is always a possibility. If, as Chairman Greenspan suggested, investor emotions can swing from undue pessimism to irrational exuberance, then the equity risk premium and the level of stock prices will do the same.

There is one other aspect of the relation among the risk premium, the discount rate, and the level of stock prices. A falling discount rate means that an increasing fraction of the value of an asset is being derived from distant future outcomes. By necessity, such distant future outcomes are more difficult to forecast and more subject to alteration when the emotional climate changes. To quote again from Chairman Greenspan's speech at the Federal Reserve Bank of Atlanta on February 27, 1998,

> ...Why do these events (market crashes) seem to erupt without some readily evident precursor? Certainly, the more extended the risk taking, or more generally, the lower the discount factors applied to future outcomes, the greater the proportion of current output (mainly capital goods) driven by perceived future needs. Hence, under such conditions, the more vulnerable are markets to a shock that abruptly triggers a revision in expectations of future needs and sets off a vicious [circle] of contraction of financial and product markets.

Despite Greenspan's views, economists quite rightly are highly suspicious of using emotions to explain movements in the equity risk premium and the level of stock prices. How often have television financial journalists uttered statements like "The market fell today as events in Russia shattered investor confidence"? Not only do such statements involve no economic analysis but they beg the question of how the journalist is measuring investor confidence other than by the level of stock prices. Nonetheless, in an echo of Thaler's warning (1993), it must be said that the overuse of pop psychology to explain movements in stock prices does not mean that all explanations based on emotion are wrong. In looking back at Japan, it is hard to argue that swings in popular emotion did not have something to do with sharp run-up and subsequent collapse of Japanese stock prices, but this is hindsight. In 1988, sophisticated investors did not widely accept the view that the lofty level of the Japanese market was evidence of an emotion bubble. Instead, Japan's stock market was seen as a reflection of the miracle of the Japanese economy and skill of Japanese managers. In fact, Japanese firms were so respected at the time that numerous books explaining how Americans could mimic Japanese management skills became best sellers in the United States.[10] Some went so far as to say that the Japanese economy should be seen as entering a "new era" or as evidencing a "new paradigm." That language sounds eerily familiar.

The behavior of the Internet stocks at the end of 1998 provides an example of possible irrational exuberance that is closer to home. During the period from July 1998 to January 1999, the prices of major Internet stocks exploded. The price of Amazon, the largest Internet retailer, rose by a factor of more than five. The price of Yahoo, the largest Internet portal, jumped by a similar amount. Other Internet companies such as E-bay, AOL, Earthlink, and Excite increased almost as much. All this occurred during a time in which the general market was largely unchanged.

From a fundamental valuation standpoint, these dramatic increases in value are difficult to explain. They were not fueled by large unexpected increases in the earnings of the companies. Most of the companies were announcing continued losses. Although revenues did rise sharply during this period, the increases were basically in line with expectations. Furthermore, no new technologies were revealed. In short, there was no new information about the companies of the sort that would lead one to predict a 500% increase in value.

One explanation put forth in the financial press was that the jump in Internet stock prices was an artifact of the irrational exuberance of Internet stock traders. Most large capitalization stocks, such as General Electric, are owned and traded primarily by institutions. One indicia of this fact is the large average trade size for these companies. Data on the trading of Internet stocks in the second half of 1998 revealed a sharply different pattern. Specifically, the trading was dominated by numerous small traders trading through on-line brokerage firms. Because most of the Internet companies had relatively few shares outstanding, and because most institutions were unwilling to take short positions in the stocks, a surge in demand from thousands of on-line traders had the power to push up prices dramatically.

[10] See, for instance, Ouchi (1982) for an early example of this literature.

As in the case of Japan, however, such dramatic price increases can be followed by equally spectacular declines. The Internet stocks proved to be no exception. In one week in January 1999, major Internet companies including Amazon, E-bay, and Yahoo dropped close to 50% on average.

There is one important distinction between the Japanese example and the Internet stock example. Whereas it is possible, though not likely, that the Japanese experience could be attributed to changes in the equity risk premium, the Internet experience is definitely unrelated to the equity risk premium. By definition, a change in the equity risk premium affects the entire market. Although there can be differences in the manner in which individual stocks, or groups of stocks, are affected by a change in the risk premium, those differences will be small relative to the change in the market generally. Consequently, variation in the equity risk premium can never explain huge increases or declines in the relative value of a certain group of stocks. Whatever caused the Internet stocks to surge and then drop, it must be something unique to investor perceptions regarding those companies.

Summary

The fundamental valuation equation makes it clear that there are three ways to explain movements in the level of stock prices generally and the U.S. stock-market boom of the 1990s in particular. The first way is rational changes in the equity risk premium. Several hypotheses were put forth to explain why a rational drop in the risk premium could have occurred in the 1990s, including a decline in the risk of common stock, changing investor beliefs regarding the risk–return properties of common stock, and changing investor demographics. None of the hypotheses was entirely consistent with the data. The changing-risk hypothesis did not work at all. The hypothesis of changing investor beliefs, although reasonable on the surface, suffered from a timing problem. The most reasonable explanation was a change in investor demographics, but the timing was still not right.

Regarding the equation's numerator, the hypothesis that higher stock prices could be explained by a permanently faster rate of growth in earnings and dividends was entertained. This new-paradigm view was strongly rejected. There is no evidence to support the contention that the long-run growth rate in potential output for the U.S. economy has risen in recent years.

Finally, emotional explanations for the increase in stock prices were considered. These explanations are difficult to disentangle from rational changes in the equity risk premium because the two are mathematically identical. In terms of Equation 5.1, an emotional run-up in stock prices, without corresponding increases in the expected dividend growth rate, is evidenced as a drop in k. For this reason, it is impossible to determine with certainty the extent to which emotional factors interact with rational ones. For example, suppose that the high level of U.S. stock prices is attributed to a combination of changing investor beliefs, changing investor demographics, and irrational investor exuberance. The only way to determine the relative importance of each explanation is by careful analysis of the premises on which the hypotheses are based and the application of reasoned judgment. Because all the hypotheses have the same impact on k, there is no way to distinguish among them on the basis of the movements of stock prices alone.

The debate about the cause of the rise in stock prices could be dismissed as an academic issue were it not for the fact that it has critical implications for what can be expected in the future. Where stocks are going from here depends in part on how they got here in the first place. The task of forecasting future long-run returns on common stocks, in light of both recent experience and the analytical work on the equity risk premium, is the subject of Chapter 6.

Appendix 5.1. International Stock Market Indices

Date	Japan NIKKE 225	England FTSE	Germany GDAX	United States S&P 500
Jan-84	10,196	N/A	N/A	163
Feb-84	10,031	N/A	N/A	157
Mar-84	10,929	N/A	N/A	159
Apr-84	10,981	1,138	N/A	160
May-84	9,940	1,017	N/A	151
Jun-84	10,378	1,039	N/A	153
Jul-84	9,999	1,009	N/A	151
Aug-84	10,584	1,103	N/A	167
Sep-84	10,649	1,139	N/A	166
Oct-84	11,253	1,152	N/A	166
Nov-84	11,429	1,181	N/A	164
Dec-84	11,543	1,231	N/A	167
Jan-85	11,993	1,280	N/A	180
Feb-85	12,322	1,261	N/A	181
Mar-85	12,590	1,277	N/A	181
Apr-85	12,426	1,291	N/A	180
May-85	12,790	1,313	N/A	190
Jun-85	12,882	1,235	N/A	192
Jul-85	12,263	1,262	N/A	191
Aug-85	12,713	1,341	N/A	189
Sep-85	12,700	1,290	N/A	182
Oct-85	12,939	1,377	N/A	190
Nov-85	12,763	1,439	N/A	202
Dec-85	13,083	1,413	N/A	211
Jan-86	13,024	1,435	N/A	212
Feb-86	13,641	1,544	N/A	227
Mar-86	15,860	1,669	N/A	239
Apr-86	15,826	1,661	N/A	236
May-86	16,739	1,603	N/A	247
Jun-86	17,654	1,650	N/A	251
Jul-86	17,510	1,558	N/A	236
Aug-86	18,821	1,661	N/A	253
Sep-86	17,853	1,556	N/A	231
Oct-86	16,911	1,632	N/A	244

(continues)

Date	Japan NIKKE 225	England FTSE	Germany GDAX	United States S&P 500
Nov-86	18,326	1,637	N/A	249
Dec-86	18,701	1,679	N/A	242
Jan-87	20,024	1,808	N/A	274
Feb-87	20,767	1,979	N/A	284
Mar-87	21,567	1,998	N/A	292
Apr-87	23,275	2,051	N/A	288
May-87	24,902	2,203	N/A	290
Jun-87	24,176	2,284	N/A	304
Jul-87	24,488	2,361	N/A	319
Aug-87	26,029	2,250	N/A	330
Sep-87	26,011	2,366	N/A	322
Oct-87	23,329	1,750	N/A	252
Nov-87	22,687	1,580	N/A	230
Dec-87	21,564	1,713	N/A	247
Jan-88	23,719	1,791	N/A	257
Feb-88	25,243	1,769	N/A	268
Mar-88	26,260	1,743	N/A	259
Apr-88	27,510	1,802	N/A	261
May-88	27,417	1,784	N/A	262
Jun-88	27,769	1,858	N/A	274
Jul-88	28,200	1,854	N/A	272
Aug-88	27,366	1,754	N/A	262
Sep-88	27,924	1,827	N/A	272
Oct-88	27,983	1,852	N/A	279
Nov-88	29,579	1,792	N/A	274
Dec-88	30,159	1,793	N/A	278
Jan-89	31,581	2,052	N/A	297
Feb-89	31,986	2,002	N/A	289
Mar-89	32,839	2,075	N/A	295
Apr-89	33,713	2,118	N/A	310
May-89	34,267	2,114	N/A	321
Jun-89	32,949	2,151	N/A	318
Jul-89	34,954	2,297	N/A	346
Aug-89	34,431	2,388	N/A	351
Sep-89	35,637	2,299	N/A	349
Oct-89	35,549	2,143	1,473	340
Nov-89	37,269	2,277	1,577	346
Dec-89	38,916	2,423	1,790	353

(continues)

Date	Japan NIKKE 225	England FTSE	Germany GDAX	United States S&P 500
Jan-90	37,189	2,337	1,823	329
Feb-90	34,592	2,255	1,810	332
Mar-90	29,980	2,248	1,969	340
Apr-90	29,585	2,103	1,813	331
May-90	33,131	2,345	1,845	361
Jun-90	31,940	2,375	1,880	358
Jul-90	31,036	2,326	1,818	356
Aug-90	25,978	2,163	1,630	323
Sep-90	20,984	1,990	1,335	306
Oct-90	25,194	2,050	1,434	304
Nov-90	22,455	2,149	1,441	322
Dec-90	23,849	2,144	1,398	330
Jan-91	23,293	2,170	1,420	344
Feb-91	26,409	2,381	1,542	367
Mar-91	26,292	2,457	1,523	375
Apr-91	26,111	2,486	1,606	375
May-91	25,790	2,500	1,704	390
Jun-91	23,291	2,415	1,622	371
Jul-91	24,121	2,589	1,622	388
Aug-91	22,336	2,646	1,651	395
Sep-91	23,916	2,622	1,607	388
Oct-91	25,222	2,566	1,582	392
Nov-91	22,687	2,420	1,567	375
Dec-91	22,984	2,493	1,578	417
Jan-92	22,023	2,571	1,688	409
Feb-92	21,339	2,562	1,745	413
Mar-92	19,346	2,440	1,718	404
Apr-92	17,391	2,654	1,734	415
May-92	18,348	2,708	1,803	415
Jun-92	15,952	2,521	1,753	408
Jul-92	15,910	2,400	1,615	424
Aug-92	18,061	2,313	1,541	414
Sep-92	17,399	2,553	1,466	418
Oct-92	16,767	2,658	1,492	419
Nov-92	17,684	2,779	1,544	431
Dec-92	16,925	2,847	1,545	436
Jan-93	17,024	2,807	1,572	439
Feb-93	16,953	2,868	1,684	443

(continues)

Date	Japan NIKKE 225	England FTSE	Germany GDAX	United States S&P 500
Mar-93	18,591	2,879	1,684	452
Apr-93	20,919	2,813	1,627	440
May-93	20,552	2,841	1,632	450
Jun-93	19,590	2,900	1,698	451
Jul-93	20,380	2,927	1,803	448
Aug-93	21,027	3,100	1,945	464
Sep-93	20,106	3,038	1,916	459
Oct-93	19,703	3,171	2,069	468
Nov-93	16,407	3,167	2,058	462
Dec-93	17,417	3,418	2,267	466
Jan-94	20,229	3,492	2,178	482
Feb-94	19,997	3,328	2,092	467
Mar-94	19,112	3,086	2,133	446
Apr-94	19,725	3,125	2,246	451
May-94	20,974	2,971	2,128	457
Jun-94	20,644	2,919	2,025	444
Jul-94	20,449	3,083	2,147	458
Aug-94	20,629	3,251	2,213	475
Sep-94	19,564	3,026	2,012	463
Oct-94	19,990	3,097	2,072	472
Nov-94	19,076	3,081	2,048	454
Dec-94	19,723	3,066	2,107	459
Jan-95	18,650	2,992	2,021	470
Feb-95	17,053	3,009	2,102	487
Mar-95	16,140	3,138	1,923	501
Apr-95	16,807	3,217	2,016	515
May-95	15,437	3,319	2,092	533
Jun-95	14,517	3,315	2,084	545
Jul-95	16,678	3,463	2,219	562
Aug-95	18,117	3,478	2,238	562
Sep-95	17,913	3,508	2,187	584
Oct-95	17,655	3,529	2,168	582
Nov-95	18,744	3,664	2,243	605
Dec-95	19,868	3,689	2,254	616
Jan-96	20,813	3,759	2,470	636
Feb-96	20,125	3,728	2,474	640
Mar-96	21,407	3,700	2,486	646
Apr-96	22,041	3,818	2,505	654

(continues)

Date	Japan NIKKE 225	England FTSE	Germany GDAX	United States S&P 500
May-96	21,956	3,748	2,543	669
Jun-96	22,531	3,711	2,561	671
Jul-96	20,693	3,703	2,473	640
Aug-96	20,167	3,868	2,544	652
Sep-96	21,556	3,954	2,652	687
Oct-96	20,467	3,979	2,659	705
Nov-96	21,020	4,058	2,846	757
Dec-96	19,361	4,119	2,889	741
Jan-97	18,330	4,276	3,035	786
Feb-97	18,557	4,308	3,260	791
Mar-97	18,003	4,313	3,429	757
Apr-97	19,151	4,436	3,438	801
May-97	20,069	4,621	3,563	848
Jun-97	20,605	4,605	3,767	885
Jul-97	20,331	4,908	4,406	954
Aug-97	18,229	4,818	3,920	899
Sep-97	17,888	5,244	4,155	947
Oct-97	16,459	4,842	3,754	915
Nov-97	16,633	4,832	3,972	955
Dec-97	15,259	5,136	4,224	970
Jan-98	16,628	5,459	4,443	980
Feb-98	16,832	5,767	4,694	1,049
Mar-98	16,527	5,932	5,097	1,102
Apr-98	15,641	5,928	5,107	1,112
May-98	15,671	5,871	5,569	1,091
Jun-98	15,830	5,833	5,897	1,134
Jul-98	16,379	5,837	5,874	1,121
Aug-98	14,108	5,249	4,834	957
Sep-98	13,406	5,064	4,475	1,017
Oct-98	13,565	5,438	4,671	1,099
Nov-98	14,884	5,744	5,023	1,164
Dec-98	13,842	5,883	5,002	1,229

Chapter 6

The Equity Risk Premium and the Long-Run Outlook for Common Stocks

So that there is no suspense, here is the bottom line: The future will not be as bright as the past. The data of Ibbotson Associates showed that over the period from 1926 to 1997, the average equity risk premium was 7.4% over treasury bonds and 9.2% over treasury bills. Investors cannot reasonably expect equities to produce such large premiums going forward. Instead, premiums are much more likely to be on the order of 300 to 400 basis points lower. Reasonable forward-looking ranges for the future equity risk premium in the long run are 3.5% to 5.5% over treasury bonds and 5.0% to 7.0% over treasury bills.

This relatively pessimistic conclusion is based on two considerations. The first is an overall assessment of the empirical data and theoretical arguments presented in Chapters 1 through 4. The second is the analysis of the level of stock prices presented in Chapter 5. Although forecasting future stock returns, even over the long run, is hazardous at best, when all the evidence is taken into account, the conclusion that the future will be less rosy than the past has strong support.

It is worth noting at the start that this does not mean that common stocks are a bad investment. Premiums of 4% over bonds and 5.5% over bills are still highly significant when compounded over long periods of time. In fact, such premiums could be considered generous if the future long-run risk differential between stocks and bonds is minimal.

Weighing the Empirical and Theoretical Evidence

There are three pieces of evidence that support the argument in favor of a large forward-looking equity risk premium. The first and most persuasive is the historical evidence itself. The argument for projecting long-run historical averages forward has been compellingly made by Ibbotson Associates in their annual publication of *Stocks, Bonds, Bills and Inflation*. In the 1998 version, they said:

> More generally, the 72-year period starting with 1926 is representative of what can happen: it includes high and low returns, volatile and quiet markets, war and peace, inflation and deflation, and prosperity and depression. Restricting attention to a shorter historical period underestimates the amount of change that could occur in a long future period. Finally, because historical event-types (not specific events) tend to repeat themselves, long-run capital market return studies can reveal a great deal about the future. Investors probably expect "unusual" events to occur from time to time and their return expectations reflect this [p. 153].

The second piece of evidence is the internal rate of return (IRR) studies of Kaplan and Ruback (1995) and Fama and French (1998). As noted in Chapter 3, this evidence is not related to the historical average returns. Rather than looking at the history of stock returns, however, Kaplan and Ruback and Fama and French worked with the rate of return of corporate capital. The Kaplan and Ruback study, which inferred the equity risk premium from the forecasts of buyers in high-leveraged transactions between 1983 and 1989, produced estimates close to the Ibbotson historical averages. The Fama and French study, which computed the equity risk premium from the actual cash flows of nonfinancial corporations, produced an estimate only slightly less than the Ibbotson average.

The third piece of evidence is the theoretical work on the equity risk premium puzzle. Theorists of various stripes have shown that if sufficient alterations are made to the standard consumption-based asset pricing model, it will produce predicted risk premiums equal to the Ibbotson average.

Although these three points carry some weight, the evidence on the other side of the scale is more convincing. Perhaps the strongest point is that the historical data are influenced by survival bias. From a theoretical standpoint, Brown, Goetzmann, and Ross (1995) showed that the impact of survival bias can lead to an overstatement of the U.S. equity risk premium by 400 basis points. Findings from a detailed international study by Goetzmann and Jorion (1997) support the theoretical work. On the basis of a study of equity returns in 39 countries, the authors concluded that the U.S. historical data overstate the forward-looking risk premium by about 350 basis points.

In addition, the historical record itself is not unambiguous. Because of the variability of stock returns, the measurement error in mean equity risk premium is large, even when large sample periods are employed. This implies that the historical average will be sensitive to the period over which the average is calculated. The evidence bears this out. The mean premium during the last 25 years has been approximately 250 basis points less over the full period from 1926 to 1997. Furthermore, when Schwert (1990) and Siegel (1998) extended that data backward in time to 1802, they found lower risk premiums. Over the years from 1802 to 1925, the average premium over both treasury bills and treasury bonds was approximately 400 basis points less than it was during the Ibbotson data period. From the standpoint of survival bias, this earlier period, when the U.S. performance was not so extraordinary relative to that of other developed countries, may be more representative. At any rate, the results are remarkably consistent with the theoretical analysis of survival bias by Brown et al. (1995) and the international findings of Goetzmann and Jorion (1997). Finally, it is possible that the entire exercise of projecting historical averages to estimate the future risk premium is misguided because the risk premium is changing over time. Unfortunately, the huge variation in stock returns makes it impossible to tell, on the exclusive basis of a historical analysis of returns, if this is the case. Furthermore, attempts to model nonstationarity by taking account of possible variation in the riskiness of common stocks have proved to be largely unsuccessful.

The estimates of the equity risk premium produced by the Kaplan and Ruback and Fama and French research are not independent of the historical estimates. This is most clear in the work of Fama and French. Rather than averaging past equity returns, they calculated the actual IRR earned by America's nonfinancial corporate sector over the 47-year period from 1950 to 1996. Because stock returns are driven fundamentally by corporate earnings, over long periods of time the Fama–French estimate should be approximately equal to the average stock return. This turns out to be almost precisely the case. The historical average return on Standard & Poor's (S&P) 500 (measured as 12 times the monthly average) over the period from 1950 to 1996 is 13.0%. The Fama–French results imply that the IRR on corporate equity was 12.8%. Therefore, the Fama–French work is best interpreted as a replication of the historical analysis using a different data set, not an independent analysis of the equity risk premium.

The Kaplan–Ruback results are less dependent on historical performance because they are based on the projections of purchasers of companies in highly leveraged transactions over the period from 1983 to 1989. Nonetheless, the results are still historical in the sense that they are based on expectations developed in the past. Furthermore, those expectations were undoubtedly influenced by the strong economy that characterized the period from 1983 to 1989. Limiting the study to such a short, bullish sample period adds an element of upward selection bias to the estimate of the expected return.

The best way to avoid all the problems of selection bias, survival bias, and nonstationarity associated with continually mining the same historical data set is to develop truly forward-looking estimates of the equity risk premium. The most direct forward-looking procedure is to apply the discounted cash flow (DCF) approach to the market as a whole. This can be done either by applying the DCF to the aggregate index or by applying it to the individual firms in the S&P 500 Index and then aggregating the results. Both approaches were implemented in Chapter 3. The results consistently indicated equity risk premiums on the order of 5.5% over treasury bills and 4.3% over treasury bonds, approximately 350 basis points less than the historical estimates and remarkably consistent with findings of the work on survival bias.

More exotic extensions of the basic DCF approach produced even lower estimates of the risk premium. Extension of the model developed by Blanchard (1993) produced equity risk premiums of less than 2% over treasury bonds as of June 1998.

The implications of the theoretical work on asset pricing depends on how the record is interpreted. From this author's perspective, the overall thrust of the theoretical work is consistent with an equity risk premium significantly less than the historical averages. To start with, application of the standard consumption-based asset pricing model produces equity risk premiums of no more than 2%, even with the most generous assumptions. It is true that clever theorists have been able to suggest alterations to the standard model that result in predictions more consistent with the historical premium. However, it is important to bear in mind the process behind that line of research. The theorists began with the *assumption* that the historical premium was the appropriate measure of the future expected premium. Then some of the best minds in economics spent over a decade searching for clever ways to alter the standard model to make it consistent with the assumption. Given the substantial ingenuity that they brought to the task, it is not surprising that they were eventually partially successful. However, as noted in Chapter 4, some of the alterations that were suggested were not only far-fetched but also inconsistent with other economic data.

The bottom line on the theoretical work is that it seems more reasonable to adjust downward the assumption regarding the expected equity risk premium than to accept obscure alterations to standard models. If the expected equity risk premium is reduced, then the equity premium puzzle can be explained with only minor alterations to the basic consumption-based asset pricing model.

Finally, and perhaps most dramatic, assuming that the future equity risk premium will be as large in the future as it has been in the past, or even as large as 6%, leads to some nonsensical predictions. The most compelling is Welch's extrapolation (1998) of the ratio of the aggregate value of the stock market to gross domestic product (GDP). Using an estimated equity risk premium of 6% over treasury bonds, Welch projected that in the period from June 1998 to June 2048, the ratio of the value of equities to GDP will rise to 10 : 1. This implies that that the return on the stock market by 2048 will equal the entire GDP!

What Does the Stock Price Run-Up of the 1990s Augur for the Future?

In Chapter 5, numerous theories were suggested to explain the stock price boom of the 1990s. The surprising fact is that with one exception, all of them predict that future long-run stock returns will be below the historical average. Recall that the theories can be grouped into three categories:

- Explanations based on a rational decline in the risk premium associated with reduced equity risk, changes in investor beliefs, or changes in investor demographics
- Explanations based on higher earnings and dividend growth—the new paradigm
- Explanations based on an irrational decline in the risk premium due to investor exuberance or other emotional factors

The Impact of a Rational Drop in the Equity Risk Premium

Regarding the explanations based on a rational decline in the risk premium, it is important to make the distinction between permanent and temporary drops. Consider first the case in which the decline is permanent. A permanent drop might be attributed, for instance, to the change in the inflationary environment associated with the collapse of the gold standard. Presumably, any change in the relative risk to stocks and bonds caused by the collapse of the gold standard will not be reversed.

The good news about permanent declines in the risk premium is that they imply that stock prices are not too high. The high level of the market in July 1998 simply reflected the new lower level of the equity risk premium. Because the equity risk premium is expected to remain permanently lower, the high prices are in no way indicative of future declines. The bad news is that expected returns in the future will be lower than they have been in the past. To say that the equity risk premium is lower is equivalent to saying that equity investors cannot expect to earn the differential over bonds that they have earned in the past. Unfortunately, the good news has a bad side. If the equity risk premium is lower and if the benefit of the drop is already incorporated in stock prices, then going forward, stockholders must resign themselves permanently to significantly lower average returns relative to bonds than they have earned in the past. This is a point that journalists such as Glassman and Hassett (1998) seem to have missed, or at least to have failed to highlight. They have been enthusiastic about a lower equity risk premium because it means that high stock prices are not indicative of a coming correction. They have failed to recognize that a lower equity risk premium also implies lower future returns.

In Chapter 5, it was estimated that a permanent drop of about 250 basis points in the premium was necessary to explain the dividend yield and price-to-earnings (P/E) ratios observed during the summer of 1997. If that drop actually occurred, then investors who bought stock in July 1998 would have to be satisfied with expected returns that were 250 basis points less, relative to bonds, than during the Ibbotson period.

It may seem that the foregoing implies that the expected risk premium would be approximately 5% (range, 7.4% to 2.5%), but that is not necessarily correct. If past investors were aware of the impact of survival bias, then their expectations for the future risk premium would have been less than the historical average of 7.4% over treasury bonds. The drop of 250 basis points should be deducted not from the historical average risk premium but from the past *expected* risk premium, which could be a good deal less. For example, if the expected risk premium was 5.5% before the drop, it would be only 3% afterward.

If the drop in the risk premium is only temporary, as predicted, for example, by the baby boom investment model, things get a little trickier. At the start, it is necessary to specify whether investors recognize that the drop is going to be temporary. As a first case, assume that they do. This means that investors expect k to be lower for a while but then return to normal levels. Under such circumstances, the initial drop in the equity risk premium must be larger than 250 basis points to explain the high level of stock prices in 1998. For the sake of argument, assume that a temporary drop of 500 basis points is required and that the equity risk premium returns to normal over the course of 20 years. Because the temporal variation in the risk premium is recognized by investors, there are, by definition, no unexpected changes in the risk premium. Therefore, there are no further unexpected movements in stock prices associated with the equity risk premium. Each year, the expected return on the market equals the treasury bond rate plus the equity risk premium for that year. This means that for the next 20 years, or however long it takes the equity risk premium to return to normal, the expected return on the market will be less than it has been in the past. In the early years, the premium will be significantly lower than it would have been had the drop been permanent. Once the adjustment is over, however, equity returns should be comparable, on average, to what they were during the Ibbotson data period.

The second possibility is that the decline in the risk premium is temporary but that investors incorrectly conclude that it is permanent. If this is the case, the market must be inefficient because investors have failed to correctly process the information that the drop is temporary. As a result of this inefficiency, the future path of the equity premium must be divided into three stages. In the first stage, no new data arrive to inform investors of the error of their ways and the equity risk premium behaves as if the drop were permanent. During this period, expected market returns will be less than during the Ibbotson data period. Next, investors begin to see the error of their ways and the equity risk premium rises unexpectedly. This is the reverse of what Glassman and Hassett argued occurred in the 1990s. During the adjustment period, there will be downward pressure on stock prices and returns could turn negative, even in nominal terms. The process can be approximated by reversing the calculation performed to illustrate the impact of an unexpected drop in the equity risk premium. While the adjustment is occurring, stock returns are low not only because the equity risk premium is below its historical average but also because the premium is rising. Once the adjustment has been completed, the premium will return to its previous historical average.

To summarize, explanations for the bull market of the 1990s based on a drop in the risk premium lead to three related predictions for future stock returns. First, if the drop in the equity risk premium is permanent, stock returns, compared to bonds, will be lower into the indefinite future than they have been in the past. However, no correction in the level of stock prices is implied. Second, if the drop is temporary and investors recognize that it is, stock returns will be even lower than if the drop were permanent in the immediate future. Eventually, as the risk premium returns to normal, expected stock returns will rise. Once again, no correction in the level of stock prices is implied. Third, if the drop in the premium is temporary but investors think that it is permanent, the prediction is more complicated. Until investors recognize the error of their ways, expected stock returns will behave as if the drop were permanent. That is, they will be below historical averages, but there will be no correction in stock prices. When investors begin to recognize that the drop was temporary, the equity risk premium will rise unexpectedly. During this adjustment period, returns will be even lower. If the adjustment occurs relatively quickly, stock prices will drop. Once the adjustment process is over, expected returns will settle down at levels consistent with the historical average.

The point is that no matter to which version of the story one ascribes, the future will not be as rosy as the past. Either (1) future stock returns will be permanently lower by 250 basis than they have been in the past, (2) future stock returns will be more than 250 basis points less than they were in the past for an extended period but will recover eventually to historical levels, or (3) future stock returns will be much lower than they have been in the past, and probably negative, for an adjustment period before returning to historical levels. Consequently, an investor who buys as of this writing, or whenever stock prices are at a similar level relative to dividends and earnings, cannot expect to earn returns relative to treasury bonds commensurate with the Ibbotson averages.

The Impact of Permanently Higher Growth

The only theory that explains the level of stock prices as of July 1998 and simultaneously holds out the hope that the future equity risk premium will be as high as it has been in the past is the new paradigm. If future long-run real economic growth exceeds past growth by 250 basis points, the DCF valuation model given by Equation 5.1 can hold without any change in the real discount rate or the equity risk premium. The problem is that despite all the hype, there is no way that the real growth potential of the U.S. economy could be increased by 250 basis. That would amount to more than doubling the current real growth rate of approximately 2%. In fact, it is unreasonable to suggest the real growth potential of the economy could be increased by even 100 basis points. Real economic growth is determined by a combination of growth in the labor force and growth in productivity. Neither of these variables can change very much or very quickly. Furthermore, to the extent that there is a long-run trend in either of these variables, it appears to be downward. After the movement of women into the labor force, which can only occur once, labor-force growth rates began to drop. In addition, despite the economic boom since 1991, productivity growth in the 1990s was less than it was in the 1960s. The fact is that there was considerable slack in the economy coming out of the last recession. The economy was able to grow at above sustainable rates for over 5 years by taking advantage of that slack. As of July 1998, the slack was gone.

In short, the new paradigm is a highly optimistic but almost certainly incorrect theory. It would be wonderful to conclude that not only are stock prices high but future returns on equities will exceed returns on bonds by margins equal to those of the Ibbotson data period. However, to do so requires turning the other cheek not only to standard macroeconomic theory but also to available data on economic growth.

The Implications of Overvaluation

The long-run implications of overvaluation are straightforward: Somehow stock prices must move back into line with such underlying determinants of value as dividends and earnings. The short-run implications are a good deal more murky. A return to more normal levels can occur in several distinct ways. First, there can be a sharp but relatively short-lived drop in stock prices. The last two examples of such drops are the crash of 1987 and the bear market of 1973–1974. Prices dropped more quickly in the crash, but the decline was not as steep. In 1973–1974, prices declined more than 50% in real terms over the course of 18 months.

In this respect, a simple calculation is insightful. In July 1998, the Dow Jones Industrial Average (DJIA) stood at about 9,300 and the P/E ratio for the S&P 500 was at a record of approximately 25. Suppose that the extraordinary P/E ratio represents overvaluation. How far would stock prices have to fall for the ratio to drop back to its postwar average? The answer is to approximately 6,000 on the DJIA (= 9,300 · 16/25). Consequently, one rough-and-ready prediction of the overvaluation theory is that if there is a sharp, short-term "correction," then stock prices could well fall to the 6,000 level on the DJIA. If the calculation is based on dividend yields, an even larger correction is required.

Another possibility is a long period of stagnation similar to the experience of Japan from the period after the crash of 1989 to this writing. Over time, if earnings and dividends continue to rise faster than stock prices do, prices will eventually fall back into line without a major correction. However, without a sharp drop of some type, a significant period of subpar returns would be required to get P/E ratios and dividend yields back to the average levels.

Of course, the foregoing are simply the two extremes. Any combination is possible. The only certainty is that if the market is overvalued and if it eventually returns to proper valuation, then the equity risk premium will be below historical averages—and below even the lower forward-looking estimates—during the period of adjustment.

It is worth stressing that if the correction comes as a sharp drop, then the timing of that drop must be unpredictable. Even though overvaluation, by definition, implies that the market is not perfectly efficient, it would have to be grossly inefficient for large future declines to be predictable. As noted earlier, a large predictable drop in prices is internally contradictory. Given the prediction of a crash, it is always better to sell the day before the predicted drop—but to beat the drop that early sellers will cause on the day preceding the crash, it is necessary to sell 2 days in advance. Therefore, there will be a drop 2 days before the crash, which means savvy investors must sell 3 days in advance. Carrying this argument forward, the prediction of the crash unravels. The drop that was supposed to occur in the future occurs today. If the prediction is for a long period of below-average returns, the contradiction is not so stark. The imperative to sell is much less when the prognostication is for subpar returns over the next 10 years as opposed to a 50% drop next year. In fact, a long period of apparently subpar returns is difficult to distinguish from a drop in the equity risk premium. If an investor observes that over the next 10 years the ex-post equity risk premium is less than it was during the Ibbotson data period, does this mean that the market is correcting for past overvaluation or that the equity risk premium has dropped? There is no way to tell from observation of the returns alone.

The key point is that no matter what form a correction takes, if stocks are overvalued today, the risk premium earned in the future will be lower than that earned in the past, on average, until the overvaluation has been eliminated.

Summary

The conclusion stated at the start of this chapter is worth reiterating: In comparison with bonds, future equity returns will not be as high as they have been in the past. Economic theory, analysis of historical returns, consideration of international data, analysis of potential statistical biases, DCF analysis, and consideration of the level of stock prices as of July 1998 all point in the direction of a lower equity risk premium in the future.

Implications of a Lower Equity Risk Premium in the Future

In Chapter 1, it was observed that the equity risk premium plays a particularly important role in three areas of finance: investment decision making (especially asset allocation), corporate capital budgeting, and pension and retirement planning. How, then, is a lower equity risk premium in the years ahead likely to affect these three areas of finance?

Investment Implications

The investment implications of a lower future equity risk premium depend on why the premium will be lower. Specifically, it depends on whether the lower future risk premium will arise because the market is currently overvalued or because the equilibrium risk premium has fallen and that has led to higher prices. The market overvaluation theory has an obvious implication. Equity holdings should be reduced until the overvaluation is eliminated. The hard part is implementing the advice. Given the fact that there is an unresolved debate regarding current overvaluation, how is an investor to decide by how much the market is overvalued at the present and when that overvaluation has been eliminated? Furthermore, how much should equity holdings be reduced for any given perceived level of overvaluation? The answer to the second question clearly depends on the type of correction that the investor fears. More generally, financial economic theory is not particularly helpful for dealing with perceived overvaluation of the stock market. Because virtually all financial models assume that markets are efficient and investors make rational decisions, they are not well designed for modeling under- or overvaluation or predicting market corrections.[1] For these reasons, no specific advice is offered here as to how to deal with a perceived overvaluation.

From the standpoint of financial economic theory, a more reasonable explanation for the high stock prices of July 1998 is not market inefficiency but a lower equity risk premium. In such cases where the decline in the equity risk premium is economically rational, the lower expected returns on stock relative to bonds does not imply that equity holdings should be reduced. That is because the smaller premium is due to some beneficial characteristics of either equities that did not exist in the past or equities whose existence was not appreciated in the past. The benefits associated with those characteristics compensate investors for the lower expected returns on common stocks going forward. For instance, the lower premium may be due to the long-run inflation-hedging characteristics of common stocks in a post–gold standard world. In that situation, the lower risk premium is fair.

It is also worth noting that even with a lower risk premium, stocks still remain an excellent long-run investment in comparison to bonds. Figure 6.1 compares the results of investing in 30-year treasury bonds with a yield of 5.75% to investment in stocks as-

---

[1] The exceptions are the behavioral models mentioned earlier. See Thaler (1993) for a collection of articles on the subject.

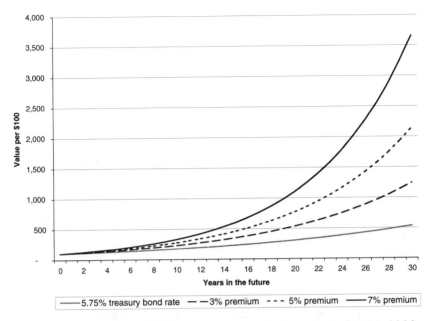

Figure 6.1. Value of $100 investment over the period of 1999–2028 as a function of the risk premium.

suming that the future risk premium is 3%, 5%, and 7%. Even at the lowest risk premium of 3%, the end of period wealth from investing in stocks is twice that from investing in bonds. If the equity premium is 5%, still well below the Ibbotson average, stocks outperform bonds by a factor of 4.

Implications for Corporate Financial Decision Making

The financial models on which corporate finance is based assume that the market is reasonably efficient. Therefore, the overvaluation theory has little to offer other than to say that companies ought to issue equity whenever they think stock prices are too high and avoid selling equity when prices are depressed. A rational decline in the risk premium, on the other hand, does have important implications for financial decision making. In particular, it implies that the cost of equity capital for U.S. companies currently is lower than historical data on equity returns indicate. Companies that fail to recognize this fact will unwittingly use a cost of equity that is too high and may therefore forgo projects with positive present value.

Implications for Pension and Retirement Planning

Pension planning, either from the point of view of a pension plan or its beneficiaries, involves the same issues as does asset allocation. Proper decision making depends on not only the expected future risk premium but also the reasons why it might differ from the past. If the ex-ante risk premium is lower because investors now realize that the long-run riskiness of investing in stock is less than they previously thought, then a lower risk premium may not have a large impact on pension investing. Nonetheless, it must, by definition, affect pension planning. To the extent that expected returns on common stocks decline, fixed-benefit funds face two choices: they can increase (1) funding for the plan or (2) the fraction of the fund invested in common stocks. Notice that the second alternative need not increase the overall risk of the fund if the reason for the drop in the risk premium is a decline in the riskiness of common stocks relative to bonds.

Employees on fixed-contribution plans or who are funding their own retirement plans face the same tradeoff. To achieve an expected dollar standard of living in the face of declining expected returns on equity, they must either save more or increase the fraction of their portfolio allocated to common stocks. Investors who plan for their retirement in the belief that the future equity risk premium will equal its past levels are likely to be unpleasantly surprised.

References

Arzac, Enrique R., and Matityahu Marcus (1981). Flotation cost allowance in rate of return regulation. *Journal of Finance* 36(5):1199–1202.

Bakshi, Gurdip S., and Zhiwu Chen (1994). Baby boom, population aging and capital markets. *Journal of Business* 67(2):165–202.

Behzad, Deba T., and Herschel I. Grossman (1988). Rational bubbles in stock prices? *American Economic Review* 78(3):520–530.

Benartzi, Shlomo, and Richard H. Thaler (1995). Myopic loss aversion and the equity risk premium puzzle. *Quarterly Journal of Economics* 110(1):75–92.

Blanchard, Oliver (1993). Movements in the equity premium. *Brookings Papers on Economic Activity* 75(2):75–118.

Black, Fisher (1976). Studies of stock price volatility changes (pp. 177–181). In: *Proceedings of the 1976 Meetings of the American Statistical Society, Business and Economics Statistics Section*.

Breen, William, Lawrence R. Glosten, and Ravi Jagannathan (1989). Economic significance of predictable variations in stock index returns. *Journal of Finance* 44(4):1177–1189.

Brewer, Elijah, and George G. Kaufman (1994). Exploring the real interest rate puzzle. *Quarterly Review of Economics and Finance* 34(4):363–373.

Brown, Lawrence D., and Kwon-Jung Kim (1991). Timely aggregate analyst forecasts as better proxies for market earnings expectations. *Journal of Accounting and Economics* 29(2):382–385.

Brown, Stephen J., William N. Goetzmann, and Stephen A. Ross (1995). Survival. *The Journal of Finance* 50(3):353–873.

Brown, Lawrence D., and Kwon-Jung Kim (1991). Timely aggregrate analyst forecasts as better proxies for market earnings expectations. *Journal of Accounting and Economics* 29(2):382–385.

Brown, Lawrence D., and Michael S. Rozeff (1978). The superiority of analysts. Forecasts as measures of expectations. *Evidence from Business* 33(1):1–16.

Campbell, John Y., and John H. Cochrane (1997). By force of habit: A consumption-based explanation of aggregate stock market behavior. Unpublished working paper, Graduate School of Business, University of Chicago, Chicago.

Campbell, John Y., and Ludger Hentschel (1992). No news is good news: An asymmetric model of changing volatility in stock returns. *Journal of Financial Economics* 31(2):281–318.

Chamberlain, Lawrence, and William W. Hay (1931). *Investments and Speculations*. New York: Henry Holt.

Cochrane, John H. (1997). Where is the market going? Uncertain facts and novel theories. *Economic Perspectives* 21(6):3–37.

Cole, Kevin, Jean Helwege, and David Laster (1996). Stock market valuation indicators: Is it different this time? *Financial Analyst Journal* 52(3):56–64.

Constantinides, George M., and Darrell Duffie (1996). Asset pricing with heterogeneous consumers. *Journal of Political Economy* 104(2):219–240.

Copeland, Tom, Tim Koller, and Jack Murrin (1994). *Valuation Measuring and Managing the Value of Companies*. New York: John Wiley & Sons.

Cornell, Bradford (1993). *Corporate Valuation*. New York: Business One Irwin.

Cornell, Bradford, John I. Hirshleifer, and Elizabeth P. James (1997). Estimating the cost of equity capital. *Contemporary Finance Digest* 1(autumn):5–26.

Cowles, Alfred (1939). *Common Stock Indexes: 1871–1937*. Bloomington, IN: Principia Press.

Damodaran, Aswath (1994). *Damodaran on Valuation*. New York: John Wiley & Sons.

Dow Jones & Co. (1972). *The Dow-Jones Averages, 1885–1970.* Edited by Maurice L. Farrell. New York: Dow Jones.

Eiteman, Wilford, J., and Frank P. Smith (1962). *Common Stock Values and Yields.* Ann Arbor, MI: University of Michigan Press.

Fama, Eugene F. (1970). Efficient capital markets: A review of theory and empirical work. *Journal of Finance* 25(2):383–417.

Fama, Eugene F. (1975). Short-term interest rates as predictors of inflation. *American Economic Review* 65(3):269–282.

Fama, Eugene F. (1991). Efficient capital markets: II. *Journal of Finance* 46(5):1575–1618.

Fama, Eugene F., and Kenneth R. French (1988a). Dividend yields and expected stock returns. *Journal of Financial Economics* 22(1):3–27.

Fama, Eugene F., and Kenneth R. French (1988b). Permanent and temporary components of stock prices. *Journal of Political Economy* 96(2):246–273.

Fama, Eugene F., and Kenneth R. French (1989). Business conditions and the expected returns on stocks and bonds. *Journal of Financial Economics* 25(1):23–50.

Fama, Eugene F., and Kenneth R. French (1992). The cross-section of expected stock returns. *Journal of Finance* 47(2): 427–466.

Fama, Eugene, F., and G. William Schwert (1977). Asset returns and inflation. *Journal of Financial Economics* 5(2):115–146.

Ferson, Wayne E., and Campbell R. Harvey (1991). The variation of economic risk premiums. *Journal of Political Economy* 99(2):385–415.

Fleming, Martin (1997). The new business cycle: The impact of the application and production of information technology on U.S. macroeconomic stabilization. *Business Economics* 32(10):36–37.

French, Kenneth R., and Richard Roll (1986). Stock return variances: The arrival of information and the reaction of traders. *Journal of Financial Economics* 19(1):2–29.

French, Kenneth R., G. William Schwert, and Robert F. Stambaugh (1987). Expected stock returns and variance. *Journal of Financial Economics* 17(1):5–26.

French, Kenneth R., and James M. Poterba (1991). Were Japanese stock prices too high? *Journal of Financial Economics* 29(2):337–364.

Glassman, James K., and Kevin A. Hassett (1998). Are stocks overvalued? Not a chance. *Wall Street Journal* March 30. p. 28, Section 1.

Glosten, Lawrence R., Ravi Jagannathan, and David E. Runkle (1993). On the relation between the expected value and the variance of the nominal excess return on stocks. *Journal of Finance* 48(5):1779–1801.

Goetzmann, William N., and Philippe Jorion (1997). A century of global stock markets. Working paper 5901. New York: National Bureau of Economic Research.

Heaton, John, and Deborah J. Lucas (1996). Evaluating the effects of incomplete markets on risk sharing and asset pricing. *Journal of Political Economy* 104(2):443–487.

Ibbotson, Roger, and Rex Sinquefield (1976). Stocks, bonds, bills and inflation: Year-by-year historical returns (1926–74). *Journal of Business* 49(1):11–43.

Ibbotson Associates (1998). *Stocks, Bonds, Bills and Inflation: 1997 Yearbook*. Chicago: Ibbotson Associates.

Jagannathan, Ravi, and Zhenyu Wang (1996). The conditional CAPM and the cross-section of expected returns. *Journal of Finance* 51(1):3–53.

Kaplan, Steven, N., and Richard S. Ruback (1995). The valuation of cash flow forecasts: An empirical analysis. *Journal of Finance* 50(4):1059–1094.

Keynes, John Maynard (1936/1965). *The General Theory of Employment, Interest and Money*. New York: Harcourt Brace and World.

Krugman, Paul (1997). How fast can the U.S. economy grow? *Harvard Business Review* July/August: 75(4):123–129.

Lakonishok, Josef, Andrei Shleifer, and Robert W. Vishny (1994). Contrarian investment, extrapolation, and risk. *Journal of Finance* 49(5):1541–1578.

Lewellen, Wilbur G., and S.G. Badrinath (1997). On the measurement of Tobin's Q. *Journal of Financial Economics* 44(1):77–122.

Lintner, John (1965). The valuation of risky assets and the selection of risky investments in stock portfolios and capital budgets. *Review of Economics and Statistics* 47(1):13–37.

Lorie, James H., and Lawrence Fisher (1964). Rates of return on investment in common stocks. *Journal of Business* 37(1):1–21.

Macaulay, F.R. (1938). *The Movements of Interest Rates, Bond Yields and Stock Prices in the United States since 1956.* New York: National Bureau of Economic Research.

MacKay, Charles (1852/1980). *Extraordinary Popular Delusions & the Madness of Crowds.* New York: Three Rivers Press.

Marshall, David, and Kent Daniel (1997). The equity premium puzzle and the risk-free rate puzzle at long horizons. *Macroeconomic Dynamics* 1(1):452–484.

Markowitz, Harry (1952). Portfolio selection. *Journal of Finance* 7(1):77–91.

Mehra, Rajnish, and Edward Prescott (1985). The equity premium: A puzzle. *Journal of Monetary Economics* 15(2):145–161.

Merton, Robert C. (1980). On estimating the expected return on the market: An exploratory investigation. *Journal of Financial Economics* 8(3):323–361.

Nelson, Daniel B. (1991). Conditional heteroskedasticity in asset returns: A new approach. *Econometrica* 59(2):347–370.

Ouchi, William (1982). *Theory Z: How American Business Can Meet the Japanese Challenge.* New York: Avon.

Porter, M.E. (1992). Capital disadvantage: America's failing capital investment system. *Harvard Business Review* (September-October): 70(5):65–83.

Poterba, James, and Lawrence J. Summers (1986). The persistence of volatility and stock market fluctuations. *American Economic Review* 75(5):1142–1151.

Ross, Steven A. (1976). The arbitrage theory of capital asset pricing. *Journal of Economic Theory* 13(3):341–360.

Schwert, William G (1990). Indexes of U.S. stock prices from 1802 to 1987. *Journal of Business* 63(3):399–426.

Sharpe, William F., Gordon J. Alexander, and Jeffery V. Bailey (1995). *Investments* (5th ed.). Englewood Cliffs, NJ: Prentice-Hall.

Sharpe, William F. (1964). Capital asset prices: a theory of market equilibrium under conditions of risk. *Journal of Finance* 19(3):425–442.

Shiller, Robert (1981). Do stock prices move too much to be justified by subsequent changes in dividends? *American Economic Review* 73(3):421–436.

Shoven, John, and Sylvester Scheiber (1993). *The Consequences of Population Again on Private Pension Fund Saving and Asset Markets*. Pub. no. 363. Center for Economic Policy Research. Stanford University, Stanford CA.

Shulman, David, Jeffery Brown, and Mari Narayanan (1997). Share repurchases: Less than meets the eye. New York: Salomon Brothers.

Siegel, Jeremy (1992). The real rate of interest from 1800 to 1990: A study of the U.S. and U.K. *Journal of Monetary Economics* 29(2):227–252.

Siegel, Jeremy (1998). *Stocks for the Long Run* (2nd ed.). New York: Irwin.

Smith W.B., and A.H. Cole (1935). *Fluctuations in American Business, 1790–1860*. Cambridge, MA: Harvard University Press.

Thaler, Richard (1993). *Advances in Behavioral Finance* Russell Sage Foundation. New York, NY.

Turner, Christopher M., Richard Startz, and Charles R. Nelson (1989). A Markov model of heteroskedasticity, risk and learning in the stock market. *Journal of Financial Economics* 25(1):3–22.

Tversky, Amos, and Daniel Kahneman (1992). Advances in prospect theory: Cumulative representation of uncertainty. *Journal of Risk and Uncertainty* 5(4):297–323.

Vander Weide, James H., and Willard T. Carleton (1988). Investor growth expectations: Analysts vs. history. *Journal of Portfolio Management* 14(3):78–82.

Welch, Ivo (1998). Views of financial economists on the equity premium and other issues. Unpublished working paper, Anderson Graduate School of Management, University of California, Los Angeles.

Index

American Stock Exchange, 8
American Telephone and Telegraph
  (AT&T), 103, 107, 109
"America's Bubble Economy" *(Econo-
  mist),* 158–159
Arithmetic averages, 36–39
Asset allocation decision making, 27–28
Asset returns, inflation and, 29–34. *See
  also* Historical analysis
Autocorrelation in returns, 149–150

Baby boomer investing, 177, 178
Behavioral theories, 156–157
Benartzi-Thaler model, 148–149, 155
Bills:
  annual holding period data on,
    13–17
  annual real returns on, 23–25
  long-term holding period returns, 68
  monthly historical data for, 79–100
  returns before 1926, 67–68
Blanchard extension of discounted cash
  flow approach, 114–115, 124
*Bluefield Water Works v. Public Service
  Commission,* 103
Bonds:
  annual holding period data on, 13–17
  annual real returns on, 23–25
  future investment value and, 214–215
  inflation impact on, 33, 74–77
  long-term holding period returns, 68
  long-term viability, 70–74
  monthly historical data for, 79–100
  returns before 1926, 67–68
Book-to-market ratios, 50
"Bubbles," financial, 185
Buffett, Warren, 159

Business cycle variation, risk premium,
  54–55

Campbell-Cochrane model, 146–148,
  155
Capital asset pricing model (CAPM),
  28–29, 133–135, 136, 139, 150
Center for Research in Security Prices,
  7–8, 172
Chamberlain, Lawrence, 171
Compounding interval, discounted cash
  flow models and, 104–105
Compustat database, 120
Constant-growth model, *see* Discounted
  cash flow model
Constantinides-Duffie model, 153–154
Consumption:
  asset pricing and, 138–140
  growth of, 144, 146–147
  utility of, 127–129
Corporate decision making, 28,
  215–216
Corporate earnings, high stock valuation
  and, 178–183

Data Resources Incorporated, 107
Discounted cash flow analysis, 102–114
  Blanchard extension of, 114–115
  calculation of expected return on mar-
    ket, 110–112
  compared to historical estimates,
    113–114
  constant-growth form, 102–106, 179
  Cornell application of, 124
  estimating risk premium and, 135,
    205
  multistage form, 106–113

Discount rate, stock valuation and, 151, 165–168
Dividend yield:
estimating time path of, 105
high stock valuation and, 178–183
models based on, 52–53
risk premium and, 49–50
stock value and, 159–161, 163
Dow Jones Industrial Average, 6–7
boom of the 1990s, 158
Drexel, Burnham, Lambert, 117

Earnings yield:
market risk premium and, 121–122
models based on, 52–53
Economic growth, impact of permanently higher, 210–211
Efficient market hypothesis, 2–3
Empirical data, risk premium puzzle and, 141–142
Equity capital, market risk premium and, 135–137
Equity risk premium:
calculating historical, 26–27
definition of, 18–19
estimates of, *see* Estimates of risk premium
high stock valuation and, *see* High stock valuation
historical measurement, *see* Historical analysis
importance of, 19–20
long-run outlook on, *see* Long-run outlook
modeling changes in, *see* Model changes
uses of, 27–29
Estimates of risk premium:
Blanchard extension, 114–115
comparison of, 124
discounted cash flow model, 102–114
earnings yield approach, 121–122
Fama-French analysis, 117–121
Kaplan-Ruback study, 115–117
Welch survey, 122–125
Ex-ante returns, 10–11
Expected returns, 151
calculations for individual companies, 110–112
Ex-post returns, 10–11

Ex-post risk premium:
regressions on dividend yield, 52–53
survival bias and, 63
Extraordinary Popular Delusions & the Madness of Crowds, 185

Fama-French analysis, 117–121, 124, 204
Federal Communications Commission, 135–137
Federal Power Commission v. Hope Natural Gas Company, 103
Federal Reserve establishment, 75
FinEcon, 113
Fisher, Lawrence, 172
Fixed-income investments, inflation and, 32–22
Flotation costs, discounted cash flow models and, 105

Galbraith, John Kenneth, 4
Geometric averages, 37–39
Goldman Sachs, 108–109
Gold standard, 75, 175
Great Depression, 69, 74, 156, 171–172
Greenspan, Alan, 159, 183, 190, 192
Gross domestic product:
ratio of stock-market value to, 164
ratio of value of equities to, 206

Habitat model, 147
Heaton-Lucas model, 153
Heterogeneity, investor, 151–154
High stock valuation, 164–194
discount rate and, 165–168
fundamental value equation and, 164–165
higher growth in earnings and, 178–183
investor demographics and, 170–178
irrational exuberance and overvaluation, 183–194
stock-market risk and, 168–170
Histograms, for equity premium, 40–43
Historical analysis:
annual holding-period returns and, 12–18
average premiums over sample periods, 45

computing average premium and, 36–39
discounted cash flow model compared, 113–114
equity risk premium and, 18–20
estimating future stock-market performance and, 20–27
inflation and, 74–77
investor returns and, 9–12
long-run outlook and, 202–204
monthly data (1926-1997), 79–100
nonstationarity and, 45–48
risk premium accuracy and, 39–45
stock market indexes and, 6–8
survival bias and, 60–70
Holding-period returns:
defined, 9–11
market performance and, 12–18, 184
Human-capital risk, 152–153
Hyperinflation, 65

Ibbotson and Associates data, 12–18, 114, 124, 172–175
Inflation:
asset returns and, 29–34
equity returns and, 32
expected *vs.* realized, 22—23
in financial analysis, 20–23
historical, 13–17
impact on stocks and bonds, 74–77
as investment risk, 175–176
measuring rate of, 30
monthly historical data for, 79–100
statistics before 1926, 67–68
Information technology, 180
Interest rates, risk aversion and, 142–144
Internal rate of return analysis, 117–121, 202–203, 204
International analysis:
Japanese stock prices, 186–193
rate of stock appreciation, 134
stock market indices (1984-1998), 196–200
survival bias and, 63–65
trade volume, 180
International Brokers' Estimating System, 106–107
Internet stocks, 193–194
Investment banks, multistage discounted cash flow and, 108–109

Investment demand, stock prices and, 178
Investment implications, of lower equity risk premium, 213–215
Investment years, maximum, 177
Investor beliefs/demographics, 170–178
Irrational exuberance, 183–195
Irrational pricing, 190

Japanese stock prices, 186–193

Kaplan-Ruback study, 115–117, 124, 204
Keynes, John Maynard, 184

Labor force growth, 180–181
Labor income risks, 153
Lifetime utility, 143
Long-run outlook, 70–74, 201–216
empirical and theoretical evidence, 202–206
lower equity risk premium implications, 213–216
overvaluation implications, 211–213
permanently higher growth impact, 210–211
rational decline in risk premium, 206–210
Lorie, James, 172
Loss aversion, 148–149
Lynch, Jones, and Ryan, 106–107

MacKay, Charles, 185–186
Market risk premium:
cost of equity capital and, 135–137
earnings yield approach to, 121–122
Milken, Michael, 183–184
Model changes in risk premium, 49–60
dividend and earnings yield models, 52–53
nonstationarity and, 53–55, 59–60
permanence change impact, 55–59
variability of returns models, 51–52
Multistage discounted cash flow, *see* Discounted cash flow model

New York Stock Exchange, 8
Nonstationarity:
bottom line on, 59–60

in estimating long-run risk premium, 53–55
historical risk premium estimates and, 45–48

Output per worker, 180–181
Overvaluation, 183–195
implications of, 211–213

Path of wealth:
annual real returns on, 23–25
historical data, 13–17, 19–20, 21
Pensions, equity risk premium and, 28, 216
Permanent *vs.* temporary declines, 206–209
Portfolio theory, 130–135
Price-to-earnings ratio (P/E), 160, 162–163, 167
Price-weighted indexes, 6–8
Productive potential, economic growth and, 180–182
Prospect theory, 148, 149

Real dollars, 30–31
Real price, calculation of, 31
Real returns, historical, 22–27
Retirement planning, equity risk premium and, 28, 216
Returns:
in assessing stock-market performance, 9–12
autocorrelation in, 149–150
time variation and, 150–151
Risk aversion:
changing investor characteristics and, 170–171
defined, 129
economic theory of, 126–130
historical equity risk premium and, 137–141
risk premium puzzle and, 142–145
Risk premium puzzle, 141–154
autocorrelation in returns and, 149–150
combining explanations and, 154
empirical data and, 141–142
heterogenous investors and, 151–154
high risk aversion and, 142–145
long-run outlook and, 203

nonstandard utility functions and, 145–149
time variations and, 150–151
Risk-return tradeoff:
defining risk and, 131–132
stocks vs fixed-income assets, 176

Schwert index, 66–68
Separability, 147–148
Sharpe ratio, 140–141, 143
Siegal yield analysis, 121–122, 124
Siegel, Jeremy, 173–174
Standard of living, consumption and, 146–147
Standard & Poor's 500 Index, 7–8
annual historical returns, 13–17
boom of the 1990s, 158–159
dividend yield 1946-1998, 161
five-year rolling standard return deviations, 169
monthly historical data for, 79–100
price-to-earnings ratios 1946-1998, 162
Stocks:
analyzing valuation, 159–164
annual holding period data on, 13–17
annual real returns on, 23–25
boom of the 1990s, 158–159
compared *vs.* fixed-income assets, 176
crash prediction, 212
discounted cash flow models and, 104
earnings yield and, 122
estimating return on, 34–35
future investment value and, 214–215
high valuation of, 164–194. *See also* High stock valuation
inflation and, 33, 74–77
international indices, 196–200
long-term holding period returns, 68
long-term viability, 70–74. *See also* Long-run outlook
market indexes for, 6–8
monthly historical data for, 79–100
1987 crash, 176
nonstationarity of, 46–48
permanent *vs.* temporary declines, 206–209
predicting risk premiums and, 55
price corrections, 211–213
price movement of, 4–5

returns before 1926, 67–68
risk premium impact on price, 55–69
survival bias and, *see* Survival bias
U.S. and Japanese compared,
    186–193
"Stocks, Bonds, Bills and Inflation: Year-
    by-Year Historical Returns (1926-
    1974)," 172–173
Survival bias, 60–70, 142, 155, 157
    bottom line on, 69–70
    impact of, 60–69
    risk premium results and, 124
Systematic/nonsystematic risks, 133

Time preference, in economic models,
    143–144
Time variation, returns and, 150–151
Tobin, James, 163–164

Tobin's Q, 163–164
Treasury bills, inflation and, 76

Utilities, discounted cash flow model ap-
    plications for, 103–104
Utility functions, nonstandard, 145–149

Value-weighted indexes, 7–8
Variability of returns, models based on,
    51–52
Volatility, stock price, 168–170

WEFA Group, 107
Weighted average cost of capital,
    118–119
Welch survey, 122–125, 124, 206

Zachs Investment Research, 106